WOMEN AND HEALTH

WOMEN AND HEALTH

Cross-Cultural Perspectives

Patricia Whelehan and Contributors

BERGIN & GARVEY PUBLISHERS, INC.
MASSACHUSETTS

To Ed Hosley
You have been my mentor, my friend,
and my guide through this project.
Thank you.

First published in 1988 by
Bergin & Garvey/Publishers, Inc.
670 Amherst Road
Granby, Massachusetts 01033

89   987654321

Printed in the United States of America

Library of Congress Cataloging-in-Publication Data
Whelehan, Patricia.
    Women and health : cross-cultural perspectives / Patricia Whelehan
and contributors.
        p. cm.
    Bibliography: p.
    Includes index.
    ISBN 0-89789-138-4 (alk. paper) : $49.95. ISBN 0-89789-139-2
(pbk. : alk. paper) : $18.95
    1. Women—Health and hygiene—Cross-cultural studies. 2. Women—
Medical care—Cross-cultural studies. I. Title.
RA564.85.W44 1988
306.4—dc19

CONTENTS

Preface

Women and Health examines a range of health issues currently confronting Western and non-Western women. This book originated from a session on Women's Health which was held at the American Anthropological Association Meetings in Denver in 1984. At that time, I was asked by Dr. Lynne Goldstein, program chair, if I would lead the session. Four papers, which served as the genesis of this volume, were given. Audience participation and response to the presentations were enthusiastic.

What both impressed and excited me about this session, however, was the sense of coherency and connectedness the papers shared, despite their topical and ethnographic diversity. The papers included an examination of the stress experienced by a group of clerical employees who work on a university campus in the United States; an analysis of a depression-reducing mechanism used by a group of impoverished, Mexican-American single mothers living in Detroit; a discussion of an extreme example of pseudocyesis and mythic stillbirth experienced among a group of Pakistani Moslem women in the Himalayas; and the strategies used to locate new health services by a group of immigrant Turkish Moslem women living in Berlin.

Given this diversity, it was surprising to find common themes. The themes illustrated women's concerns for their health and their role as active participants in dealing with various health care issues. The women discussed in this session tried to maintain a state of well-being, despite a lack of economic resources, the presence of stress and sex-role conflicts. Women were shown as capable of both using culturally sanctioned strategies to meet their health care needs and redefining those strategies to do so. The papers illustrated the adaptability and flexibility women have in resolving their health care concerns.

Given the energy and rapport experienced by the participants, the suggestion was made to publish the papers collectively. The question then became "where." This question was answered about three weeks later when Jim Bergin contacted me after having read a press release on the session. He suggested I send him a book prospectus to consider.

From there, with the continuing guidance and support of Dr. Edward Hosley, and the encouragement of the publishers, this project was undertaken. The major sections of the book—"Variations in Traditional Life-Cycle Concerns"; "The Effects of Culture Change on Women's Health"; and "Health Care Concerns Related to Stress"—emerged from the original session. Networking through letters, phone calls, and a "call for papers" in the *Anthropology Newsletter* brought in additional manuscripts for consideration. The thirteen papers, which include two from the original session and eleven solicited papers, that comprise this volume are a genuinely collaborative, cooperative effort of time, energy, and hard work. The papers address some of the major continuous and relatively new aspects of women's health. This book contributes to the existing literature in the field by making a positive statement about Western and non-Western women's involvement with their changing health care needs.

* * *

The publication of this book is due to the efforts of numerous people. I would first like to thank Dr. Lynne Goldstein, who asked me to chair the session on women's health which formed the seed for the book. Without her initial request, the book would not have been initiated in this form and at this time. Second, I would like to thank Jim Bergin, for asking me to edit this book. Both of these people gave me a professional opportunity for which I am deeply appreciative. Ms. Ann Gross, book editor at Bergin & Garvey, patiently provided constructive criticism and support during the final stages of manuscript preparation.

Each of the contributors has worked hard to produce a chapter which meets high professional standards and will be of interest primarily to undergraduates and other new acquaintances to anthropology. To those authors who were scrupulously conscientious about deadlines and also offered support to me as an editor, I extend additional thanks.

I would also like to thank the Anthropology Department, and Administration of Potsdam College for granting me released time for the Spring 1986 semester in order to work on this project. That time has proved to be invaluable. Our department secretary, Ms. Patricia Beaulieu, not only devoted selfless time to manuscript preparation, numerous revisions, and file drawers full of correspondence, but remained calm and upbeat even when I didn't. The Clerical Center at the College has processed numerous drafts of this manuscript, for which I am deeply grateful. Dr. Edward Hosley filled the roles of mentor, guide, and friend. All I've learned about editing a book is due to him; the flaws and errors are completely mine.

Lastly, I would like to thank Bill, and my daughter, Rachel, for their patience, encouragement, and support.

Introduction

Medical anthropology is a well-established, broadly based subdiscipline within anthropology. A variety of publications, research topics, and courses have been developed within this field (e.g., a number of undergraduate courses and graduate programs in medical anthropology, the *Medical Anthropology Quarterly: International Journal for the Cultural and Social Analysis of Health*, and numerous books of which Foster and Anderson 1978; Woods 1979; and Romanucci-Ross, Moerman, and Tancredi 1983 are examples). Paralleling this growth is an increasing anthropological interest in women from cross-cultural, evolutionary, and biosocial perspectives (e.g., Rosaldo and Lamphere 1974, Ortner 1981, Reiter 1975, Schlegel 1977, and Friedl 1975). In contrast, issues in women's health, aside from gynecologic and affective disorders, have not received much anthropological attention until recently.

Outside anthropology, the interest in women's health has increased over the past fifteen years. As with anthropology, however, much of this interest on both a lay and professional level has been directed towards gynecologic/reproductive concerns and affective disorders. In addition, most of the nonanthropological studies focus on Western women as opposed to a wider ethnological approach. These biases are evidenced in the number of self-help books as well as the articles which appear in medical, sociological, and psychological journals (e.g., Boston Women's Health Collective, *Our Bodies Our Selves* 1976, 1984; Goodman 1980). Views of women as people who are basically tied to their biology and who are the more passive, dependent, and affective members of their larger social groups, extend to the treatment of women's health issues within and outside anthropology. This volume is a move away from these foci, towards a more comprehensive appraisal of various aspects of women's health.

The chapters in this volume share a common research approach. Almost every chapter is based upon participant observation and interviews. Each one incorporates both a theoretical orientation and a discussion of a specific health-related problem. Thus, there is an integration of theory, behavior, and problem resolution, a feature which distinguishes this volume from most other works on women's health (e.g., Stewart et al. 1979; Lettvin 1980).

The focus of the book is health—how women achieve it, maintain it, and deal with threats to it. The book makes a positive statement about women's active, deliberate involvement in meeting their health care needs, including the ability to adapt to those culture change and stress situations affecting health.

Women in many cultures use a number of similar strategies to meet their health care needs. These strategies appear as shared themes found

ix

throughout the book. In Part I, women meet their life-cycle experiences through deliberate, rational decision-making processes, syncretizing traditional and Western medical beliefs and practices, and applying a sense of satisfaction achieved in earlier life to deal with health and status concerns of later life.

The impact that Western-induced culture change has on various aspects of health is the focus of the second part of the book. These chapters discuss women's search for new health care services after migrating to a city, coping with negative economic and social changes as a result of urbanization and Westernization, and integrating traditional birthing practices with Western ones. In trying to meet these challenges positively, women redefine cultural expectations of appropriate female behavior, rely on female-based social support networks, and expand definitions of their role boundaries. They are not simply passive receptors of both the negative and positive effects of culture change.

Social, political, and economic changes—on local and global levels—affect the individuals living through them. One effect of larger culture change is stress for the individual members of the group. Women are not immune to culturally induced stress, as is addressed in the third part of the book. They experience stress in their work environments, in their roles as single parents, as overburdened wives and mothers, and as economic participants in the larger, changing society. Much of the stress described in these chapters is related to changing and conflicting definitions of appropriate sex-role behavior and relationships with men. In order to reduce or avoid negative stress, women manipulate traditional beliefs about power and male-female relationships, redefine concepts of kin, adopt the sick role or become assertive. Again, women are active, deliberate, rational participants within their specific cultural systems. They act to meet their needs, adapt to change, and cope with stress.

PART I

VARIATIONS IN TRADITIONAL LIFE-CYCLE CONCERNS

A common perception of women's health is that it deals almost exclusively with such topics as menarche and menopause, birth control, pregnancy, childbirth and lactation, or more recently, sexuality. There is, in fact, an extensive social science literature on such issues (e.g., Barbach 1976; Brown and Kerns 1985; Hatcher et al. 1976 continuous; Hite 1976; Laderman 1983; *Medical Anthropology* 1981, V 5; Raphael 1976). These continuous, biological givens comprise a large but not all-inclusive part of women's health. Other aspects of women's health, to be discussed later in this volume, include the effects of work, migration, and stress on women's well-being. In addressing the universal aspects of women's health, there are both shared and culture-specific means of responding to life-cycle concerns. In addition, as societies change, culturally managed health issues also change.

These chapters address a variety of gynecologic concerns spanning the life cycle. They involve a discussion of syncretic midwifery practices, the symbolic dimensions of menstruation, birth control choice and menopause, the psychological effects of hysterectomy, and the social status of postmenopausal women.

1

The topics discussed also reflect the effects that increased Westernization has on traditional health care issues. This theme of culture change as a factor in women's health is introduced here and appears throughout the book. Change is reflected in the synthesis of traditional, rural Mexican and Western birthing practices, as well as in the technological innovations in birth control available to a group of Newfoundland women. Less directly, the social perceptions underlying elective hysterectomy and the criteria used by a group of postmenopausal women in Peru as a measure of role satisfaction also exemplify culture change.

In Chapter 1, Dona Lee Davis discusses how a group of Newfoundland women's perceptions of "blood" influence their attitudes toward menstruation, new and traditional methods of birth control, and menopause. Blood symbolism, a common theme, extends to attitudes about appropriate female sexual behavior, definitions of being a good wife and mother, states of health, and when to seek the services of a physician. Blood symbolism weaves together the threads of a woman's gynecologic life.

Betty B. Faust examines syncretic midwifery practices in a Mexican Maya village. Traditional midwives seek training in Western obstetric practices. When these practices are perceived to result in the death of an infant, suspicions of witchcraft surface. These suspicions result in changes in traditional midwifery practices. Midwives continue to give pre- and postnatal care, but no longer assist in childbirth; a local, trusted Western-trained obstetrician now attends childbirth. The merging of traditional and Western birthing practices supports indigenous beliefs concerning female modesty, childbirth, life, and death, while also bringing new medical procedures to the group.

Elyse Barnett discusses the factors which contribute to a sense of well-being among a group of postmenopausal Peruvian women. She challenges the common beliefs that while American women suffer status and role deprivation during menopause due to the "empty nest" syndrome, their peers in non-Western societies experience increased status due to the high value generally accorded the elderly in traditional societies. Barnett incorporates Bart's (1969) observations that, cross-culturally, the status of menopausal women rarely is continuous—it either increases or decreases. Barnett relates the menopausal woman's social experiences and status to the personal satisfaction with having fulfilled major roles earlier in life. In her work among Puente Piedre Peruvian women, she finds that those women who are satisfied with what they have accomplished in their primary roles, either as mothers or employees, experience greater self-esteem and view menopause positively.

Hysterectomies, one of the most commonly performed major surgical procedures in the United States, generally are elective (i.e., nonemergency) operations. Despite this, women who have elective hysterectomies experience a range of social and psychological changes after the surgery. Linnea

Klee's chapter discusses factors involved in how well women cope postoperatively. Most importantly, their perceptions of themselves as wives, mothers, sexual partners, and women influence how they respond to the hysterectomy. In addition, the perceptions the medical profession holds toward women and the surgery influence both these women's decisions to have the hysterectomy and their postoperative experiences.

1

"BAD BLOOD" AND THE CULTURAL MANAGEMENT OF HEALTH IN A NEWFOUNDLAND FISHING COMMUNITY

Dona Lee Davis

Davis examines the importance of blood symbolism in the sexual and reproductive lives of a group of coastal Newfoundland women ranging in age from their late teens to their fifties and sixties. Blood symbolism, based on an image of limited good and humoral medicine, is incorporated into their attitudes towards menstruation, birth control choice, decisions concerning PAP smears and hysterectomies, as well as general states of health. Since concepts of blood influence these women's health care decisions and practices, medical workers need to be sensitive to these beliefs when developing treatment plans.

This is a study of *community* health. A community is a geographically bounded settlement, which includes at least three generations, and where every resident knows or has personal knowledge of every other resident (Mead 1978). The subject of this study is Grey Rock Harbour, an isolated fishing community. The purpose of this study is to explain how the ethos of limited good, popular blood lore, and idiosyncratic experiences combine to shape collective action and the dissemination of health related information and how these, in turn, affect the cultural management of health. The study focuses on popular beliefs about "blood" and "bad blood." Local blood beliefs are related to three female health issues: birth control, cervical cancer, and hypertension. The chapter concludes with a discussion of how local factors which limit the assumption of leadership roles can hamper the effectiveness of a province-wide women's health education program.

Located on the southwest coast of Newfoundland, Grey Rock Harbour (a pseudonym), population 766, is a homogeneous community. All villagers are of English descent, Anglican faith, and share similar lifestyles as well as socioeconomic and occupational status. A year-round inshore fishery dominates both the occupational and emotional life of the community. The history of Grey Rock Harbour is a chronicle of poverty, isolation, and the struggle for survival in a harsh environment. However, since confederation with Canada in 1949, material conditions have steadily improved. In the mid 1960s, a dirt road was built connecting the village to larger population centers where service facilities and consumer products are more readily available.

Locals take a great deal of pride in the tradition of the fishery. Their stoic endurance of hard times past and preservation of valued traditions are seen as elements intrinsic to the Newfoundland character (Davis 1983c). The daily life of Harbour folk is continually shaped by their long heritage of common experience and a shared belief that survival of the community rests on everyone remaining the same or equal (Davis 1983b, 1986b).

Harbour folk have traditionally relied on a vast array of home treatments for a wide variety of complaints. The last doctor to reside in the community died in the 1930s. Locals tend to seek medical care only when a crisis stage is reached, or when they are unable to perform daily duties (Davis 1983a, 1984). In the mid 1970s, a "Wednesday clinic" was established in Grey Rock Harbour. For the first time in their history, on every other Wednesday, weather permitting, residents had freely available clinical services within walking distance of their homes. The clinic was staffed by a local practical nurse and a doctor on rotating duty from a nearby town.

The introduction of modern health care services has stimulated interest in the health of individuals, personalities of health care practitioners, evaluation of treatments, and the quality of various kinds of health services. Each of these is an important and frequent topic of village conversation (Davis 1984). In an attempt to make sense of this confusing proliferation of health services, and to meet changes on their own terms, locals have combined information garnered from the new biomedical services with more traditional beliefs to form a new lay health lore. The analysis which follows focuses on the notion of "blood." Blood and bad blood are associated with menstruation, reproduction, overall female health and temperament, and are rooted in the social contexts of poverty and isolation that continue to characterize Harbour life.

The data for this study were collected through participant observation. From October 1977 to December 1978, I lived in two different households and actively participated in the domestic and public activities of Harbour women. The original purpose of the study focused on assessing the effects of women's status on their experiences of menopause and middle age (see Davis 1986a, 1986b). Data on menstruation, contraception, and hysterectomies came, in part, from a standardized questionnaire, which was administered to thirty-seven women ages 35–65. Because I had lived in the field for nine months previous to the first interview, I immediately realized that the interview schedule was not appropriate for eliciting local women's views of their own bodies and physiogical functioning. Interview data were supplemented with additional, more open-ended discussions about blood and nerves designed to elicit women's own explanatory models of biological processes (see Davis 1983a). The accounts described in this chapter are based both on responses to directed questioning and conversations recorded in my field notes.

The recent province-wide availability of birth control information and devices, hypertension education campaigns, and cervical cancer screening programs have combined to stimulate an active reevaluation of the traditional importance of blood, especially menstrual blood, as an indicator of a diverse range of health states. In 1969, it became legal to distribute contraceptive information and devices in Newfoundland. Large family size, high illegitimacy rates, early age of marriage, high unemployment, and low per capita income make the prospect of fertility regulation very appealing (Alderdice et al. 1973). Tubal ligation rapidly became the preferred means of fertility regulation among young women in the Harbour. During the 1960s and '70s, Newfoundland had, and continues to have, the highest mortality rates from cervical cancer in Canada (Miller 1981). In 1962, a provincial cervical cancer screening program was developed. Coincident with this program was a rapid rise in hysterectomy rates for the entire province. Five village women had hysterectomies between 1970 and 1978. Although they entered relatively late into the screening program, Grey Rock Harbour women soon became very concerned with the problem of cancer and other "states" of the womb. Hypertension, which was called the new blood disease or the "new blood," became recognized as a major health problem in Newfoundland in the 1970s. Rates are especially high for those residing in fishing as opposed to inland villages (Fodor, Abbott, and Rusted 1973).

Extensive female communication networks, social, economic and emotional support systems, together with the assumption of personal responsibility for one's own health are commonly accepted as social factors which can function to aid in the delivery of health care services (Presser and Bumpass 1972). These three factors characterize Harbour women. However, regarding three recent developments—availability of contraception, inception of a province-wide cervical cancer screening program, and the "discovery" of abnormally high hypertension rates among outport Newfoundlanders, especially middle-aged women—these female coping strategies actually acted as impediments to effective health management.

New knowledge is transferred through oral communication and assimilated into either existing folk categories or newly formulated popular beliefs. The following section demonstrates how collective features, such as the nature of female communication networks and support systems along with an understanding of the limits of personal responsibility, relate to the complexity of lay beliefs about women's health complaints and the nature of "blood." The analysis which follows demonstrates that these beliefs should not be dismissed as old wives' tales or benign, out-dated survivals of earlier

Harbour or English folk traditions. Rather, they continue to play an active role in shaping individual and collective action, and are intrinsically related to the rules of conduct that govern Harbour social interaction. The importance of these beliefs needs to be considered both by health care planners when introducing new technology or programs and by health care providers in their dealings with Harbour residents.

BLOOD SYMBOLISM AND COLLECTIVE IDENTITY

In Grey Rock Harbour, "blood" describes a wide variety of bodily states and governs a wide range of beliefs and behaviors involving health and other matters. Blood is more than just the "red fluid" in one's veins and arteries. Blood includes "natural" or "vital" juices (e.g., hormones). Harbour concepts of blood are elaborated into various properties and shape a person's sense of biological functions, personality or character, and health/illness status. Women's health, especially in terms of female reproductive processes, figures prominently in local blood lore.

Good blood is essential for good health. Yet people seldom accentuate the positive or refer to good blood. Instead they are mainly interested in the negative aspects of bad blood with its numerous harmful varieties and potentially dangerous qualities. The color, volume, or viscosity and quality of blood are frequent topics of conversation among women. Blood may be described in terms of the following characteristics: "red," "orange," or "black"; "high" or "low"; "thick" or "thin"; "too much" or "too little"; "good" or "bad"; "mixed" or "poison." However, when asked to explain these terms, locals generally disagree. One individual will state that "red blood" denotes health while another will state that "black blood" does. Loss of blood through menstruation can be "bad" since it may leave the blood volume low and result in energy loss. Yet, heavy periods can also be "good" as a release for the excitable woman who suffers from "too much" blood. Informants can rarely provide clear definitions of their own concepts of the various characteristics of blood, but their views are revealed in reference to a person who suffers from the ailment (e.g., "I'm not sure, exactly [what is meant by thick blood], but Cassie Bunt over in Crow Cove got it"). It is important that the nature of a blood complaint be consistent with the person who experiences it; for example, locals will agree on the nature of "Betty's low blood" or "Hazel's thick blood." There are no universally agreed upon "textbook" definitions of blood. When asked to define "blood" (e.g., what does too much blood mean?), informants' responses are likely to be highly variable and often contradictory. In addition, some talk to a great extent about one type of blood (thick, poison) and claim little knowledge about others.

There are three types of explanations for confusion over blood beliefs. First is the village tradition of dependence on oral rather than written means of information exchange. Second is the intimate nature of social interaction.

However, the natures of oral communication and intimate social interaction are inseparable from the third type of explanation, which is the moral order of the community where social levelling and an image of limited good set standards of appropriate behavior and impression management. Before further analysis is possible, an expanded consideration of each of these explanations is necessary.

The various interpretations of blood states rest on oral communication in a basically nonliterate population which has always based cognitions on experience rather than formal or textbook learning. This lack of consensus over the nature of blood may frustrate a researcher who hopes to diagnose medical equivalents for bad blood. It is tempting for the outsider to view these beliefs as illogical or backward. However, to the Harbour women the rationality of blood is based in a series of individual- or situation-specific contexts, which include her own actions and experiences and the actions and experiences of those with whom she has long-term, intimate contact. Each context or situation has its own underlying logic. Each person's blood problem is its own case, its own type or prototype. Generalized rules are not necessary. Each woman is aware of all blood cases because of the limited size of the village. In addition, the meaning of cases can be renegotiated through casual conversation at any time, and there is no felt need for consensus. The meaning of the term *blood* varies according to the context in which the term is used.

The saliency of blood lore is based on two rather different social processes. First is the enhancement of personal identity rooted in the face-to-face nature of social interactions which characterize small communities such as Grey Rock Harbour. Second are the strong social forces which subvert individual identity to a collective village identity (e.g., "We're all the same here"). Each member has full knowledge of one's fellows, their personalities, their families and family histories, their life histories, and their daily activities. Individual identities emphasize a range of diversity in personalities that present constant topics for village gossip and spice up the more humdrum aspects of daily life. Public restraint and embarrassment at personalized attention also typify Harbour lifestyles. A collective ethos dominates the individual ethos. Limits on individual variation are severely enforced, and the expression of individuality is highly codified. Despite pressure to live up to a collective ethos or ideologically defined community identity, individuals can express their individuality in terms of blood. Thus if Cassie fails to live up to the collective ethos, it is not Cassie's fault, but something beyond her conscious control—her blood— that is responsible. To the extent that the social order inhibits individuality, concepts such as blood allow for its expression.

As the foregoing discussion illustrates, an egalitarian ethic and a "judge not lest you be judged" mentality lie at the moral core of Harbour life. Public assertiveness as an expression of individuality, especially in terms of bragging or "acting uppity," is frowned upon. Inappropriate behavior is negatively sanctioned through gossip, shunning, and even vandalism. The egalitarian ethic of Grey Rock Harbour stultifies individual expression. Because they share in the occupational traditions of fishing life, all women as fishermen's wives must be hardworking, stoic, self-sacrificing individuals. Women derive status through suffering, yet they must not blow their own horn. They let their bodies do it for them. The biology of blood absolves a woman from responsibility for her complaints and provides her with a trial to overcome, something to stoically endure. This belief influences a woman's choice of birth control, decisions regarding hysterectomies, self-treatment of hypertension, and evaluation of health care providers. Locals believe that "we all come up together, or we don't come up at all." This belief influences individual and collective action and may be referred to as "the image of limited good."

The phrase was originally coined by Foster (1965) to refer to a belief characteristic of, but not limited to, peasant societies. According to the image of limited good, all the desired things in life exist in finite quantity, are always in short supply, and one individual or family can improve themselves only at the expense of others. Such beliefs occur in conservative societies where individual progress is seen as a threat to community stability, the maintenance of traditional society, and traditional ethos. This view of the environment which guides and structures behavior is a basic, unquestioned premise of Harbour life. It acts as an integrating principle which can be used to account for and explain diverse and seemingly unrelated or irrational forms of behavior.

By focusing on the patterns of oral communication and the nature of face-to-face interaction and intimate knowledge of one another, the image of limited good can serve as a theoretical focus with which to explore the relationships among seemingly unrelated or diverse behavior patterns. Local reactions to birth control, cancer, and hypertension as health issues illustrate three dimensions of the concept of limited good. In Grey Rock Harbour, locals believe that too much convenience will weaken the Newfoundland outport race, whose strength and identity are drawn from the continued adjustment to adversity. The relation between blood beliefs and limited good can be illustrated by local rejection of convenient, effective forms of birth control as too easy. Cervical cancer screening programs failed because locals accused outside professionals of treating them unfairly. Locals think that intracommunity roles of fair treatment should also govern the administration of extracommunity or provincial and national policies. Finally, local reaction to hypertension education was based on a strong desire to be inconspicuous in their behavior, or like everyone else. Locals incorporate new information into preexisting knowledge and beliefs in order to derive a consensus for determining uniform standards of appropriate behavior. The ethnographic examples that follow illustrate that the belief patterns and behavioral predispositions of Harbour women have a rationale of their own which may be quite different from the logical assumptions of biomedical health care providers.

BIRTH CONTROL

In 1969, it became legal to distribute literature on contraception and sell contraceptives in the province. Surgical sterilization rapidly became the preferred means of birth control among women in their twenties and early thirties. "Tying the tubes," "tubals," or "tubal 'gations" were done in the hospital of a nearby village. Through self-admissions and gossip, one can conservatively estimate that over one-half of the village women between the ages of twenty and thirty-five have been "fixed."

Provincial family planning advocates cite large family size, high illegitimacy rates, early age of marriage, high unemployment, and low per capita income as good reasons for increased use of fertility regulation methods in Newfoundland (Alderdice et al. 1973). The preference for tubal ligation in Grey Rock Harbour is analyzed as "ritualistic surgery," or surgery in which the relationships between means and ends is not intrinsic (Bolande 1969). The image of limited good is an important determinant of contraceptive preference. Limited good is reflected in numerous beliefs, including community egalitarianism. Bodily suffering is viewed as good for the soul. A positive valuation of self-sacrifice and stoicism enhances female status. A distrust of anything new, an unwillingness to tamper with fate, and a belief that easy achievement cannot ultimately be good for you are also aspects of the image of limited good.

Despite rumors that "local doctors hand them out like candy," young women are fairly ignorant of the various methods of contraception. Although hesitancy to use effective birth control methods rests on both a moral ("good girls don't plan ahead") and rational ("it is bad for your body") basis, older and younger women are very interested in birth control. It is a frequent topic of conversation among them. Since few young women read magazines or have any access to extra-village sources of information, local gossip and oral lore remain the major sources of contraceptive knowledge.

Tubal ligation is the preferred means of contraception because it is the lesser of evils—the "least worst"—of the contraceptive alternatives. Although people know about the Pill, their understanding of how it works is erroneous, and attitudes towards its use are negative. Young women who use the Pill are considered immoral. They usually start to date early, at ages eleven through thirteen, choosing boys two to four years older. Sexual intimacy is thought to be a natural consequence of romantic attraction and marriage occurs at an early age. Courting females depend on males for contraception, which usually consists of withdrawal or condoms, the latter of which are unavailable for purchase in the village. The belief prevails that "if he loves you and respects you, he will use something [i.e., a condom]." Furthermore, since contraception is the man's responsibility, if his methods fail and a woman becomes pregnant, it is his fault and he is obliged to marry her. Use of condoms is not considered a dependable form of contraception, and their use implies a recognized risk of pregnancy. A young woman who uses the Pill and is sexually active forfeits the "if it fails, I'll marry you" commitment from her lover, and is considered loose or wayward in her behavior. The reasoning behind this is that the use of an extremely effective means of contraception would mean that a woman could risk having sexual relations with someone she was not committed to marrying. Sex without love conditional to a promise of marriage is frowned upon.

Everyone in town knew a story about a woman who, after using the Pill, bled to death during a "regular" (routine) operation; supposedly her blood would not clot. Details about which girl, which village, and what kind of operation have been lost. When I asked how the Pill could possibly have caused such bleeding, I was told that "the doctor told her mother the Pill caused the bleeding, so he must have been right." In the local view, "that poor dear, who bled to death" provides sufficient proof of the assumption that the Pill interferes with blood clotting. The Pill is also believed to be dangerous because it interferes with hormones. It is thought that anything strong enough to "kill all those germs [sperm]" cannot be good for the rest of your body or for your unborn babies. The credibility of oral contraceptives was also undermined by reports about a man who was prescribed the Pill. People resent doctors who "push" any kind of contraception so that "their kind" (us poor and ignorant folk) will not reproduce. Yet, the most commonly reported reason for avoiding the Pill was the belief that if you start taking the Pill too early you may somehow use up its "magical" properties, and will be unable to plan your family when you really want to do so.

Other fertility regulating devices are also unacceptable. Intrauterine devices (I.U.D.s) are called "the loop." The major "loop" horror story involved Esther "over in the bottoms who went to the doctor and got one of those loops. Next thing you know, she's pregnant!" This was confirmed by Esther herself, who blames the doctor for using her in "some kind of experience [experiment]." Diaphragms are unknown. The reason for this is probably due to the fact that local doctors fail to recommend them. Foams and jellies, although messy and inconvenient, are used by some women. However, they are considered to be too dangerous for regular use, since, as with the Pill, anything that kills sperm is thought to be bad for your body. Women who depend on these methods of birth control use them only when "I think I could get pregnant." Emic explanations of birth control need to be understood by health care providers in order that clear, accurate information about contraceptive use and effectiveness can be given to villagers.

Although part of the hesitancy to use convenient/effective means of birth control stems from misinformation, education alone would not result in changed patterns of contraceptive use. This is because the ambivalence displayed toward more convenient methods also reflects a continuity of values between mothers and their grown daughters. In the local ethos, bodily suffering is good for the soul. In the past, women derived character and high status from unquestioning acceptance of an unexpected or undesired pregnancy. Older women believed that it was their fate to have children and any tampering with that fate would be wrong. Resources were limited. These locals believe that those who practice birth control, which is considered to be good and desirable, must pay a price; using highly effective birth control is an unfair way to get ahead.

If the Pill is rejected as too easy, withdrawal and rhythm are acceptable because they have built-in costs. A woman who practices withdrawal sees herself as a strong woman, a woman who can control herself in spite of sexual pleasure. Similarly, a woman who practices rhythm also sacrifices sexual pleasure by avoiding "her man," usually "sometime around the middle of the month." These women realize that they run a greater risk of pregnancy. The mothers of daughters who practice withdrawal and rhythm generally approve of these methods, and feel that their daughters have not been "weakened" by the changes that have accompanied modernization. A closer look at the relations between mothers and their grown daughters is necessary to further explain rejection of the Pill.

Today's young and middle-aged mothers are characterized by different reproductive patterns. Young women complete childbearing early in their marriage, usually in their early twenties, whereas many middle-aged women in their late thirties and forties continue to have children. Young women have different attitudes towards birth control than women whose reproductive careers began over twenty years ago. Although older women are ambivalent about the ethics of "being so selfish," younger women feel that limiting family size is a key to an improved lifestyle, mainly in terms of less work and better material conditions. While their mothers and grand-mothers frequently voice negative attitudes towards birth control, young women are not as resigned to their fate as childbearers as their mothers were (are). In fact, many women justify the early termination of their re-productive careers by pointing to their mother's misery. In choosing sterili-zation, a young woman shows rebellion against her mother's narrow perspective on birth control and at the same time outdoes her in terms of self-sacrifice. Having your "tubes tied" is considered to be the most effective method. It is convenient and safe, yet one can also emphasize the suffering aspect: one must go to the hospital to be "cut up" and one sacrifices the option of having children in the future. "Tying the tubes" also "blocks off" or "prevents the flow of 'natural juices'," and can result in long-term "wom-en's problems" such as cramps or abnormal periods, and make one more prone to disease and bad moods. In addition, it is believed that tubal ligation necessitates that a hysterectomy be performed later, which will cause weight gain.

How do younger women maintain the status of "good woman" and operate within the system of limited good, so that their personal boon (fewer children) does not adversely affect the luck and circumstances of others? In my view, it is not merely coincidence that the preferred means of birth control among the younger women have built-in sacrifices or prices to pay. By choosing a method that allows them to maintain an image of martyr to their reproductive capacity, younger women achieve a compromise between the beliefs of their mother's generation, and their own desire to limit their family size. Withdrawal, rhythm, and sterilization are all practiced at some cost to self and challenge to strength of character. The Pill is condemned precisely because it is easy, convenient, and effective. As one woman aptly phrased it, "Having no children today is sinfully easy."

The potential exists for intergenerational conflict centering around the introduction of new contraceptives. The extent to which daughters avoid this conflict by not using more effective, yet reversible, contraception needs to be assessed. Emphasizing the sacrificial aspects of Pill or I.U.D. use in terms of their risk factors may encourage their adoption while supporting local norms and avoiding the ultimate sacrifice of fertility which accompanies tubal ligation.

CERVICAL CANCER AND HYSTERECTOMY

The discussion of birth control shows how collective beliefs can shape individual actions. However, individual events can also generate collective action. A series of seemingly unrelated, idiosyncratic events undermined a very promising preventative health care program. Here, we see the image of limited good shaping social action in the guise of fairness and equitable treatment of all individuals. Although not mentioned by Foster (1965), Harbour notions of fairness can be viewed as a local manifestation of limited good. The egalitarian structure and social levelling that characterize Harbour life stem not so much from fatalism as they do from an expectation of being treated fairly. Just as someone or some family should not use unfair means to get ahead, such as refusing to help out less fortunate relatives, it is also unfair to persecute someone or put them down. Just as everyone has the same obligations, they should also have the same opportunities. Expectations of fairness govern intravillage relationships, but they are also expected to govern villagers' relations with outsiders. This notion includes local provincial and national government agencies, which are expected to deliver their services with equal consideration to all citizens, rich or poor. Yet, experience has shown that these expectations of fairness are not always met. Harbour folk sometimes feel themselves to be the victims of unfair and callous treatment by governing officials and agencies. Villagers recognize their greatly improved lifestyles. Since confederation with Canada, they have become the recipients of numerous health and welfare benefits. However, things do not always work out as planned. This leads to a curious hope-hate relationship with the outside. A closer look at what happened during a cervical cancer screening campaign illustrates this point.

Many Harbour women have participated in province-wide cervical cancer screening programs. The screening program is partially responsible for the fact that the Newfoundland hysterectomy rates rose by 28 percent between 1973 and 1977 to become the second highest rate in Canada (Miller 1981). Initial acceptance of the program was extremely positive since it fit well with local notions of bodily health. Initially women welcomed the health-check and tended to be favorably disposed towards hysterectomies. However, the effectiveness of the cervical cancer screening program was seriously undermined by a series of chance events.

Local beliefs underlying positive attitudes toward cervical screening and hysterectomy were based in traditional beliefs. It is considered normal that women who have low blood go through puberty at a late age. Similarly, a woman with thin blood will continue to menstruate until late in life. Both menstruation and menopause may be viewed as healthy bodily cleansings. The heavier your period, the cleaner you become. Excessive or prolonged bleeding at midlife (menopause) is a healthy sign that both present and future menstrual blood is being eliminated, and has the same function as purging the blood or relieving the body of stored impurities. Many postmenopausal difficulties are blamed on the fact that the body did not sufficiently clean itself out at menopause (e.g., menses became too sparse or terminated too early). The postmenopausal period is sometimes referred to as being clean or clear, as in the phrase "I'm clear." Hot flashes are also beneficial to the menopausal woman because they prevent the accumulation of "too much blood," and are also said to purify the blood. Women traditionally purge themselves (take laxatives) to clean the blood every spring and fall.

A hysterectomy can be a form of surgical purge. The phrase "the doctor cleaned me out, took all of it" refers to a hysterectomy. Four out of the five village women with hysterectomies prior to my visit reported that their operations were voluntary. The fifth woman said she had cancer of the uterus and reportedly had no choice. Each woman had sought medical intervention after a period of prolonged or excessive bleeding. When I suggested to one woman that the physician may have performed an unnecessary operation, she angrily replied that I "should have to wash them rags out every night before [I] talked like that again." Only one of these women had their operation locally. The rest went to the mainland or a larger population center. Local doctors were not to be trusted for such an important operation. None of the women could tell me why they bled excessively (e.g., "The doctor never said; I guess it was the change of life."), nor could they tell me whether or not their ovaries as well as their uteri had been removed. Not all women who are plagued by excessive or prolonged flow go to a doctor, especially if it occurs at menopause. Local critics have implied that some women will "jump at the chance for a hysterectomy for fear of having a change-of-life baby."

Despite the initial acceptance of the cervical cancer screening program, eventual rejection of screening was brought about by a series of incidents which led women to believe that they were being treated unfairly by local medical personnel. One woman, after providing a smear, received a letter in the mail saying her smear was positive. She kept waiting to be called back by the doctor to have an appointment scheduled. No "invitation" came. After suffering irregular, heavy bleeding for three years, which she felt must be cleaning out the cancer if there was any, she began to feel quite ill and finally went to the doctor. He checked her records and told her that she had indeed had cancer for the last three years. Frustrated and disappointed by the provincial medical system, the young woman went to Nova Scotia for her operation. The delay, worry and fear that accompanied this woman's waiting made other local women resentful of what they perceived to be a callous medical profession. The adverse experience of one person left the local women with not only a negative outlook on the screening program, but also with a heightened awareness of their wombs and the potential dangers of cancer. Women angrily resented the fact that doctors created anxiety about the problem of womb disease and then abandoned them. There is poor communication between physicians and their patients as to the nature of their medical condition and recommended treatments. Just as rumors are used to sanction local misbehaviors, women began to gossip about the motives of the doctors, speculating that they must get extra pay for performing more hysterectomies.

An additional, unrelated case made matters worse. A young woman died of cancer of the bowel when she was thirty-five years of age. Although she had had troubles for a long time, the doctor's diagnosis of cancer was followed by death in six months, sudden from the locals' point of view. There was a general cancer scare among village women of similar age. Fearing heredity as a factor in the genesis of cancer, the deceased woman's sister went to the doctor for a check-up. She was found to have uterine cancer, and a hysterectomy was performed. Many women at this point went to the doctor requesting a cervical smear, convinced that they were to be the next "sudden death" victim.

Faith in the medical profession as sympathetic to women's problems was finally, totally undermined in the eyes of local women by the case of a young Harbour woman who went to the local clinic to complain of irregular periods and pain at intercourse. She was convinced that she, like her dead relative referred to in the previous paragraph, had cancer. The doctor told her that there was nothing wrong with her, that she was probably having sex too often (e.g., he made some reference about "behaving like a civilized woman" and "not a wild animal"), and that she ought to practice self-control. He did not examine her in any way, nor did he ask her any questions about her sex life or symptoms. She was devastated, ashamed, and more sure than ever that she had cancer, but there would be no help for her. Harbour women were outraged by her unfair treatment ("I'd die before I gave that creamer [the doctor] the time of day"). Such resentments function to renew reliance on more traditional means of treatment and turn women away from Western physicians who may be insensitive. Physicians clearly need to keep their own biases under control and recognize that gynecology, as a field, addresses some of the most intimate and personal dimensions of one's sense of self. Physicians need to be sensitive to this aspect in their verbal and clinical dealings with their patients.

Everyone knew about these events. Extensive gossip initially defended the doctors, eventually defense and accusations were balanced, and finally the need for collective consensus overrode the view of the medical defenders. Initially hoping for the best, locals came to believe that they were being treated unfairly by outsiders who did not understand them. As poor, backward[1] outporters, they were not accorded the respect by the doctors that they earned during lifetimes of hardship. The end result was community action in the form of boycotting the local doctors in matters of gynecological health. Women refused to seek treatment or traveled to other communities with their gynecological health problems.

HYPERTENSION

Local notice of hypertension originated from a combination of factors. Epidemiological studies of hypertension in a nearby island community during the 1960s first alerted locals to a "new blood disease" found to affect large numbers of people in that village. Thirty-three percent of the population was found to suffer from elevated arterial blood pressure; only 10 percent was being treated (Gerson and Fodor 1978). Rates were particularly high for middle-aged women. Locals began to speculate whether or not they, too, were suffering from the new disease. The nature and severity of symptoms appropriate for presentation at the clinic became popular topics of discussion. Local awareness was heightened when area doctors, alerted to the extent of the illness, began taking the blood pressure of their clinical patients, providing them with hypertension literature, and suggesting they cut down on salt intake.

Hypertension, like cervical cancer and hysterectomy, can be related to the concept of limited good, where there is a desire on the part of villagers to look and act like everyone else and to be inconspicuous in their behavior (Foster 1965). This, when combined with the belief that you should only resort to doctors when you really need them, inhibits impulsive individual actions. Unlike the longer-standing concerns of cancer and birth control, hypertension presented the locals with a new disease to which they did not know how to respond. Not wanting to bother the doctor about something they might not even have, locals exchanged information about the new disease among themselves. For example, a woman who was worried about suffering from the new blood would call all her friends and relatives in order to decide whether or not she had sufficient or proper symptoms to report to a doctor. A consensus about the nature of new blood symptoms and their amenability to home versus clinical treatment began to emerge and became self-perpetuating.

Hypertension in Grey Rock Harbour has not resulted in a new folk syndrome, but has magnified or renewed the traditional concerns with blood. Since the "h" sound is difficult for locals to pronounce and "tension" refers to another folk syndrome, "nerves," locals substitute the term "too much blood." Medical diagnoses of blood pressure as high or low are equated with having "too much or too little blood" in the body, and not with the muscular efficiency of the heart or pressure on vascular walls. Locals use the common-sense overlap of hypertension and blood beliefs to treat themselves or present themselves for treatment at the clinic. Yet the cognitive bases of their decision making is not always conducive to effective treatment of hypertension.

In the local view, "too much blood" (the new synonym for hypertension) is a minor complaint which can result in headaches, backaches, dizziness, swelling of the feet, and nose bleeds. Since these are not complaints likely to interfere with daily tasks, they are regarded as amenable to home treatment. The traditional cures include ingestion of hot water, sugar, soda and vinegar to "dry up the blood" or control blood volume. Red jello will also dry or thicken the blood. With home remedies readily available, there is no need for further consultation with the physician.

Yet people who feel that they suffer from low or thick blood go to the doctor. "Not enough" or "low blood" is equated with anemia ("she's got no blood" or "her blood is run down"). In this condition, a person who has "got no color," is tired, weak, sickly, and has no appetite, is at risk for a serious disease. Any kind of bleeding, puncture wound, or copious menstruation at this time is very bad. Cod liver oil and special tonics were once taken to "build the blood up." Men are felt to have thicker blood than women. Thick blood also refers to heart problems, especially "the angina heart." In this sense, the blood is so thick (viscous) that the heart has a great deal of difficulty pumping it through the vessels ("tubes").

Menstrual bleeding is a good indicator of the states of "too much," "low," "too thick" or "thin" blood. The women whose blood is perceived as "too much" or "too heavy," or whose cycles of bleeding are prolonged, wait for the body to cure itself of "high blood" on a monthly basis. Heavy, prolonged, or irregular bleeding in this sense is not seen as a reason to go to a doctor, especially if it occurs at middle age. It means the body is taking good care of itself. However, the woman with little or no menstrual bleeding or clotted "black blood" will report to a doctor.

People will consult with each other, exchange symptoms, and derive a consensus of which symptoms are best treated at home and which symptoms require medical intervention. The community would frown on the villager who visited the doctor for problems that could be treated at home. Unfortunately, individuals with "too much blood" (i.e., hypertension, whether diagnosed by self or doctor), or with particular menstrual problems that could benefit from medical care, may not feel that they have complaints the community has determined as acceptable to present to the physician for treatment.

CONCLUSION

In summary, this study shows that popular lay beliefs about the nature of blood are related to a wide range of beliefs and behaviors, which may or may not have negative consequences for the delivery of health care services to the women of Grey Rock Harbour. Borrowing on traditional notions of biology which do not draw firm distinctions between body, society, and self, women's communication networks have created a unique contraceptive folklore. A series of unforeseen events undermined the effectiveness of the cervical screening program. Hypertension education attempts stimulated local reevaluation of blood complaints which acted to obscure, rather than clarify, the danger signals of hypertension.

Birth control, hypertension, and cancer, all recent health concerns, are not well understood by Harbour folk, or, for that matter, by college professors. Each of these concerns involves abstract and confounding notions of health and illness. The multidimensional nature of these health and social problems has made them a popular topic of conversation, as locals attempt to make sense of a confusing array of health-related phenomena. Here, blood complaints are seen as a unifying theme in local beliefs concerning birth control, hypertension and cervical cancer. However, one does not need to look far for unifying themes in Grey Rock Harbour, where isolation, shared occupation, historic traditions, and an egalitarian social ethic dominate and integrate diverse realms of village life. It is not surprising that the rationales and beliefs surrounding these complaints have filtered through oral communication networks and face-to-face social interactions to merge with the image of limited good and its cognitive and structural correlates. In their attempt to become informed, responsible, health care consumers, locals are fusing notions of mind, body, and society with past and present.

The introduction of new contraceptive technology, hysterectomies as a means of dealing with menopausal symptoms, and a Western medical concern about hypertension are received ambivalently by Harbour residents. These medical changes are evaluated in terms of indigenous beliefs about blood and normal body functioning. Culture conflict exists between Harbour residents and medical personnel over perceptions of health. In addition to these conflicts, health workers have difficulty interacting with the residents, resulting in Harbour women rejecting some aspects of Western medical technology.

Western health care planners and practitioners need to keep several things in mind when bringing medical change to any area. Clear, accurate information needs to be disseminated through traditional communication channels. In this case, for example, an oral tradition prevails. Reversible means of birth control as well as the option of a tubal ligation should be offered in a manner which reflects local beliefs about sacrifice and stoicism. Improved communication between the physicians and the women regarding the side effects of procedures, surgical risks, and contraceptive use and its effectiveness is important. Physicians' assistants, nurse practitioners, or other groups may help alleviate communication problems. Doctors also need to be aware of and to control their personal and professional biases. Lack of sophistication in Western medical practices by the patients is not an excuse for insensitive treatment by the physicians. As widespread as the complaint is, physicians need to be more adept in responding to the sociopsychological dimensions of their patients, in addition to caring for their physical symptoms.

NOTE

1. Harbour folk refer to themselves as backward.

2

WHEN IS A MIDWIFE A WITCH? A CASE STUDY FROM A MODERNIZING MAYA VILLAGE

Betty B. Faust

A rural Maya village in Mexico is experiencing technological change. Part of the change is reflected in midwifery practices. In this region, traditionally there have been both male and female midwives. Government programs train only female midwives in Western[1] obstetrical practices. There are free village clinics in which a doctor is available most days. Women's preferences for midwives are discussed relative to the sociopsychological support, massage, and herbal knowledge midwives provide. Village perceptions that doctors are better able to save lives in the event of serious complications is tempered by concerns for female modesty and for the status differences between doctors and their patients. Traditional beliefs affect evaluation of both midwives and doctors. When a midwife's use of new methods was followed by the unexpected death of an apparently healthy newborn, a village evaluation process began to consider the possibility of witchcraft. The communication processes resulted in change in obstetric practice and choice of birth attendant.

About a modernizing midwife they said:

> You know, she has books. She reads things. She knows things. She sits there at night in her house and reads things. She must be a witch. She needed some bodies. That is why she killed the baby and tried to kill the mother. Only the mother is stronger and she's fighting it off. . . . You know, they say witches have a contract with the Devil. They just have to deliver a certain number, every so often. So many bodies they have to give him.

The midwife in question has been a participant in a Mexican government training program for traditional midwives. It is her practice of modern techniques, not traditional ones, that is associated with the suspicion that she may be a witch. Witchcraft suspicion surfaced after an apparently healthy newborn, whose birth she had attended, died several hours after birth.

21

ECONOMIC MODERNIZATION AND ORAL TRADITION

Here in Taj (a pseudonym), a village of fifteen hundred people in Southeast Mexico, traditional beliefs are strong, and modernization of production is occurring rapidly. The social structure is not egalitarian. The rich families (*ricos*) are more likely to include individuals of somewhat European appearance, which is referred to locally as *bonito* (pretty or handsome), but their predominantly Maya heritage is not denied. Many of the older men in these families still offer *zacá* (a traditional ritual beverage of corn and honey) to the local spirit-owners of the land, the *aluxes*, even before starting up their tractors to plant their hybrid corn with fertilizers. Some of them send their sons to school to become veterinarians, teachers, or engineers. Some of their daughters are becoming teachers and nurses. There are consanguineal, affinal, and fictive kinship bonds between these rich families and the poor ones in this town. Yet there is also a strong sense that the village *presidente* (mayor) should take care of everyone equally, and there is great resentment when he does not, although it is not expressed publicly.

In this modernizing Maya town, witches, miracles, spirit-beings, and the souls of the dead are all part of ordinary reality. Descriptions of experiences with these are told and received as ordinary, matter-of-fact, unsurprising occurrences. They do not happen every day, certainly, but they are not cause for great astonishment, nor are they a challenge to people's conception of reality. They are simply part of the real world. It is known that outsiders make fun of these things, but that is because they do not "know." Within the village, it is understood that miracles and witches exist side-by-side with tractors, television sets, and penicillin.

Suspicions that the *partera*, the traditional midwife, may be a witch follow the same pattern of communication as criticisms of the *presidente*. The fears are not shared with the doctor, nor are they aired in the town plaza, nor around the neighborhood stores where other gossip concerning family quarrels and romantic scandals is exhaustively discussed. Distrust of people like the mayor and the midwife, people in positions of power, is voiced only in very special circumstances, behind closed doors, in the family or with persons of *confianza* (confidence)—people in whom one can confide, trustworthy friends, tried-and-true. However, in the case of the modernizing midwife, these networks of private communication criss-crossed the village so completely that within a few months consensus had formed: the village had come to public judgment which was observable in behavioral change.

This case study is part of a larger research project which examines the interactions of economic modernization and oral traditions in a Maya village of Campeche, Mexico. Data for this case study were collected from May 1985 to September 1986 through participant observation and interviews. I have not attended a birth, since no one except the mother-in-law and the midwife normally attend, but after four different births I have been an accepted member of the group of women who surrounded the parents and the new baby with advice, sympathy, support, and care. Acceptance was probably facilitated by my age (42) and experience as a mother and grandmother. In addition, I was the only person in the village with a camera, and thus able to offer the valuable service of photographing the infants.[2]

The baby boy, who was expected to live, died less than twenty-four hours after birth. I attended the wake and the burial and three of the Maya ceremonies for the dead, which are repeated at given intervals. Interviews were conducted with the village doctor, the baby's mother, her mother, a retired midwife, and the baby's aunt, who was in charge of the traditional ceremonies, the *bixes*. The midwife involved had been interviewed previously about her practices.[3]

THEORETICAL ISSUES

This chapter describes village communication concerning the evaluation of care for mother and baby during the birthing process and the postpartum period. It shows that, from the point of view of the local people, the traditional midwife's use of modern medical technology contributed to the evaluation of her as a witch. This is the case despite their own utilization of and respect for the local medical clinic and the regional hospital and their increasing acceptance of the need to boil water for infants and young children in order to protect them from dysentery. Family planning has also been widely accepted in the village; two and three-child families are becoming the norm for people in their twenties.

The explanation offered for these apparent contradictions and for their eventual resolution in a combined system of birth care relies on concepts developed within the interpretive tradition in anthropology. This approach focuses on how traditional symbols are interpreted and used in transactions by actors seeking to fulfill their perceived needs (cf. Geertz 1973, 1983). The case for the explicit treatment of traditional medical beliefs and practices as a cultural system has been strongly presented by Kleinman (1980). Using this approach Tedlock (in press) has critiqued the existing literature on the hot-cold categorization of Latin American folk medicine. My research with midwives of the lowland Campeche Maya area is consistent with hers on traditional healers of the highland Guatemala Maya. In both cases the hot-cold classifications were not important concepts used in the medical system of the trained, traditional expert. Tedlock's descriptions of the difference between the knowledge of the community in general and that of the traditional expert are similar to the situation I found. This difference provides us with a means to understand the events described in this chapter; i.e., since the community does not "know" either medical system, it must rely on empirical assessment of the trustworthiness of practitioners. One part of confidence in an expert is the perceived effectiveness of his or her techniques and tools; another is assessment of moral character. The latter is critical since medical knowledge is power: power to cure or to kill. When we do not share the knowledge of the practitioner, we are placed in a dependent situation and must rely on our perceptions of their trustworthiness.

In this case study, analysis of the process through which traditional beliefs effected community action is modeled on a similar analysis by Gossen of a Chamula case (1986). Concepts embedded in oral tradition were used by the Chamula to assess Protestant missionary activity. Concepts of moral order encoded in the oral tradition redirected a gradually increasing course of change. Symbols from myth became action symbols in the hands of community leaders, affecting social transactions which resulted in the expulsion of Protestants from the community and the community's conversion to a local variant of Greek Orthodoxy.

Oral tradition is both a record of judgments concerning past events and a symbolic expression of the moral code which will judge new experiences with modernization. Traditional beliefs do not prevent or inhibit change per se; they channel it. These beliefs contain the society's underlying principles of jurisprudence (Gluckman 1965). They form the basis of public judgment (Yankelovich 1987) concerning social consequences and potential risks in the early stages of modernization. It is possible that this is also the case for the majority of the population in later stages as well (Horton 1967:103–6). Gmelch's analysis of "baseball magic" (1978) is a potent reminder of common uses of magic in our own society.

The use of witchcraft to explain the nonrational, larger-than-life reasons for events, particularly misfortunes, is well documented in the anthropological literature (e.g., Evans-Pritchard 1937; Bowen 1964; Kluckhohn 1962; Gluckman 1964; Mair 1969). Evans Pritchard's classic analysis of the functions of witchcraft in situations of illness and death applies to this case. As summarized in Gluckman:

> Beliefs in witchcraft explain why particular persons at particular times and places suffer particular misfortunes, accident, disease and so forth. Witchcraft as a theory of causation is concerned with the singularity of misfortune. . . . Witchcraft explains "why"; the "how" is answered by common sense empirical observation (1964:84, 85).

Thus, the unexpected death of an apparently healthy infant born after a normal labor had to be specifically explained. The traditional beliefs concerning witches' use of poisons and insertion of evil substances in order to cause death affected the evaluation of the injections the midwife gave the woman during labor.

Concepts developed by Douglas in *Purity and Danger* (1966) describe the sense of danger and pollution associated with the crossing of boundaries between conceptual categories. In the case of the midwife, the domains of

Western medicine and traditional midwifery have crossed. The midwife is now using techniques learned in a government training program as well as continuing some traditional practices. Following Douglas' model, we might expect that anxiety concerning the midwife's competence would focus on those practices she has taken from another domain, that of Western medicine. In addition, her status as a midwife makes her particularly vulnerable to accusations of witchcraft. Douglas specifically discusses the perinatal state as "marginal and undefinable" and observes that suspicions of witchcraft are most likely to occur in "symbolically ambiguous and inarticulate" areas, in the "non-structure" (1966:95, 102).

Oral traditions are used in the village evaluation of all available alternatives. Although this evaluation is expressed in symbolic forms foreign to the modern world, these forms are pragmatic attempts to evaluate what techniques and which caregiver is most appropriate for what type of health problem. The local conceptual scheme may not separate experience into objective and subjective, nor separate analytic techniques into rational and intuitive as does modern university culture. Types of analysis and descriptions of observed events are integrated through a dialectic process within an objective/subjective, rational/ intuitive, holistic system (Tedlock 1982). Understanding the differences in analytic framework, communication style, and symbolism allows us to understand the processes involved both in the evolution of an eclectic practice of obstetrics and in the suspicions of witchcraft which surfaced in the case.

THE MIDWIFE AS A WITCH

The baby was born without complications, healthy, large, beautiful, and died ten hours later on the way to the hospital. Was the midwife therefore a witch? Some women thought so. Most of the evidence they considered important was not associated with her traditional methods, but rather with her use of techniques and material from a government program to improve the practice of midwifery in rural areas. Yet no one expressed the slightest doubt about the importance of taking the baby to the city hospital, if only they had been able to get there in time. This is not a simple case of distrust of Western medicine. These people are in the process of adopting many practices of the modern world, but they chose those practices which the midwife had adopted from the government program as indications that she is a witch. From the villagers' point of view, she is anomalous, belonging to two categories at once. She is neither purely one nor the other. She is therefore an entity who should, according to Douglas' model, be seen as dangerous. The potential to see her that way was there. The unexpected death of an apparently healthy newborn triggered the suspicion: perhaps she is a witch.

Evaluation of the midwife included assessment of the possibility that the baby might have simply died of natural causes. This was not considered likely for the following explicit reasons: the mother had three previous, normal births; there were no unusual symptoms during the pregnancy; labor and delivery were normal; the baby was large, strong, and apparently healthy; and there were no problems in the first hours after birth.

The events leading to the death were carefully reviewed. Several hours after birth the baby began to complain without stopping. Some say he died from so much complaining. The family finally decided to take him to the doctor, even though they could see no reason for his complaining. It was fiesta time, still Christmas vacation for the rural doctors who go home to their own families in the cities. Since there was no doctor in Taj, the family borrowed a truck and took the baby to the woman doctor in the next town. This doctor said that she could not help them because they needed special equipment and oxygen. She sent them to the nearest city.

About five kilometers outside of the city, the baby died after they went over a bump in the road. "He vomited yellow stuff and died right after the bump." This detail was repeated in every telling of the story of the baby's death. Repetition of detail seems to reflect a general, understandable belief that any of the events immediately preceding a death may have caused it and therefore deserve to be preserved in memory and carefully examined. The women said that probably the "yellow stuff" was poison. Someone remembered that the color of the injection that the midwife had given the mother the night before was yellow. "That witch probably tried to poison both of them, but the mother is bigger and she's fighting it off. Everybody knows it takes poison a while to work." This explained why the baby appeared fine and then became ill.

Consideration of the possibility of witchcraft continued. It was said that the midwife used to live with a man from somewhere else and that he was strange. "He probably taught her these things [i.e., specific techniques in witchcraft]." They used to quarrel, and one day, they say, "He shot her in the hip with his gun. That is why she limps. She got him though. She poisoned him." This is the consensus among the women. The conversation continued with comments to the effect that when the midwife, Doña Sus, was attending this birth she would not use *hierba buena*, the name for the local variety of mint, nor *ruda*, a local variety of rue. She would not use tobacco leaves either. All of these plants traditionally relieve the discomforts and pain associated with labor and delivery. She said, "We do not need those things any more. The injection is better." Doña Sus then gave the mother the injection. She has not rejected all traditional practices, however. For eight to fifteen days after the birth, she continues doing the traditional massage and binding which is believed to reposition and secure the mother's bones and internal organs so that she may resume her normal work.[4] She uses herbs for other forms of curing, but in childbirth she has come to believe that this shot has replaced the need for other, traditional treatments.

The day after the wake the father's family took the mother to the hospital in the city. She was still bleeding badly and had a fever. After the birth, she had received from her mother-in-law traditional treatments for pain with tobacco leaves, and for healing with rue.[5] The tobacco is a native, local variety which is said to be good for the relief of postpartum pain (Furst 1976). Rue is frequently used in curing because of its pleasant smell, reputed medicinal qualities, and its symbolic associations. The small green leaves of this herb emerge from the tips of its branches in the form of a cross. The color green is associated with the vertical direction, one of the five cardinal directions of the three-dimensional Maya cosmology. The cross is a symbolic representation of those directions and of the sacred tree which connects the celestial world with the underworld. The winds of the four directions are potential causes of illness and are propitiated in traditional curing rituals, as well as being propitiated in times of drought, for they also bring the rains. Orientation with the cosmos is important to the maintenance of health in traditional Maya thought, as it is in the iconography of ancient Maya civilization (Tedlock 1984).

An additional herbal symbolism was used in the attempts to cure the mother at home. A cross of green maguey leaves was placed under her bed, and another on her front door. The latter serves as both a religious symbol and as a sign to the community that a person in the family is very ill and only close kin should visit. Maguey and rue, as green crosses, have reference to the religiously understood world and are not unlike the crucifixes hung above the beds of the sick in hospital rooms. These visual symbols, along with the communications involved in the traditional massage, may be symbolic means of curing which access somatic levels through emotional transference, as discussed by Dow (1986).

The mother's hemorrhaging did not stop, and the village doctor had not returned from vacation. It was time to take her to the city hospital. It was expected that her in-laws would take her to the hospital, to find someone with her blood type or find the money to buy blood, and to choose the doctor and hospital and pay for the treatment.

It was after the mother was taken to the hospital that we buried the baby, at sunset. After the burial we returned to the father's brother's house where the wake had been held. Subdued talk about the midwife continued among three local women who had had children and me. One of these women who had had complications in labor had received a similar injection from her attending midwife, yet there was no suspicion of witchcraft in her case. That midwife, following traditional lines of communication, received permission from the laboring woman's husband and in-laws to administer the drug, and both baby and mother survived. On the other hand, Doña Sus, the midwife in this case, was suspected of giving an unnecessary drug to a woman in normal labor without first consulting the woman's kin group. Since she had been drinking as part of a fiesta, it was believed she gave the injection in order to speed up the labor so that she could return to the celebration with her family. Questions of ethics and judgment were involved in this interpretation.

Suspicions about the midwife being a witch did not lead to confrontation or any official action; however, the evaluation of her services did result in changes in behavior. In the months that followed this incident, news of it unofficially spread throughout the village. Initially upper- and middle-class families (by local standards), like the one whose baby died, did not go to this midwife for help with childbirth. Gradually the more marginal, poorer families also became reluctant to come to her for help with childbirth. The other official (government-trained) midwife in town encouraged her patients to go to the clinic for help with the birth itself out of fear that she, too, would be seen as a witch. During this period a new doctor, married to the daughter of a relatively wealthy, local family, came to town. He charged for his services (according to his own sliding scale) but was willing to come to people's homes to attend childbirth. The mother-in-law and other close female relatives could be in attendance with him. As the husband of a local woman he was not seen as a threat on a social level. He permitted the traditional massage and the use of herbs by the older women, some of whom had been midwives. He was also in a position to arrange transportation to the city hospital in emergencies. His services came to be greatly valued. The midwife suspected of being a witch continued to serve the community, as did the second government-trained midwife, both assisting with conditions not as potentially dangerous as childbirth. The poorer women continued seeing them for help with prolapsed uteri, massage and binding, herbs to encourage conception, and the like. These changes in village behavior have substantially affected midwives' earning power, although they continue to practice.

According to the ex-midwife I interviewed most extensively (one who had never gone to a government training program), there was always the fear that people would think a midwife was a witch. Perhaps it is a little like worrying about a malpractice suit but without the insurance. The midwives' charges for services may reflect that risk. They charged ten thousand pesos for a delivery in March 1986; this was equivalent to eight days of work for the average man in Taj. Midwives charged only one to two hundred pesos, however, for a massage session. Midwives who have not gone to the training programs are no longer willing to take the risks involved in attending childbirth, a defining characteristic of the term midwife (*partera, -o*). They are no longer called midwives, but everyone knows which of the women know how to do massage and binding. They continue to provide services, as do their male colleagues who were never given the opportunity to attend the training courses. They are referred to as "former" *parteras*, or *parteros*, and continue to give prenatal and postnatal care for a fee. What may be lost is knowledge of how to position the fetus during labor and delivery without resorting to a cesarean. Doctors do not allow this practice, seeing it as dangerous. I would propose that it might be useful to empirically ascertain if in fact this positioning might reduce the need for cesareans.

Whether the massage works through physiological processes to reduce tension, fear, and resulting tension in the birth canal is unknown. It seems reasonable that the massage can reposition the fetus. It is possible that the herbs used have pain-reducing properties. It is also possible, following Dow's (1986) work on universal aspects of symbolic healing, that the ritual of the massage and the symbolic aspects of the herbs are communication systems capable of accessing unconscious mechanisms which control somatic functioning.

TRADITIONAL BIRTH ATTENDANTS, THEIR TRAINING AND THEIR TECHNIQUES.

Before the baby died and the community began to see the midwife as a witch, I had an interview with the clinic doctor. He explained why, at that time, many village women preferred to pay the local midwife for help with the birth although the clinic was free and they attended the clinic for prenatal visits. In his words, it was a question of "*verguenza, pudor*" roughly translated as "shame, female modesty." This was not meant as shame in the North American sense, but shame in the Mediterranean sense. Women were embarrassed to have a strange man look at them "there," and besides, their husbands were jealous. The doctor did not know that in this area there are male traditional birth attendants, called "parteros," and that women express no sense of shame in visiting them.

The doctor was not alone in his ignorance; other local professionals were also unaware that some traditional birth attendants are male. I was surprised to find this practice since the existence of male *parteros* in the Maya area has not been previously reported in the anthropological literature, indeed male midwives are relatively unknown worldwide.[6]

My consultants did not think of male midwives as particularly unusual, although it was acknowledged that they were not nearly as common as female ones. Several male midwives in the local area were remembered; one is a kinsman of my adopted family. I was told to go see him if I had problems with my uterus. It is commonly understood that all women who have had children may have problems with the position of the uterus. I have interviewed this man and he says he worked as a *partero* when his wife was alive to help him as assistant. I asked if she was the *partera* and he was her assistant, thinking I had misunderstood him. No, he was the *partero* and she was his assistant. Other local consultants corroborated this. He was the one who knew how to assist with the birth, who actually repositioned the baby when necessary.

The local traditional healer, the *hmen*, told me in a taped interview about his father's work both as a *hmen* (shaman) and as a *partero*. His father taught him, but he no longer does this work, except with his wife. He says the doctors have forbidden it. He is quite critical of Western obstetrics, especially of cesareans and of the overprescribing of vitamins, which he sees as connected. Vitamins given in excess "spill over" from the mother to the baby in her womb. This causes the baby to grow too large to fit through her pelvic opening, since the mother reached adulthood without vitamins and thus is relatively small. Cesareans and tubal ligations cause women to have internal scars which weaken them and give them pain. This makes it difficult to do their traditional work which requires substantial physical exertion. Work is locally considered essential for human health. Anything which interferes with a person's capacity to work further predisposes that person to ill health.

The shaman's beliefs concerning Western obstetrics are reasonable deductions based on observed realities. They do not reflect a general antagonism toward Western medicine. They were explained to me during the course of a bus trip he was making to the city pharmacy to buy asthma medication for his wife; he said that it works better for her than any of the herbal cures he has been able to find. Survey questionnaires of medical histories and medical examinations of scientifically constructed samples might prove useful to test empirically his hypotheses concerning Western obstetric practice in the Campeche Maya area.

On another level, it is important to understand why a population of women who traditionally felt no sense of shame in front of a male midwife do so in front of a male doctor. I suggest that this sense of shame has to do with the well known history of Latin males' exploitation of Indian women (e.g., De la Fuente 1967:444; Farriss 1984:106; and Paz 1961:79—88). It is suggested that this historical reality has informed Maya oral tradition, which cautions women concerning associations with male strangers. Village women express apprehension and caution concerning the approach of any male stranger. Within the connotations provided by Maya oral tradition, it is not possible for a woman to allow a male stranger even to converse with her without arousing doubts as to her intentions. His are assumed to be predatory, especially if he differs greatly in social class, power, or ethnic background from her family. Although some exceptions are made for doctors, permitting genital contact is clearly problematic.

The typical village doctor is a recent graduate of medical school doing his mandated year of social service in the countryside. He is a young man away from family, from parents, from wife and/or girlfriend, who are all back in the city. His intentions toward young village women are suspect, while at the same time he is an object of fantasy for these young women. The village assesses this situation as a potentially dangerous one.[7]

The degree to which the village worries about, gossips about, and attempts to control this situation is initially somewhat difficult to understand for those of us who came of age in the sixties or later in the United States. An example may convey the local reality. A few months before I arrived in Taj, a daughter of a local family who is a nurse was rejected by her fiancé because of her association with the doctor with whom she worked in a nearby town clinic. The fiancé had been spying on her through the clinic windows and one day saw the doctor put his arm around her shoulders and give her a quick hug. Whether this was a comradely gesture of caring for a member of the team or something more was never determined, nor even asked. The gesture was enough; the engagement was off. It was feared by this young woman's friends and family that she would never marry as a result of the implications of this for her reputation. Such incidents confirm and contribute to the oral tradition of suspicion of male strangers, thus women avoid male doctors for obstetric and gynecological care. Doctors should be made aware in their training programs that their social behavior affects local acceptance of their medical services and may have devastating affects on their assistants. Reluctance to accept the doctor's examinations or help with childbirth may be publicly explained to the doctor in terms familiar to his Latin cultural concepts of shame and honor, but the social realities are more complex.

Prenatal visits in the village clinic do not include a pelvic examination because doctors believe that women are afraid of them and will not come in at all if they are required. Therefore, it is common that a woman facing her first birth has never had an internal examination, although she has normally had prenatal care in the clinic. In their training programs midwives are taught to bring their patients to the local clinic for prenatal consultations. These include advice concerning nutrition, dangers of alcohol and tobacco use to the fetus, monthly weighing to supervise weight gain, analysis of urine, and monitoring of pulse and blood pressure.

During her pregnancy the woman continues to visit the TBA for abdominal massage, on a monthly basis (from the third month) or whenever suffering from discomfort. The common complaints of pregnancy (indigestion, heartburn, constipation, nausea, water retention) are treated by the TBA with home remedies which are approved as harmless by the doctor. Between eight and fifteen days after the birth, TBAs do the traditional massage and binding described above. In addition, the TBAs can put back a fallen womb (prolapsed uterus) and know which herbs to use for those who have trouble getting pregnant. If, on the other hand, a woman does not wish to get pregnant, that currently requires the specialties of the doctor and the clinic.[8] Midwives are trained to bring their clients to the clinic for information concerning various methods of family planning, as well as for prenatal visits. When the doctor was asked about the indigenous practices of massage and binding and treatments for fallen wombs, he responded that massage and binding are physically harmless and perhaps psychologically reassuring, but fallen wombs should be corrected surgically.

My visit with the midwife of this case study, Doña Sus, occurred before the death of the baby which was ascribed to her. The visit began with a description of the treatment for fallen womb, which she had just given the patient who was leaving as I arrived.[9] She told me that sometimes fallen wombs require surgery. They are caused by doctors and by traditional birth attendants who are in a hurry and give "that shot" (*sic*). This would seem a clear indication that she was aware of the potential harm done by the shot she herself later gave in the case described in this chapter.

The interview with Doña Sus included a discussion of childbirth. She knows how to move the baby, to change its position within the womb if necessary, but now believes it is better to take the mother for an operation (i.e., a cesarean), when possible, if repositioning is required. She says that her government training program taught her not to attempt to reposition the fetus as she could be held responsible for its death. Before there was a village clinic and a highway enabling people to reach the city hospital in three hours, the midwife had to position the fetus herself. In one instance the baby's arm had come out first and had to be put back in. This was accomplished by using her hand to push the baby's arm back up inside the womb. Then the baby had to be turned by skillful abdominal massage so that the head could emerge. Another time the baby's feet were on either side of the mother's "bone," and the midwife had to pull both feet out and tie them together, push them back in, and turn the baby around so that the head was down. The baby is turned by external massage of the abdomen. These manipulations of the fetus are talked about as common practices.

One consultant told me about the terrible pain she experienced after one such birth, pain so severe she could not put her legs together for days but lay in her hammock with legs apart, knees bent. Despite her clear memory of terrible pain, she is very glad that there were no doctors[10] in those days, because if there had been they would have ". . . cut me up, and then I would probably be useless like my daughter-in-law. Those doctors would have cut me up and left big, big scars." They might even have killed her! There are frequent complaints of disabling pain due to cesareans and tubal ligations. It is not known if this results from some problem with abdominal surgery as performed in the rural medical system or with the psychological insecurities women have about these operations. Fears expressed by the grandmothers and complaints by other mothers do not, however, prevent women from having these operations, when they are believed to be needed.

In this region, traditional birth attendants (TBAs) include both male and female midwives. Only the female traditional birth attendants have been invited to attend government training programs. As well as the midwife, Doña Sus, could remember, her government training program for midwifery lasted two to three weeks; that for birth control, two to three weekends. At the end of the training program, the midwives are governmentally licensed to practice and receive a certificate. Literacy is not a requirement for the program, since the government is aware that many traditional midwives are not literate.

In addition to the training program, the government provides a free village clinic where pregnant women are encouraged to visit the doctor for prenatal care. Villagers value techniques and medicines of both the traditional and the Western systems and seek to use elements of both, in the situations they feel appropriate and with practitioners they feel are trustworthy.

According to the village doctor, the government training programs for midwives are designed to give these birth attendants a better understanding of the physiology of the birth process as understood by Western medical science, to teach them basic hygienic practices to reduce the incidence of infection, and to give them some medications for use in emergencies which do not allow time to reach a doctor. He said that government-trained midwives are competent to handle a normal birth and in case of complications are to refer the pregnant woman to the local clinic, doctor, or hospital. The midwife is provided with the following equipment to use during labor and birth:

1 pair of rubber gloves
2 clamps for the umbilical cord
1 pair of scissors for cutting the cord
string for tying the umbilical cord
1 rubber bulb with nozzle for removing mucous from the nose and throat of the
    newborn
sterile gauzes
medication for pain: *dipirona* (a type of analgesic not used in the U.S. because
    of its toxic properties; it is made in Mexico for local sale, according to a
    doctor in the city) and *ápido apetyl salicílico* (aspirin)
medication for uterine involution after birth of the placenta: *oxytocina* (oxytocin)

The oxytocin injection is a synthetic hormone, one of whose brand names is Ergotrate Maleate. *The Physician's Desk Reference* gives the following contraindications:

Ergotrate Maleate is contraindicated for the induction of labor. . . . Because of the high uterine tone produced, this drug is not recommended for routine use prior to the delivery of the placenta unless the operator is versed in the techniques described . . . and has adequate facilities and personnel at his disposal (1976:941).

Midwives are told not to use it prior to delivery; however, according to a village doctor, they logically infer that something which increases the strength of contractions after birth will also increase the force of contractions prior to birth, thus speeding delivery. The possible effects on the fetus may not have been explained to them in a manner they understand. However, my prior interview with Doña Sus indicated that she had at least been told that this shot could contribute to the mother's risk of having a prolapsed uterus. Whether or not she entirely believed it is another matter.

The village doctor said that he saw no negligence involved in the midwife's management of the birth of the baby who died. He was new in the area and perhaps did not want to jeopardize his relationship with the residents of Taj, and it is also possible he did not want to discuss the possibility with a researcher from the United States. As a Western-trained doctor, he dismissed any ideas of witchcraft. He stated that unforeseen postpartum complications caused the baby's death and that pieces of unexpelled placenta caused the mother's uterine infection and blood loss.

Later in the city I discussed the case anonymously and in confidence with a pediatrician, an obstetrician, and a general practitioner who has experience in rural medicine. From these conversations, the following medical interpretation of the baby's death emerged. The shot was possibly given before the fetus had descended in the birth canal. The oxytocin given in the injection results in an initial prolonged and intense contraction of the uterus, which is followed by other strong contractions. These intensified contractions could have cut off the blood supply from the placenta to the fetus, causing fetal distress due to oxygen insufficiency. Fetal distress commonly results in the release of meconium into the amniotic fluid and can also result in the fetus attempting to breathe prematurely. The inhalation of meconium can introduce bacteria to the lungs resulting in the development of a lung infection. Breathing difficulties could occur hours after birth, producing labored, distressed breathing, locally interpreted as "complaining." This series of events may have occurred with the baby who died but cannot now be proven.

In this village, a combination of traditional and Western technologies is being used. Perceptions of a local midwife as a witch, which resulted from her (possible) misuse of an injection provided in a government training program, have contributed to the preference for a locally trusted doctor's care. Acceptance of a doctor as a birth attendant thus is not village rejection of traditional techniques as necessarily inferior in themselves but rather a reflection of village evaluation of the relative safety of alternative practitioners available to them. Given the choice of including as much as possible of the traditional technologies of care with the perceived greater safety of the Western-trained doctor's care in emergency cases, they choose the combination. Ideally they would prefer that the doctor allow the midwife to try positioning the fetus, in the hope that this would avoid resort to a cesarean. However, once having chosen the doctor as an attendant, the traditional technology of positioning the fetus is no longer an option. Yet this is balanced by an appreciation of the other technologies, medicines, and facilities which the doctor can provide: stronger medications for severe pain; forceps; and access to the hospital with its resources, including blood and oxygen. These things are believed to increase chances of survival for mother and baby in difficult childbirth situations.

That the doctor permits massage, binding, and herbal remedies is greatly appreciated, since villagers have found nothing more effective in Western medicine with which to replace them as aids in normal childbirth. The strong medicine of the doctor is seen as potentially harmful, as having some risks associated with it, while at the same time being often effective in cases where all else has failed and death is imminent.

PREFERENCE FOR TRADITIONAL MIDWIVES: POLICY IMPLICATIONS.

Some Western medical practices are adopted because they are perceived to be more effective than traditional ones, however, some are adopted because of the influence of other factors. While Western obstetrics may result in a decreased mortality rate for childbirth compared to midwifery by either government-trained or traditional midwives, it still may be the case that in the traditional system there is knowledge of effective techniques such as massage, herbal medicines, and manual positioning of the fetus which could be important contributions to obstetrical science, were it not for the Western medical bias against the empirically based knowledge embedded in traditional medical systems.

Certain aspects of this case have a bearing on theories concerning motivation for the use of traditional birth attendants when doctors are available (Velimirovic and Velimirovic 1981). One reason frequently given for the popularity of traditional midwives has been that they are female (Sukkary 1981; Schwarz 1981). However, some traditional birth attendants in Taj have been male. This has always been the case here, according to my consultants. In addition, in two of the neighboring towns there are clinics with female doctors, one of whom resides in Taj. Thus the preference for midwives cannot be a tradition-based preference for a female helper in this culture.

Another explanation for the popularity of the traditional helpers has been that they are less expensive. But in Taj the services of the medical doctor and nurse in the village clinic are free, while the midwives charge ten thousand pesos, which is more than the average agricultural worker can earn in eight days. Despite the expense, the fears that the midwives may be witches, and the fact that some of the midwives are male, women continued to prefer their traditional birth attendants, except in cases involving serious complications. This preference changed in response to the case history analyzed here.

CONCLUSION

This chapter concludes that the traditional techniques, together with the emotional support received from the continuous presence of the midwife, are the primary positive motivations for this preference. These techniques include: (1) the use of herbs to relieve the discomforts of pregnancy, labor, and delivery; (2) massage of the abdomen, done monthly after the third month (or moon) of pregnancy to position the fetus; (3) abdominal massage during labor, to ease contractions and correct any problem with the position of the fetus; (4) manual reinsertion of the fetus' arms or legs which have emerged prior to the head (followed by massage to correct positioning) so that normal birth may occur and a cesarean be avoided; and (5) massage which is done eight to fifteen days after birth in order to reposition bones loosened in the birth process, and binding which is kept in place for the following forty days of recuperation.

The oral tradition affects decision making and evaluation of both doctors and midwives. Medical training programs for traditional midwives and for rural doctors need to teach students the importance of studying the beliefs of their clients since these beliefs will certainly be real in their consequences and may result in tragic communication errors, potentially involving program failure or intense hostility directed at practitioners.

Understanding many of the biases and shortcomings of Western medicine, many Western-trained Mexican doctors reserve judgment concerning traditional practices and treat them with respect. This attitude of constructive skepticism is well supported by evolving theory concerning the sociology of knowledge and may contribute improvements to the training program. It might also contribute to improvement of obstetric practice in very developed countries. It may be that traditional Maya massage can correctly position the fetus for the birth process in many cases. It may also be true that prenatal vitamins should be given in smaller amounts so that the fetus is not too large for the pelvic opening, in cases where the mother is small. At the same time, it is probably the case that many problem births cannot be avoided by either of those approaches and will result in maternal and/or infant deaths unless there is recourse to Western medical facilities. Therefore, all possible efforts should be made to make such medical care available and to avoid communication problems which result in misunderstandings and underuse of available facilities. At the same time, improvements could perhaps be made in surgical procedures in order to lessen the risk of adhesions and other complications which cause long-term discomfort and disabilities.

Currently many villages are often without doctors two or three days a week. A system of accountability could perhaps be instituted since many government employees stationed in rural areas (not just doctors, but school teachers and agricultural technicians as well) find it difficult to wait until Friday afternoon to leave and to return Sunday night or early Monday morning, from families in the city. Doctors working in village clinics perhaps could be encouraged to bring their wives and children with them. Provisions might be made for relief by other qualified doctors, so that a doctor would be available at all times. Encouraging doctors to study the local village culture might help them become more comfortable and more appreciative of the people they are to serve. In addition, explicitly teaching midwives to both value their traditional knowledge and incorporate some new knowledge might result in a greater improvement in medical care than either alone.[11]

NOTES

This 1985–86 research project was funded by a grant from the Shell Foundation. The 1985 preliminary study was made possible by a grant from the Benevolent Fund of the State University of New York, Albany. The author wishes to express her gratitude for these grants; for the support of her family, friends, colleagues; and for the assistance of the Centro de Investigaciones Históricos y Sociales of the Universidad Autónoma del Sureste which generously made available research facilities throughout the period of field work. She would also like to thank the municipal president of Campeche, the honorable Mr. José Medina Maldonado and family; his personal secretary, Mr. José Aranda Alpuche and family; her Mexican colleagues: the anthropologists Dr. Juan Manuel Sandoval Palacios and Mr. Abel Morales Lopez; the pediatrician Dr. Santiago Gonzales Ambrosio and family, and the obstetrician Dr. Manuel Gantús Castro; and her American/Canadian colleagues, anthropologists Dr. William J. Folan and his wife Lynda Florey. There are many others who cannot be named without jeopardizing the anonymity of Taj. Finally, she would very much like to thank Dr. Susan Wadley, Dr. Bruce Derr, and Dr. Barbara Tedlock for their helpful suggestions. The author acknowledges sole responsibility for any errors.

1. The term "Western medicine" is used in this chapter to denote the system of medical science which has developed in the United States and those countries which share the broad outlines of that cultural tradition. It is used for the sake of consistency in the book; however, its use in Latin America is clearly problematic. Since many traditional elements of folk medicine in Latin America are of European origin (coming from Spanish folk customs), to contrast Western with traditional is misleading and gives the impression that: (1) Latin American folk medicine is entirely indigenous, and (2) all people in Western Europe believe in, accept, use, and understand the medical system which has evolved in response to scientific research of the last two centuries. Neither of these implied assumptions is true. In addition, to hold that Latin America is other than Western is equally problematic. It is as far west geographically as the United States and just as much a former colony of a Western European country.

2. Photographing infants carries far greater significance than would be expected. The use of photographs of deceased family members on the family altar has become incorporated as a traditional component of the Maya ceremony (*bix*) which honors the dead with special dishes, beverages, flowers, candles, and incense. It is preferable to have a photograph of the person taken before death. In one case, I was asked to photograph a baby who was thought to be dying. In another, I was asked during a wake to photograph the baby who had died.

3. I did not attempt to interview her again since my own anomalous status within the community made me feel vulnerable to charges of witchcraft, and the principle of guilt by association had been made quite clear to me (cf. Bowen 1964:246–63).

4. The binding serves as a kind of brace, holding her in the right position while she gradually takes on her normal household duties, which were temporarily assumed by her mother-in-law and sisters-in-law. The binding is kept in place for forty days. The massage and binding practiced in Taj is the same as that described in detail for the Yucatec Maya by Fuller and Jordan (1981).

5. It is the mother-in-law who is expected to care for a woman before, during, and after childbirth because of the patrilocal tradition of residence. Older women have a great deal of knowledge about home remedies and only call in the midwife for specific skilled services: birthing, massage, binding, and herbal treatments for complications which do not respond to home remedies.

6. There are two aspects of Maya culture which may be seen as supportive of male midwives. One is that other specialties of the Maya curing tradition are practiced by both men and women. For example, daykeepers, the shamanic healers of the highlands, may be either male or female (Tedlock 1982). Second, the separation between male and female spheres in the Maya culture is not rigid. A number of local men fondly and proudly recalled having been the only available assistant when their wives had given birth. Elmendorf's discussion of midwifery in Chan Kom makes it clear that the husband was supposed to be present and assist with childbirth (1976). My own observations of intrafamily joking and discussions of health problems revealed no sense of separate, gendered spheres of medical or physiological knowledge. Men and women of the same extended family discussed together problems of childbirth, menarche, menstruation, breastfeeding, and the like. There is no apparent sense of shame or modesty in discussions within the family nor even with the local *hmen* (shamanic healer).

7. A rather large literature concerning the psychological consequences for women patients of being seduced by their doctors has been published during the last ten years in the United States. Codes of professional ethics, legal cases, and classes in medical schools are mechanisms which are being used to try to correct this problem. Village fears may thus be seen as realistic rather than as the result of ignorance, backwardness, or mistrust of the modern world.

8. According to one older male consultant, traditional birth control involved abstinence during the waning phase of the moon (after full moon) and for forty days after the binding which occurred between the eighth and the fifteenth postpartum days. Prolonged nursing of infants was understood to prevent conception in most women. In addition to the above, a middle-age male consultant insisted that in his parents' time, ". . . men were more considerate of their wives and their children and did not have as many children. They controlled themselves [se controlaron]. They did not just grab [agarrar] their wives whenever they felt like it." This implies some acceptance of abstinence as a means of family planning.

9. In that early interview, Doña Sus told me that to treat a fallen womb that is inflamed, she soaks rags in water boiled with castor oil pods. They must be clean, white rags, or course. The protruding part of the womb is soaked until the swelling goes down. Then, it is pushed gently back up again. The woman's abdomen is wrapped and bound as in the process described for postpartum care by Fuller and Jordan (1981). The woman is to stay in her hammock for eight days and not lift anything heavy. If the womb begins to descend, the woman should go back to the partera. After eight days, the binding is removed for massage and then replaced. The woman is to stay bound for forty days and be very careful. After this treatment, she is never again to lift anything heavy.

10. The words "doctor" and "doctora" are locally used only for those who have been the recipients of Western medical training.

11. This etic analysis of implications of the case for health care policy was developed in consultation with Mexican physicians trained in local medical schools, some of whom had also received part of their training in the United States.

3

LA EDAD CRITICA: THE POSITIVE EXPERIENCE OF MENOPAUSE IN A SMALL PERUVIAN TOWN

Elyse Ann Barnett

Postmenopausal women living in Puente Piedre, Peru were observed and interviewed concerning their perceptions of their role, status, and satisfaction with their lives. In challenge to the Western medical and psychological stereotypes of the "empty-nest syndrome" and negative views of menopausal women, Barnett found most of these women to be relatively satisfied with their current situation. This satisfaction is linked to several sociocultural factors, including the cultural recognition of adulthood, generally only granted to women and men over forty, and the end of the daily, direct responsibility of caring for their biological children, accompanied by the satisfaction of filling the role of grandmother. In addition, role satisfaction achieved earlier in life as a mother or worker is internalized as part of these women's identity and contributes positively to their current sense of well-being.

Explanation of women's experiences of menopause traditionally has focused on the importance of role and status at midlife. The designs of prior studies have been motivated by observations of sociocultural changes typical in the United States that commonly affect middle-aged women. Because women in the United States generally reach menopause when their children are leaving home, they face an "empty nest" (Spence and Lonner 1971; Lowenthal et al. 1975). At the same time, they frequently lose the status and prestige that Western culture reserves for its young (Silverman 1967; Flint 1975; Freedman, Kaplan, and Sadock 1976). Several anthropologists have concluded that the negative consequences of menopause might more accurately reflect these unfavorable sociocultural changes than any physiological changes associated with aging (Deykin et al. 1966; Flint 1975; Van Keep 1976). No hypothesis to explain the relationship between specific female roles and statuses at middle age and women's symptoms and emotional distresses at menopause has gone unchallenged.

40

My own research in Peru (1986) suggests that the wide variation in women's responses to menopause might be explained by identity continuity theory. Stated briefly, this theory suggests that persons who have found satisfaction in their principal life role continue to identify with that role, despite any changes in role performance. Identity continuity theory evolved from work by Atchley (1971) on "successful" retirement among men. Atchley found that men who were satisfied with their previous work role continued to identify with that role, even after retirement. Thus, a happily retired railroad worker referred to himself as a "railroad worker" many years after he last actively performed in that role. However, a railroad worker who had no sense of satisfaction with his work accomplishments saw himself as a "retired man" with no sense of identity with his former work role.

In many societies, the role of homemaker is not an option for men. Unlike men, however, some women can choose between the role of traditional mother or that of a worker outside of the home. Others must work outside the home due to economic necessity. Like men, women's sense of satisfaction with their principal life role might give them a continuing identity in the face of possible role changes. It may be that, like men, women who are not satisfied with their accomplishments in their principal life roles at menopause or retirement are less likely ever to view themselves as successful. Individuals who have not considered themselves successful in their principal life role attempt to maintain a tenuous role identity by continuing to perform various tasks. Thus, even in societies in which women's roles are active and continuous throughout their lives, women who are not satisfied in their principal life roles at the onset of menopause are less likely to experience well-being during the climacteric years.

Identity continuity theory, supported by my recent research in Peru (1986), may be important in determining the effects of the presence, absence, or loss of various roles to women during middle age. The theory may be equally useful for explaining the contradictory findings on factors which might affect women's well-being at menopause, specifically the empty nest syndrome and outside work.

THE NATURE OF MENOPAUSE: PSYCHOLOGICAL THEORIES

In the United States, explanations of the negative consequences of menopause have focused on involutional psychosis and the empty nest syndrome; until the present decade, involutional psychosis was an internationally recognized label used to describe the "mental disorder of midlife transition," which primarily affected menopausal women (Freedman, Kaplan, and Sadock 1976). Recognition of involutional psychosis, which was characterized by depression and accompanying somatic complaints, evolved from Freudian psychoanalysis. Helene Deutsch, a protégé of Freud, asserted that menopause was "narcissistic mortification" for women (1945). Deutsch believed that a woman's sense of worth was tied to reproduction, and that loss of fertility was synonymous with "partial death." The term *involutional psychosis* was dropped from the psychiatric nomenclature in 1980 (APA 1980). Middle-aged women who experienced difficulties with the transition to non-reproductive years were no longer labelled as "mentally ill." If women experienced a depression at midlife, it was not considered to be clinically different from depressions which affect women at other ages.

The depression associated with menopause is now commonly called the "empty nest syndrome." This term refers specifically to the difficulties women encounter when their children leave home to go to college, gain employment, or get married. Unlike involutional psychosis, empty-nest syndrome has never been sanctioned as a psychiatric term (APA 1980). Nonetheless, the phrase is used widely by both professionals and the general population. It emphasizes the loss of the mothering role over any other losses faced by middle-aged women.

Alternative theories to explain the consequences of maternal role loss among middle-aged women have been proposed. Erikson (1969) refers to the years surrounding menopause as a period of "generativity versus stagnation." He states, "all human beings need to be needed," and this desire often translates into productivity. When women are not needed, they may become so preoccupied with self as to preclude growth. The inherent threat of the empty nest is clear: women who are no longer needed by their children may stagnate and become pathologically self-absorbed.

Other investigators of human behavior suggest that psychomotor energy is released at the time women relinquish traditional maternal functions (Benedek 1950; Prados 1967). If this new energy is not used in creative pursuits, it becomes the source of neurotic behaviors and misery. Prados believes that "ego maturity and stability," rather than any new symbiotic relationships, maintain the woman's sense of identity. He suggests that women who are able to enjoy pursuits outside of mothering can escape the negative consequences of the empty nest.

In addition to loss of fertility and of the maternal role, women's variable responses to menopause traditionally have been attributed to the presence or absence of alternative roles at midlife, particularly roles involving outside work (Maoz et al. 1978). Women with employment away from the home are thought to have various advantages over women whose prior undivided attention was focused on mothering (Deykin et al. 1966; Jacobson and Klerman 1966). Dennerstein and Burrows (1978) suggested that women with outside employment are able to redirect their energies gradually as their maternal responsibilities lessen.

No prior studies, however, have addressed the relation between women's job satisfaction and attitudes toward menopause. Work satisfaction has either been tacitly assumed in prior research (Van Keep and Kellerhals 1975), or not considered at all (Deykin et al. 1966).

Medical practitioners and anthropologists turned to studies of women in other cultures to understand the empty nest syndrome (Freedman, Kaplan, and Sadock 1976; Bancroft 1976). They have suggested that society may dictate the degree to which women invest themselves in the roles of homemaker and mother, as well as the availability of substitute roles at midlife. Consequently, there have been many hypotheses about the nature of menopause for women who have active and continuous maternal roles throughout life (Bart 1969; Flint 1975).

THE NATURE OF MENOPAUSE: ANTHROPOLOGICAL THEORIES

Many researchers have focused on the quality of life for women before and after menopause in various cultures. Brown (1985) attempted to present a general theory of the nature of middle age. Bart (1969) proposed a model to divide cultures into those that are likely to increase women's status at midlife and those that do the reverse. The construct validity of these proposals has not been proven in anthropological research.

Brown (1985) notes that middle-aged women in nonindustrialized societies frequently are freed from many personal restrictions, given authority over specified younger kin, and allowed eligibility for special status. Brown supports her findings with ethnographic material. Reproductive issues are the origin of many personal restrictions for women in such societies. In addition to the restrictions of caring for many children and performing heavy household chores, the woman who is fertile often is under the protection of men. Once the woman reaches menopause, she is no longer restricted to the home by either menstrual custom, modesty, display of respect, or the responsibilities of raising a large family.

Finally, Brown notes the improved status of middle-aged women in nonindustrialized societies. In those societies where menstruating women are perceived as "dangerous" or "polluting," menopause provides a release from an inferior status. Other cultures reserve certain important roles, such as midwife or healer, for menopausal women. Thus, middle-aged women in nonindustrial societies can enter new roles that offer them greater freedom of movement than do the restrictive roles of wife and mother.

Bart (1969) drew similar conclusions from cross cultural data entered in the Human Relations Area Files.[1] Bart identified nine cultural variables that related to women's status at middle age. Women, she found, either gain or lose status during middle age; they rarely enjoy continuity of status. Bart reasoned that as women approach the climacteric, the increased social status, as commonly found in traditional cultures, offers them a measure of protection against the negative consequences of menopause.

Six of the nine cultural traits that Bart identified appear to reduce the threats to the maternal role that often accompany aging: strong ties to family of origin, extended family system, emphasis on reproduction, strong mother-child reciprocal relationship in later life, institutionalized grandmother role, and institutionalized mother-in-law role. "Strong ties to family of origin and kin," as opposed to "strong marital ties," suggests that menopausal women have enjoyed continued loyalties spanning many generations and a growing network of family support. Bart also lists three additional cultural characteristics which increase women's status at midlife: reproduction is considered more important than sex for pleasure, there are extensive menstrual taboos, and age is valued over youth.

Presumably, the family of origin should be nearby so that the woman can enjoy fully the benefits of extended network interactions. As I observed in Peru (1986), however, close ties can be maintained even at a distance. In several families in which daughters and their husbands relocated to another district, extended visitation of the daughter to the mother was customary. These visits might last six to eight months if the husband was unable to be present, and up to two years when the daughter's entire family visited. The fact that it was culturally acceptable to leave one's husband for months at a time demonstrates the lack of responsibility or lack of primary importance of the wife. The children always accompanied their mothers, however, underscoring the continued importance of the maternal role.

The identification of "extended family networks," as opposed to "nuclear families," as a marker of women's status is a natural development from ties to the woman's kin. It is important, however, to distinguish between extended families in which debilitated elderly mothers come to reside with their children and nuclear families in which expansion evolves naturally. It should be easier for middle-aged mothers to maintain their control in the latter form of family extension. In Bart's model, both strong ties to family of origin and extended family networks facilitate the development of a strong mother-child relationship that becomes reciprocal later in life. In many third world cultures that have limited resources such as housing, food, and disposable income, the mother-child reciprocal bond becomes a means of survival for new families.

The institutionalized grandmother role is generally recognized by many cultures in which the extended family is common. In these settings, the "older and wiser" grandmother assumes much of the responsibility for care of her grandchildren. The institutionalized grandmother role thus provides a natural continuation of maternal role functions for the woman beyond her reproductive years. Typically, the first grandchild is born just about the time a woman reaches the age of menopause. When there is a defined grandmother role, the most intense period of grandmother-grandchild interaction is likely to occur near the time of the grandmother's menopause.

In cultures in which the mother-in-law role has been institutionalized, the maternal role expands for women when their sons marry or become engaged. Thus, the middle-aged woman has a new "daughter" to train. Brown (1985) notes that very often the increased freedoms of middle-aged women are related to the servitude of daughters-in-law and, to a lesser extent, to control over the former's grown children. Daughters-in-law often are expected to assume most of the household chores under the guidance of the mother-in-law. Sons regularly contribute to the financial support of the mother who, in some cultures, may control all of the family's money.

Bart (1969) specifically notes a distinct contrast between these societies and Western ones, in which there is no defined mother-in-law role except a rule that mothers-in law should not interfere in their children's marriages. These five criteria—strong ties to family of orientation and kin, extended family networks, strong mother-child bonds, institutionalized grandmother role, and institutionalized mother-in-law role—all prolong the family duties of women during middle age. If, as Bart suggests, loss of the maternal role is synonymous with decreased status, these five criteria should be predictive of increased status for middle-aged women.

Bart also identified the societal trait of the importance of reproduction versus that of sex as an end in itself as a significant determinant of increased maternal status at middle age. A cultural trait of discouraging nonprocreative sex keeps the wife's role focused on parental responsibilities, and helps to elevate the status of the maternal role over that of wife. By contrast, a society that values sex as an end in itself puts the demands of the husband-wife relationship in potential competition with the demands of the mother-child dyad. In this situation, greater status also might be conferred on women who are young and attractive, as is often reported in our own society (Freedman, Kaplan, and Sadock 1976). The remaining two criteria—extensive menstrual taboos and the valuing of age over youth—might be rationalized by the increased freedoms that result for middle-aged women in societies where these traits are present. Presumably, women in societies that grant greater freedoms to them in middle age can look forward to enjoying greater status with aging.

Extensive menstrual taboos are thought to restrict younger women within a society and to make the transition to middle age synonymous with new freedoms or "rewards" (Bart 1969; Flint 1975). In Puente Piedre, women were restricted by significant taboos surrounding menstruation. They were not permitted to eat lemons or *aji* (a hot pepper), bathe, or spend extended periods out-of-doors. A different set of taboos at menopause, however, caused women to acquire more liberties in middle age. A prime example was the taboo against touching detergent after menopause, thus excusing older women from doing the family wash. Such a "restriction" presents an interesting twist to the belief that taboos in a society necessarily limit personal freedom (Barnett 1986).

Finally, the Bart model refers to the cultural value of age over youth. In many ways, this construct naturally evolves in societies with large, extended kinship networks. Typically, the oldest person in the family hierarchy controls the most resources. In societies where hard work is not necessarily equated with success, older persons are respected for the particular wisdom they have accrued as part of their survival skills. Bart did not claim that the variables she listed bore any direct relationship to women's status in middle age, but rather that the criteria did occur with regularity in those societies in which aging women held increased status.

Cross-cultural research allows anthropologists to study the relative importance of certain sociocultural variables by looking at the experiences of similar cohorts in a diversity of settings. Anthropologists have pointed to the obvious contrasts between women living in Western societies, who suffer many losses at menopause, and those in Third World cultures, who enjoy many gains. Identifying contrasts in middle age for women in different societies, of course, is simpler than proving that cultural variations actually affect women's experiences of menopause.

Flint (1975), working in India, suggested that a positive experience of menopause was more likely for women who were given rewards at midlife. She contrasted an overtly positive climacteric for women of India with a stereotypically negative experience among women of the United States. Flint argued that menopause carries a reward for Indian women, as it allows them to remove their veils and end the social isolation of *purdah*, whereas menopause is a punishment for North American women, who suffer from role loss and the empty nest syndrome.

Later work by Datan (1971) and Davis (1980), however, called into question the importance of expanded roles and increased status in influencing women's perceptions of menopause. Datan studied women from five Israeli subcultures that ranged from traditional to modern. She was surprised to find that the women who suffered most profoundly from the negative consequences of menopause were those in the transitional cultures. Datan concluded that both traditional and modern societies must offer aging women rewards that are absent in transitional cultures.

Davis (1980) studied a Newfoundland fishing village and concluded that the high status and many rewards commonly accorded to women there throughout midlife did not lessen the negative consequence of menopause. Although Davis used the model developed by Bart as the theoretical basis for her research, she was cautious about interpreting the negative findings because women of Newfoundland enjoyed continuously rewarding social roles throughout their lifetime (the Bart model assumes changing status at menopause).

PERCEPTIONS OF MENOPAUSE IN PUENTE PIEDRE

I conducted fieldwork from March 1980 through June 1981 in the Peruvian town of Puente Piedre. A small, cohesive community, its residents are actually from a more diverse economic status than originally believed. Census material from a study conducted in the 1970s suggests that approximately one hundred women are one to three years past their last menstrual cycle, making it possible to interview all women experiencing the transition to nonreproductive years. A completed study of the town was available which provided me with much background information. This same study introduced the residents to the notion of anthropological research; they felt honored by the previous attention to their town and expressed interest in cooperating with my research efforts.

The research combined participant observation with formal interviews. The Maoz-Datan interview (Datan 1971), the Menopause Index checklist (Kupperman et al. 1953), and open-ended questions were the basis of a pilot study. Later, the interview content was modified to collect data on recurring themes important to these women. This included a more comprehensive focus on the women's satisfactions with their roles as mothers and as laborers, if they held this additional role. The Bart model for classifying societies by the presence of nine criteria was reworked to measure intracultural variation among women. Questions to assess women's overall perception of menopause were also formulated.

Final questionnaire data were collected from ninety seven eligible women living in the central district of Puente Piedre, excluding any women who lived in the temporary shelters running through the middle of town.[2] Eligible women were defined as those who had missed at least two consecutive menstrual cycles attributed to menopause, but had not ceased to menstruate for more than three years. One woman who met this criterion was excluded from data analysis; this woman had never married, had no children, no outside employment, and was considered unusual by other women of the town. Among sixty-three traditional mothers, only two refused to be interviewed, each citing their spouse's objections. Only thirty-six of forty-eight laborers were interviewed; two specifically refused because of lack of time, and others were equally difficult to interview because of similar time demands. Thus, from 112 eligible women, sixty-one traditional mothers and thirty-six laborers comprised the study group.

Studying women's roles at menopause in Puente Piedre allowed for reexamination of many of the maternal role characteristics previously identified as important forces in shaping women's perceptions of menopause. Large extended families with dense, continuous maternal roles were common; none of the women interviewed were "empty nested" (Barnett 1986). The apparent variation in women's responses to menopause cannot be explained by the different responses to maternal role loss frequently referred to in studies of our own culture.

Early adulthood (*joventude*, before age forty) represented a time of uncertainty for many women interviewed. A young couple often is not officially married by the church until they have several children, leaving the woman to establish a family without the security of marriage. The custom of delaying a church wedding until after starting a family occurs among the majority of women studied. The role of wife is an obligation that is expected of all "good" mothers, but is one for which women rarely are prepared at the time they leave home to live with their partners. Women are unprepared for the period of rejection by both their parents and their husbands' parents for assuming a role that is demanded of her by society.

Thus it is not surprising that women thought that their lives were most difficult when they were twenty-five years of age. They recounted their mothers-in-law's threats of sending them back to their fathers in disgrace. They described how strenuous it was to care for a family during the early years of their marriage when they had several small children at home. Clothing was all washed by hand and every item of clothing was ironed, in the belief that this was necessary to prevent disease. A typical meal took three hours to prepare; there was no one to help with even the most menial tasks, such as cleaning rice. Stereotypically, it was acceptable for the man to feel dissatisfied by his young partner's lack of attentions and consider himself free to engage in multiple affairs, leaving the woman alone with the children for days at a time.

These women reported that their lives improved somewhat when they reach the age of thirty. After bearing several children, the women generally reconcile with their parents' family. Typically, the women's fathers then forced a marriage by threatening to reclaim their daughters and their children. After women marry in the church, the disgrace lay with their in-laws should they separate from their husbands. Once it was in the mother-in-law's interest to maintain the union, she no longer threatened to divide the couple. Life at home was then somewhat easier for the women, particularly if they had an older daughter who could assist with the care of younger children and the simple tasks involved in meal preparation. Yet the responsibilities were still numerous and the work difficult—none of the women interviewed wished to return to this stage of life either.

People are finally recorded in the Peruvian census as *adultos* (adults) once they reach age forty. This categorization suggests that women receive the recognition of maturity just prior to reaching *la edad crítica* (menopause; literally, "the critical state"). Moreover, just as the women are entering *la edad crítica*, multiple taboos are enacted. These cultural taboos, for example, forbid the older women to wash or iron clothes, or stay indoors for prolonged periods.

It was only at menopause that the women interviewed fully enjoy their children: most of the women at this age lived in large extended families; none of the women lived solely with their spouses. Older sons began to offer financial help and provided the labor to complete the family home, which often had remained unfinished because of the financial burden of caring for many small children. Daughters took over many of the household tasks and eventually assumed total responsibility for the chores of daily living—an assignment promoted by the multiple taboos observed by women reaching menopause.

Those middle-aged women who were not employed outside the home often assumed full care for the first-born grandchild. In many cases, the newly weaned infant lived continuously with the grandmother; in others, the grandmother cared for the child during the day. A grandmother who did not consider herself the primary caretaker of her grandchildren often had extensive contact with them. For example, in the author's residence, the woman of the house did not consider her four-year-old grandson to be "living" with her; in fact, the child spent six months per year in her household because it was "too cold" at his parents' home.

There is no category of "old age" in the Peruvian census. Women remain *adultos* until the time of their death. They continue to maintain their autonomy, dependent on no one person because they can rely on all who are younger. For example, older women who can barely walk have no hesitation about walking to the store alone. It is common to see an old woman arrive at a curbside and extend her arms, knowing that the nearest children will immediately run to assist her.

Many roles available to women in other cultures are also available to women of Puente Piedre; however, only the roles defined as traditional mother or laborer represent principal life roles. Traditional mothers remain in the home to care for their children on a full-time basis. Laborers are those who either work in their homes on projects for financial remuneration, or work outside the home between twenty and sixty hours per week.

At the time of menopause, women employed outside the home in Puente Piedre hold alternative roles, but often undesirable ones. Women's lack of formal education limits those who work outside the home to menial tasks, and excuses them from few, if any, responsibilities within the home. Some women interviewed enjoyed their outside employment, but apart from financial gain, they perceived it as carrying no a priori benefit. By examining the menopausal experiences of common laborers, rather than of professional women, the importance of alternative roles in influencing women's perceptions of menopause can be explored from a different perspective.

All women are mothers and wives, if only in name. The wife role is rarely important to women outside of providing a name for their children. Women said that they often remained married "for the children"; they needed their husbands "for the children." Thus, the wife role was seldom considered more than an extension of maternal role obligations. Forty percent of the women rated the wife role as "neutral" on a five-point Likert scale which ranges from all bad to all good. Given the observed predisposition of women to classify events and people rigidly as either "good" or "bad," the lack of value judgment regarding the wife role probably reflects a lack of importance of this role (Barnett 1986).

In contrast, fewer than 10 percent of the laborers rated their work as neutral, and fewer than 25 percent of traditional mothers judged their children's accomplishments, defined as a measure of maternal satisfaction, neutrally. The degree to which women discussed the roles of laborer and traditional mother suggests that these roles are more important to them.

In Puente Piedre, a traditional mother considered herself successful if during her lifetime, all her daughters came of age, married, and had children. The daughters' marriages and grandchildren were both expected and valued by the mother. Middle-aged women who either had adult, unmarried daughters, or who had doubts whether their younger daughters might ever be desirable brides, considered themselves failures as mothers.

Laborers were less affected by their sense of satisfaction in the maternal role; it therefore becomes important to study laborers separately from traditional mothers. These women were asked to judge their satisfaction in the workplace as a reflection of their principal life roles. To contrast the importance of the laborers' sense of accomplishment in their employment with their traditional maternal role, these women were also asked the same set of questions regarding their role as mother.

Attitudes toward menopause varied greatly among the traditional mothers and laborers interviewed; however, the variance in both groups is the same. Moreover, women are equally likely to find satisfaction (or dissatisfaction) in either role.[3] For both traditional mothers and laborers, severity of symptoms is highly correlated to women's attitudes toward menopause. There is no correlation, however, between symptom severity and role satisfaction, the latter of which is also highly correlated to women's attitudes toward menopause.

Principal life role satisfaction remains an independent correlate to women's attitudes toward menopause. Traditional mothers' satisfaction with children's accomplishments is positively correlated with their attitudes toward menopause. Laborers' satisfaction in the workplace—and not their satisfaction with children's accomplishments—correlates with their attitudes toward menopause.

A further analysis of the data does not support alternative hypotheses that might explain the variability in women's attitudes. The number of roles that a woman had at menopause is not significant in predicting attitude; women with employment outside the home did not view menopause more favorably than did traditional mothers; a woman's satisfaction in the role of wife did not influence her attitude toward menopause.[4] Although only four women in the sample are truly empty nested, a comparison of attitudes among mothers with all of their children at home and those with some children departed show no significant difference.[5] Bart (1969) proposed nine criteria for improved status at middle age; in the present study, none of these nine variables considered individually nor a composite scoring of them correlates with women's attitudes toward menopause (Barnett 1986).

CONCLUSION

The important cultural finding among the women I interviewed in Puente Piedre is that their attitudes toward menopause are related to their satisfaction in their principal life roles. Such attitudes are independent of the presence, loss, or status of social roles at middle age. This observation should allow for greater understanding of the variation of women's attitudes toward menopause in other cultures. The importance of role satisfaction may account for all the conflicting reports in the literature on the empty nest syndrome (Krystal and Chiriboga 1979; Lowenthal et al. 1975; Spence and Lonner 1971); the benefits of outside employment or alternative roles (Maoz et al. 1978; Poloma and Garland 1971); and the importance of a strong and positive relationship with one's spouse (Dennerstein and Burrows 1978; Van Keep 1976).

The empty nest syndrome is one of the most widely debated issues in studies of menopausal women in Western societies. Some researchers have found that women dread the transition to the empty nest, whereas others report that women actually look forward to the time alone. Authors have tried to explain these differences on the basis of whether the woman works outside of the home, or has other meaningful relationships (Dennerstein and Burrows 1978; Maoz et al. 1978; Van Keep 1976), but such perspectives miss the importance of identifying the woman's principal life role and her satisfaction in that role.

Thus, women who have committed themselves to raising their children full-time are most likely to suffer from an empty nest syndrome at the time of menopause, but not because they lack an alternative role in middle age. Rather, satisfaction of traditional mothers in their role, as measured by the way they evaluate their children's accomplishments, is the more important variable. That is to say, the triggers for the negative emotions labeled as the empty nest syndrome in Western societies is not that Johnny is leaving home, it is that Johnny isn't going to Harvard or is otherwise not meeting his mother's expectations.

It must be noted that parental expectations can and will vary among cultures and even within the same culture. In Puente Piedre, for example, most women interviewed expected their children, particularly their daughters, to marry young and to bear children. The issue is whether children meet the expectations of their mothers, rather than any inherent quality of the goals in question.

The distinction between the void left when grown children leave home and the dissatisfaction when children are either unable or unwilling to meet their mother's expectations has both academic and clinical significance. Future research on the empty nest syndrome must focus on women's contentment in the traditional mother role as measured by their sense of satisfaction with their children's accomplishments. The transition to the empty nest must be recognized as an important life event because it triggers or coexists with women's introspection on the outcome of their principal life roles (Neugarten and Kraines 1964). In the clinical treatment of emotional distress at the time of menopause, it is important to identify the trigger. If the therapist and client focus on role *loss* when the real issue is role *satisfaction*, therapy can be misdirected.

According to this theory, laborers should be less influenced by their children's accomplishments because being a "traditional mother" has not been their principal life role. Moreover, it may be incorrect to conclude that outside work per se can mollify the negative impact of children leaving home (Maoz et al. 1978), even for women who identify themselves primarily as laborers. Future studies should specifically address role satisfaction among laborers, including women who hold unskilled as well as skilled positions. The issue of whether the woman chooses work or must work out of necessity should also be considered. Anthropologists might also focus on laborers in societies that discourage women from seeking employment or assign negative connotations to working women. Of foremost importance is separating the issue of role alternatives from that of role satisfaction among laborers.

The prominent use of volunteers and selection for more educated women in prior studies on outside work may have biased past research (Rubin 1981). Certainly, women who are more educated and of higher income brackets have greater control over their positions and are more able to change work situations until they achieve a measure of job satisfaction. It may well be role satisfaction as a laborer, rather than the outside employment itself, that predisposes many Western women to be at an advantage over their non-laboring cohorts at the time of menopause. Support for this explanation is found in an International Health Foundation study of Belgian women from several socioeconomic classes: only those in the middle or high socioeconomic classes seemed to benefit from outside employment, as measured by overall attitudes toward menopause (Van Keep and Kellerhals 1974).

Cultural expectations also may help determine the importance of outside employment. For example, Maoz et al. (1978) compared menopausal women from various social classes in Israel and found that the majority of women in all socioeconomic groups viewed work as a negative experience. He concluded that, when the society does not positively view women's labors outside the home, the work role will have little benefit for working women. Maoz's study does not negate the proposition that women in professional positions are more likely to find their jobs rewarding; instead, it suggests the need to evaluate women as individuals.

Flint (1975) discussed the significance of whether society externally rewards or punishes menopausal women. Study in Peru, however, suggests that equally important rewards might be those that come from a woman's sense of accomplishment in her own principal role. It may be incorrect to conclude that society is obligated to reward middle-aged women if the latter are to escape the negative consequences of menopause. Women in various societies define role expectations differently, but this writer's findings indicate that the internal rewards that accompany a woman's sense of accomplishment in her principal life role are significant in determining individual perceptions of menopause.

Although Bart (1969) concludes that increasing status at middle age may mollify the negative influence of menopause, this may occur only when status is an accurate reflection of a woman's satisfaction. There are many societies in which women are satisfied with their principal life roles although those roles do not confer status. For example, in Puente Piedre, success in the maternal role cannot be equated with status. For traditional mothers of Puente Piedre and for women in most societies who are employed in unskilled or semiskilled positions, success in the primary role is not equated with status.

My research in Peru (1986) suggests that the wide variation in women's responses to menopause might be explained by identity continuity theory. The woman who holds a positive view of her years as a laborer will continue to see herself as a flourishing laborer. Traditional mothers who are satisfied with their performance as a mother will continue to identify themselves as successful traditional mothers. Women who do not experience a sense of accomplishment and satisfaction in their principal life role, however, may set a pattern of discontentment for themselves that will persist despite role continuity. Thus, women need more than just a role to play during middle age; they need satisfaction with the role with which they identify, a finding consistent with identity continuity theory (Atchley 1971).

If the identity continuity theory is correct, menopausal women who are not satisfied in their principal life roles will be less adaptable to changes in those roles. In the event of principal role dissatisfaction, traditional mothers will feel the need to perform perfunctory maternal role functions, whereas laborers will resist retirement. Women who have not considered themselves successful in their principal life roles need these continuing role tasks in order to maintain a sense of identity and self-worth.

In Western society, women typically reflect on their childrens' accomplishments at the time they leave home. The empty nest syndrome may thus be a cultural artifact. If mothers' expectations for their children are not met, women may be burdened by their childrens' exit from the home. However, if women are satisfied with their childrens' accomplishments, their identity as mothers remains strong and they accept their childrens' departure. Traditional mothers in Third World cultures have fewer expectations for their children then Western women. Even in more traditional societies, where women do not face the empty nest, principal role satisfaction may remain the important variable affecting women's perceptions of menopause.

Both Flint's theory (1975) on the importance of rewards and punishments and Bart's theory (1969) on the influence of status on women's experiences of menopause remain useful concepts in analyzing women's attitudes toward menopause in cross-cultural perspective. Future research could examine the relationships among external rewards granted by society, increased status at middle age, and the likelihood that women will be more satisfied with accomplishments in their principal role in life. It appears that the more control that a woman has over her principal life roles—such as work in Western societies, or parenting in traditional societies—the greater the chances are that she will experience satisfaction in that role.

Women's roles and expectations also vary from culture to culture. Although from an outsider's (etic) point of view, anthropologists may be able to say that one culture treats its women "better" than does another, from an insider's (emic) perspective, all women have the chance to be successful in their principal roles in life. An individual woman's success in her role may be more likely in one culture than another, but there always will be intracultural variation. In conclusion, a woman's perceptions of accomplishment within her principal life role may be central in explaining inter- and intracultural differences in women's perceptions of menopause.

NOTES

1. The Human Relations Area Files are a correlational composite of data relating to such topics as subsistence, kinship, socialization practices, and initiation rites, compared cross-culturally.
2. Women in this "shantytown within a shantytown" were markedly different from women who have established themselves in the larger community. Also, the one-room shacks in this area would have provided no privacy for interviewing women.
3. A pooled t-test for variance for menopausal symptoms ($f = .20$, $t = .039$, $p = .66$) and a separated t-test for attitudes toward menopause ($f = 6.2$, $p = .02$, $t = 1.6$, $p = .11$) showed no significant difference between traditional mothers and laborers.
4. Spearman's correlation $= -.049$, $p > .32$.
5. Chi-square $= .46$, $p > .5$.

4

THE SOCIAL SIGNIFICANCE OF ELECTIVE HYSTERECTOMY

Linnea Klee

Hysterectomy is one of the most commonly performed surgical procedures in the United States. Aside from medical indications, the social perceptions doctors hold towards women who are candidates for a hysterectomy, and the sociopsychological perceptions these women hold towards their bodies and surgery influence the decision to have a hysterectomy. These perceptions also affect postoperative adjustment and recovery. A discrepancy exists between the perceptions of doctors and patients relative to the need for hysterectomies. Sensitizing physicians to the patients' perceptions and concerns may reduce this discrepancy and promote a positive postoperative experience.

Surgical removal of the uterus is the most common major surgery performed in the United States today. As many as 50 to 65 percent of American women may undergo hysterectomies in their lifetimes (Bunker, McPherson, and Henneman 1977; Richards 1978). There is controversy, however, over hysterectomy as a solution to benign uterine disease, and many hysterectomies are believed to be unnecessary (Center for Disease Control 1980). In addition, the surgery is expensive and sometimes has severe physical and psychological costs. The history and present practice of this surgery symbolizes the continuing debate over interpretation and control of women's health. Childbirth research has revealed conflicts between women's views and those of health care professionals, but virtually no research has investigated these issues with regard to gynecologic illness and surgery. For example, research on childbirth has shown that women who view the uterus as an "involuntary muscle" rather than an integral part of their physical and psychological being may have more difficulty in labor (Martin 1984). Medical policies regarding hysterectomy also reveal conflicts between professional definitions of the functions of female organs and the more intangible views women hold of themselves. The following discussion will review findings from research on hysterectomy and examine controversies surrounding its indications and effects.

This study consists of my analysis, from a medical anthropologist's point of view, of medical, epidemiologic, social science, medical historic, and feminist literature published between 1960 and 1985. My intention is to determine the perspectives of these various fields on the medicalization of women's health generally, but especially with regard to hysterectomy, and to establish what we presently know about the social and psychological significance of this surgery. An anthropological explanatory framework is suggested to organize this disparate information.

Many hysterectomies are reported to be unnecessary, but physicians disagree on appropriate indications for surgery. Since women themselves may make the final decision for or against elective surgery, we need to know more about their own beliefs. Medical anthropologists have begun to examine how popular health beliefs compare with biomedical definitions of diseases such as those for which hysterectomy is recommended (Fabrega 1974). So far, we know little about where women's own interpretations of illness and expectations of treatment coincide with physicians' definitions. We know that they often differ.

The explanatory model approach in medical anthropology might be useful to examine the process women go through when facing surgery. This perspective investigates interactions between physicians' biomedical definitions of disease and patients' sociocultural interpretations of illness.[1] The explanatory model concept was developed as a clinical tool to aid medical practitioners in negotiations with their patients (Kleinman, Eisenberg, and Good 1978). It seeks to account for beliefs about five primary aspects of episodes of ill health: (1) etiology of the illness; (2) time and mode of onset of symptoms; (3) pathophysiology of the illness; (4) course of sickness; and (5) treatment (Kleinman 1980:105). Each of these areas is embedded in a particular sociocultural context that influences its interpretation. This approach is also useful as a heuristic guide for research in medical anthropology, because it provides a way to identify the meanings people attribute to an illness experience. People rarely report such attitudes and beliefs about illness directly to their physicians (Kleinman 1981). As yet, there is little research that identifies how women interpret gynecologic illnesses and their treatment by this surgery. Biomedical explanations of hysterectomy are apparent in the literature, but it is important to distinguish between the ideal and real in reading what physicians report themselves as doing as opposed to their actual practice (Lock 1982). Moreover, there is disagreement among physicians about the indications for hysterectomy.

CONTROVERSIAL SURGERY

The Center for Disease Control reports that one in seven of the 3.5 million elective hysterectomies performed between 1970 and 1979 was unnecessary. Furthermore, more than 60 percent of all hysterectomies are carried out on premenopausal women aged 15–44, thus ending their future child-bearing capacity (Center for Disease Control 1980; Easterday, Grimes, and Riggs 1983). Women's health advocates and some medical professionals criticize unnecessary gynecological surgery (see Barker-Benfield 1975; Bart 1977; Corea 1977; Kasper 1985; Keyser 1984; Marieskind 1975; Morgan 1982; Ruzek 1979; Scully 1980; Seaman and Seaman 1977). The idea of a "useless uterus syndrome" after final childbearing especially angers critics who argue that childbearing is not the only purpose of the uterus (Morgan 1982; Scully 1980; Wright 1969).

Unlike other surgeries, hysterectomy has a variety of medical indications. Most hysterectomies occur on an elective or nonemergency basis. The discretionary nature of the surgery confounds its medical indications with social and psychological factors such as the desire for further childbearing, fears of changes in sexuality, effects on gender identity, and impact on marital relationships (Richard 1978; Roeske 1978).

A review of the literature shows the following to be appropriate medical indications for hysterectomy, with estimates of their frequency (not totalling 100 percent): (1) malignancy of uterus, cervix, ovaries or Fallopian tubes, 8–15 percent; (2) large leiomyomas (benign uterine fibroid tumors), 27–33 percent; (3) uterine descensus or prolapse ("pelvic relaxation"), 14–35 percent; (4) dysfunctional bleeding 9–40 percent. Other accepted indications include chronic pelvic pain, proximity to other diseased organs, and obstetric catastrophies (see Bunker 1976; Bunker, McPherson, and Henneman 1977; Koepsell et al. 1980; Newton and Baron 1976; Paulshock 1976; Richards 1978; Thompson and Birch 1981).

Among indications criticized as unnecessary are prophylaxis against uterine cancer, sterilization, management of menopause, leukorrhea and chronic cervicitis, primary dysmenorrhea and premenstrual tension, mild urinary incontinence, abnormal vaginal or cervical cytology, cervical dysplasia, and the "useless uterus syndrome." The latter indication was described by Wright in his now classic statement, "The uterus has but one function: reproduction. After the last planned pregnancy, the uterus becomes a useless, bleeding, symptom-producing, potentially cancer bearing organ and therefore should be removed" (1969:561). Some critics would expand this list of unnecessary indications (Thompson and Birch 1981; Morgan 1982). Others charge that hysterectomies are often performed for sheer monetary gain, or for teaching purposes alone (Scully 1980). Evidence exists that fee-for-service payment and payment through insurance coverage result in greater numbers of hysterectomies than occur in settings where physicians are paid on a capitation basis (Kasper 1985; Koepsell et al. 1980).

Several studies have identified percentages of unnecessary surgery. D'Esopo (1962) found that according to pathology reports spanning six years in one hospital, about 15 percent of the hysterectomies were performed on normal uteri. Elsewhere, after a physicians' committee began surveillance of hysterectomies in seven hospitals, the proportion judged unjustified dropped from 23.7 percent to 7.8 percent in four years (Dyck et al. 1977:326). In another case, 32 percent of recommended hysterectomies were not confirmed when the cases were reexamined by a board of specialists (McCarthy and Widmer 1974:1333).

WOMEN'S EXPERIENCE OF HYSTERECTOMY

The physiologic, social, and psychological impacts of hysterectomy have not been sufficiently examined. These consequences can best be understood from women's own experiences of its psychosocial costs. We need to know more about how women themselves perceive the loss of the uterus physiologically and emotionally.

Evidence that the uterus, and certainly the ovaries, have other physiologic and psychological functions than in childbearing is only recently forthcoming. Hysterectomy, which involves oophorectomy (removal of uterus and ovaries), results in castration and premature menopause. Loss of ovarian hormones may produce a number of physiologic changes including "hot flashes," changed sexual response, and increased risk of osteoporosis. Removal of the uterus alone may also affect sexual response and produce as yet undefined hormonal changes. Loss of childbearing capacity may result in feelings of grief and lowered self-esteem. Husbands' attitudes towards their wives and women's acceptance in a social group of mothers may change when maternal potential is lost (Dennerstein, Wood, and Burrows 1982; Morgan 1982; Seaman and Seaman 1977; Webb and Wilson-Barnett 1983). Women frequently experience depression following hysterectomy. Whether this response is purely psychological or is the result of endocrine imbalance has yet to be determined (Richards 1973, 1974; Sloan 1978).

Among the sociocultural variables that have a bearing on the choice for or against elective hysterectomy and satisfaction with the surgical outcome are beliefs about the importance of motherhood and the desire for children, as well as fears about aging, loss of femininity, attractiveness, sexual response, and feminine identity. Other fears concern pain, the hospital experience, surgery, morbidity and complications, and the significance to women of the loss of menstruation as a cyclical marker of their life experience. In each of these areas the importance of husbands, children, other family members, lovers, and friends to women's perceptions and choices has been almost entirely neglected in research.

We know almost nothing of the effect of popular and folk beliefs about menstruation, pregnancy, and female organs on women's attitudes towards hysterectomy (Webb and Wilson-Barnett 1983). The surgery dramatically changes women's experiences with regard to menstruation and pregnancy, and possibly their sexuality. Whether women respond negatively or positively in these areas is determined by sociocultural beliefs and attitudes about women's accepted roles in the family and in society. We do not know for sure if the recent movement for women's liberation has redefined these perspectives in the United States to lend a positive valuation to the freedom hysterectomy provides from menstruation, pregnancy and childbirth, and the need for birth control. Nor do we know if, by increasing women's consciousness of themselves and their bodies, this movement has encouraged a greater desire to preserve gynecologic functioning through life. On the one hand, the practice of menstrual extraction, the induced removal of the endometrium at the time of menstruation, has taken on political significance as a demonstration of women's rights (Delaney, Lupton, and Toth 1976); on the other, many women angrily resist hysterectomy as an assault on gender identity (Scully 1980).

Professional medical views of hysterectomy continue to be influenced by internalization of historical beliefs about the "hysterical woman" and the central role of the uterus (Smith-Rosenberg 1972). Nineteenth-century physicians viewed the reproductive system as the principal controller of women's personalities, behavior, intellectual functioning, and social roles. Physicians believed that they had an obligation to intervene in the biologic functioning of women because of its purported psychological and social effects (Smith-Rosenberg and Rosenberg 1973). Women were also influenced by these powerful social beliefs, and experienced the illnesses expected of them (Barker-Benfield 1975). For example, the novelist Charlotte Brontë, warned by her father of the deleterious effects he believed marriage and childbearing would have on her "delicate constitution," died soon after marriage in 1855 of pernicious morning sickness (Peters 1986:410). This condition (hyperemesis gravidarum) is today believed to be at least partially psychological in origin. While much enlightenment has occurred with the professionalization of scientific medicine, the lingering impact of nineteenth century (and earlier) views should not be underestimated, for they may be all the more insidious in a newly rationalized form. The employment of female castration for psychological disorders in the nineteenth century oddly parallels modern concern about psychological disorders resulting from castration (Barker-Benfield 1975). Symptoms once attributed to malfunctions of the uterus are strangely similar to the side effects now believed to result from its removal, namely the crying, insomnia, and nervousness occurring after hysterectomy, now classified as "depression" (Wood 1973).

The following discussion will expand on some of these issues, examining hyserectomy and socioeconomic status, perceptions of maternity and the female organs, diagnosis and illness experiences, and beliefs about biomedicine and medical decision making.

Socioeconomic Status and Hysterectomy

Women's socioeconomic class and cultural background will have a bearing on their choices to undergo or avoid surgery, and their responses to elective hysterectomy. Data on socioeconomic status in relation to this surgery are scanty and conflicting. Social characteristics of women who favor or oppose elective hysterectomy have not been identified. Evidence that physicians' wives undergo hysterectomy at much higher rates than other professonal class women is cited as an indication that informed women will choose surgery (Bunker, McPherson, and Henneman 1977; Richards 1978). As physicians' wives, such women are undoubtedly more accepting of the medical model, and may additionally be influenced by their peers. In contrast, a German study found woman with higher intelligence and education more likely to oppose hysterectomies (Newton and Baron 1976). Bombardier et al. (1977) corroborate this finding, reporting a negative relationship between education and surgical utilization in the United States.

Between 1970 and 1978, most hysterectomies in the United States were performed on white women, reflecting their greater numbers in the overall population. But black women experienced a higher rate of hysterectomies during this period (972 per 100,000 for black women aged 15–44, compared to 777 per 100,000 for white women). Different geographic localities also report different rates of hysterectomies (Center for Disease Control 1980:3–4). There is a correlation between hysterectomy and both high and low socioeconomic status in the United States because hysterectomy is associated with both private insurance and Medicaid coverage, but this relationship needs further study (Kasper 1985; Koepsell et al. 1980).

The scarcity of research relating class and cultural background to hysterectomy outcomes means that no real conclusions can be drawn. One study found no relationship between emotional and attitudinal outcomes of hysterectomy and occupation or education among 254 returned questionnaires (Baron 1977). Another also found no relationship between psychiatric outcome and age or social class in a prospective study of 156 hysterectomy patients (Gath 1980). But Roeske found a positive correlation among twenty-one women between socioeconomic class, vocation or avocation, and satisfaction with surgery. She concluded, "For these women, the uterus was no longer as highly valued as during their childbearing years. They had other sources for self-esteem which had, at times, been limited in the past by child care or by the internal sexual organs' pathology" (1978:485).

Perceptions of Maternity and Female Organs

Women's attitudes toward maternity are clearly of great importance to perceptions of the uterus. The experiences of being a woman and mother have been inextricably bound and socially dictated both cross-culturally and historically (Barker-Benfield 1975; Grossman and Bart 1979; Raphael 1975). Other roles for women are only recently more socially sanctioned. The impact of change in women's self definition and the symbolic importance of the uterus for perceptions of health, femininity, and roles as woman and mother need further assessment.

Beliefs about menstruation have an obvious place in the study of the impact of hysterectomy. As in other cultures, menstrual taboos and rituals exist in modern American society, from fears of women's "weakness" during menstruation to new emphasis on the "pre-menstrual syndrome" as an explanation of a myriad of psychological and physiological symptoms (Dan, Graham, and Beecher 1980; Delaney, Lupton, and Toth 1976; Weideger 1977). Exclusion of women because of beliefs in the dangers of menstrual blood has existed cross-culturally, historically, and in present American life (Jessop 1983; Kessler 1976). Menstruation is clearly associated with an impressive variety of cultural interpretatons and rituals, yet only a few studies have looked at the impact of the sudden loss of this fundamental experience caused by surgery.

In a recent British study, 102 women who had undergone simple hysterectomies were not unhappy about loss of menstruation. Out of seventy-three responses to a question concerning future pregnancy, fifty-nine women said they were happy about not being able to become pregnant again. Seven who were unhappy about not being able to conceive were either childless or had experienced fertility problems. The majority of these women also reported that their sex life was the same or better after surgery. Poorer outcomes from hysterectomy were associated with lower levels of support from family and friends. This study also found that while lay myths or folk beliefs about hysterectomy were widespread, they were rejected by the majority of women (Webb and Wilson-Barnett 1983:100–1).

In other recent research, only eleven out of forty women reported a change in feelings of femininity after hysterectomy, and seven of those women felt *more* feminine. Seventy-five percent of this sample expressed relief that surgery was performed. Reasons for dissatisfaction were not provided (Cosper, Fuller, and Robinson 1980:334). An early study by Drellich and Bieber (1958:323–24, 329) is often cited because it is one of the few that examined women's viewpoints. These authors found that twenty-three premenopausal hysterectomy patients valued menstruation positively as a physiologic metronome giving regulation to daily life, or as a cleansing ritual important to the maintenance of health and strength. They also found that these women viewed loss of child-bearing capacity negatively, but this finding may be colored by the authors' own clear bias toward the desirability of child-bearing. The women also expressed concern about loss of sexuality, strength, and independence. They feared pain, aging, and surgical complications. This early study raised many issues that remain unexamined with regard to this surgery.

Although we know very little about how women respond to surgical loss of menstruation, some related work on women's and physicians' attitudes toward menopause exists. Weideger (1977) has argued that the gynecologist acts as a shaman in assessing and interpreting what is normal female behavior, guiding women both medically and spiritually through menopause. Lock (1982) examined the medical literature and interviewed physicians for attitudes towards menopause. She found that beliefs about menopause which physicians actually employ in their practices differ from biomedical models presented in the literature. The working models they develop are determined by such characteristics as their age and sex, type of training, subspeciality, attitudes toward women, information from colleagues and the media, and the political and economic organization of the health care system. Because menopause continues to be viewed both as a normal process and as a disease by physicians and the patients they influence, physicians and patients alike apply various interpretations to it. Townsend and Carbone (1980) reviewed cross-cultural literature on menopause to determine if its symptomatology reflects sociocultural factors. They found little useful literature on which to base their conclusions; but they suggest that menopause is a socially constructed illness in American society. They point out that its symptoms resemble those often identified in folk illnesses, such as dizziness, fatigue, anxiety, headaches, and depression.

Almost no research has been conducted on differences in response to hysterectomy among pre- and postmenopausal women. Frequency of this surgery, however, is highest among premenopausal women. The average age of menopause, the cessation of the menses, is 50. In 1978, 63 percent of women who had hysterectomies were aged 15–44, 31 percent were aged 45–64, and 6 percent were aged 65 or older (Easterday, Grimes, and Riggs 1983; *Vital and Health Statistics* 1966). An additional issue is the previous sterilization of some of these women. Richards, for example, found that among 274 women who had undergone hysterectomies, 16.4 percent had had prior tubal ligations, and 24.4 percent of their husbands had had vasectomies (1978:448). Researchers rarely distinguish women who were previously surgically sterilized or who have completed menopause when they discuss satisfaction with the outcomes of hysterectomy.

Most social research on hysterectomy concerns the incidence of depression following surgery. This work is inconclusive and conflicting (Wijma 1984). Part of the problem is that most studies have been restrospective, chronicling depression as many as four to five years after hysterectomy. A second problem is the differing definitions of depression or other psychological disturbance. Referral to psychiatrists is the most commonly used measure for incidence of depression. A few studies have used psychiatric interviewing (Kaltreider, Wallace and Horowitz 1979; Martin et al. 1977). A third problem is that even when measures are taken prior to surgery, the impact of trepidation about surgery itself is not taken into account (Gath 1980; Sloan 1978; Youngs and Wise 1976).

The significance of research on depression and hysterectomy lies in its very ambiguity. Some studies find excess psychopathology after hysterectomy, others do not. The suggestion that women who undergo hysterectomies demonstrate more psychopathology prior to surgery than other women reflects historic notions of the interplay between women's psyches and gynecologic organs. Some have also suggested that postoperative depression may result from hormonal imbalance, even when the ovaries are not removed (Richards 1973, 1974). There is an apparent association between having a hysterectomy and experiencing depression either pre- or postoperatively, or both. We do not know what influence women's perceptions of female roles has on this incidence of depression.

Anthropological work on childbirth by Stern and Kruckman (1983) suggests that the social context of illness may determine the experience of postpartum depression. They note that little attention has been given to cultural patterning in examinations of the etiology of this phenomenon. Thus, the Western deemphasis on a socially recognized postpartum recovery period may result in many women becoming depressed as they struggle unaided to accommodate new social roles and responsibilities. Clearly, the way in which the recovery period from hysterectomy is regarded and carried out might similarly have an impact on the etiology of depression.

Diagnosis and Illness

The type of diagnosis and the way in which it is presented to a woman may heavily influence her choices for or against an elective hysterectomy, but there are no previous studies relating women's choices regarding hysterectomy and their perceptions of their diagnosis and symptomatology. Cain et al. (1983) examined women diagnosed with gynecologic cancer and found differences in psychosocial reactions related to location and extent of disease. For example, women with cervical cancer were less informed and less optimistic about outcome than were women with ovarian or endometrial cancer. These differences may in part be explained by differences in incidence of disease by socioeconomic class and educational level. Similar research has not been done with women who have benign uterine disease. Fear of potential cancer may significantly influence women's views of the value of elective hysterectomy, even when this disease has *not* been diagnosed (Cosper, Fuller, and Robinson 1980).

Both uterine cancer rates and hysterectomy rates have climbed dramatically. Incidence of endometrial cancer rose 40–150 percent among middle-aged American women between 1969 and 1973. National incidence rates for hysterectomy increased 21 percent between 1970 and 1975. Increase in hysterectomies reduces the population at risk for uterine and ovarian cancer, so incidence of these cancers is actually higher than most estimates. While increased incidence rates may result from better detection of cancer through improved health awareness and health care, a number of researchers also identify estrogen replacement therapy in the etiology of endometrial cancer (Antunes et al. 1979; Lyon and Gardner 1977: 439; Weiss, Szekely, and Austin 1976: 1260). Whether increases in endometrial cancer are iatrogenic or not, hysterectomy of a nonmalignant uterus eliminates the possibility of this disease, and this can be a persuasive argument for surgery. Some gynecologists favor elective hysterectomy for cancer prophylaxis alone (Errera 1973; Paulshock 1976; Wright 1969). We have no information on the salience of this argument for women who face elective hysterectomy for benign disease.

Epidemiological studies indicate that the benefits of elective surgery for prophylaxis against cancer alone do not justify its financial costs. Hysterectomy for benign disease is similarly not cost-effective (Cole and Berlin 1977; Jackson et al. 1978). Disadvantages of surgery include operative deaths, postoperative morbidity, possible marginal estrogen deficiency even when ovaries are intact, possible increases in atherosclerotic vascular disease, and depression (Dicker et al. 1982). Estimates of the mortality rate from hysterectomy range between 0.06 percent and 0.3 percent (Cole and Berlin 1977:118; Davies 1983:34). Complications occur in about 46 percent of surgeries (Errera 1973:43). When ovaries are removed, the subsequent use of estrogen replacement therapy may be linked with breast cancer (Bunker, McPherson, Henneman 1977; Morgan 1982). If women begin to forego surgery for prophylaxis and benign disease, costs to both hospitals and patients will be reduced. Over two billion dollars were spent on hysterectomies in the United States in 1977, including hospital costs and physician fees, a cost that has not declined in ensuing years (Easterday, Grimes, and Riggs 1983:203; Kasper 1985:122).

Beliefs about Biomedicine and Medical Decision Making

Despite the disadvantages of hysterectomy, little research has examined women's beliefs about surgery or the effect of previous medical experiences on choices for or against elective hysterectomy. Only a few studies have considered fears of surgery or surgical complications in the etiology of post-surgical depression (Gath 1980; Sloan 1978). Fears of surgical mortality and morbidity may have significant influence on women's choices to avoid or postpone surgery. Morgan (1982) found that women commonly fear hysterectomy itself, its outcome and complications, and potential cancer. Drellich and Bieber (1958) found through intensive interviewing that women feared pain and complications of surgery. They were concerned about having to wear bags or bottles in the hospital and were afraid they might lose control over their excretory functions. Richards, however, reports that 90.9 percent of 274 women responding to a questionnaire said they were pleased with their hysterectomies once the surgery was over. These women felt that their elective surgeries had been necessary (1978:447). Webb and Wilson-Barnet also found that eighty-seven of ninety-five women who had undergone simple hysterectomies for benign disease reported being glad that they had had surgery (1983:101). Nevertheless, measures of satisfaction after surgery do not tell us how women's expectations of hospitalization and surgery affect their preoperative choices. Additionally, understanding of and faith in bio-medicine is a social affirmation not shared by all groups in American society. There may be socioeconomic and cultural differences in women's perceptions of what hospitalization and surgery are like.

Kasrawi, Labib, and Hathout (1984) recognize the need for research on what they call the "premath" of hysterectomy. They found that women's greater understanding of reproductive physiology before surgery was cor-related with fewer myths about the effects of hysterectomy. This research was conducted in Kuwait with eighty-two women admitted to the hospital for hysterectomies. Despite the likelihood of cultural differences in appli-cation of this research to Western women, the authors' recommendation of education prior to surgery is well-taken.

McKinlay (1975) has argued that lack of compliance with physicians' recommendations may be attributed to poor communication by physicians who assume that patients are ignorant. Additionally, the tendency to blame the patient for ignorance may serve physicians in generally unexamined ways. The patient may be kept manageable and prevented from uncovering errors in treatment if she is kept uninformed. Critics also assert that women are talked into unnecessary hysterectomies by their physicians. Through interviews and observations in a hospital setting, Scully (1980) found that the need for residents to acquire surgical skill justified performance of un-necessary hysterectomies. As part of the argument used to convince women to accept surgery, they were frightened by the use of the word "tumor," persuaded that once childbearing was completed the uterus was unneeded, and assured that the surgery was simple and quick. Keyser (1984), a gyne-cologist, confirms these observations that women are scared into surgery and that physicians deliberately underinform their patients as to alternatives to surgery.

Clearly, women's degrees of knowledge about the surgery, the sources of information they use, and the attitudes of their families and friends have an important relationship to their perceptions of elective hysterectomy, yet no studies have been conducted on information networks in relation to hysterectomy. At the same time that a woman is consulting a gynecologist or surgeon, she may be exploring holistic health approaches or vitamin therapy, or visiting a feminist clinic. Related anthropological research has examined the effects of prior medical experiences and beliefs about medical practice, and the influences of family and friends, on women's choices of childbirth place and provider, and their choices for repeat cesarean section or trial of labor for vaginal birth after a previous cesarean (McClain 1981,

1983, 1985). Additional research is needed to specify the sociocultural context of health beliefs and practices in which decision making about hysterectomy occurs.

CONCLUSIONS

The foregoing review indicates areas where research is urgently needed if we are to understand women's own thinking when they face the choice for or against elective gynecologic surgery. Given the reported rate of unnecessary hysterectomies and the social and psychological impact of the surgery, greater understanding of women's beliefs and expectations about hysterectomy is needed. We do not know enough about the effect on women of loss of organs that are closely associated with feminine gender identity and social roles. In particular, it would be helpful to understand more about the decision-making process women undergo when facing recommended surgery.

Research that has been conducted on hysterectomy informs us that the relationship between socioeconomic status and choice for or against surgery or degree of satisfaction with outcome is unknown. Clearly, more studies are needed of differences in the attitudes of women from varying socioeconomic, cultural, ethnic, and religious backgrounds towards the female organs and their functions and the impact of their loss. The few women who have been surveyed have had generally positive responses to the loss of menstruation and childbearing capacity through hysterectomy, but we know very little about women's perceptions of these key functions and whether there is a difference in responses of pre- and postmenopausal women, or previously sterilized women, who experience the surgery. Few studies have attempted to evaluate the influence of fears of cancer on satisfaction with surgery. We also do not know if varying cultural valuations of menstruation and childbearing affect surgical choices.

Depression is common in women after hysterectomy, but its relationship to the surgery is unclear. Little is understood about the etiology of postsurgical depression, and almost no research has attempted to relate it to women's attitudes about their bodies and about loss of the uterus. It is possible that women who express early satisfaction with hysterectomy later become depressed, when their initial relief from disease and discomfort is replaced by feelings of loss or mourning.

We also have no information on women's extent of knowledge about their diagnosis and illness, their expectations of surgery and its side effects, and their willingness to undergo hysterectomies and degree of satisfaction with outcome. There is often poor communication between physicians and patients concerning this surgery, and while we can assume that women use information networks, we know nothing about this process in relation to hysterectomy decision making. Some studies have suggested that women who are less well informed more readily accede to their physician's advice, but no research has addressed this question with reference to gynecologic surgery.

Research on hysterectomy could examine the utility of the explanatory model's approach in a dynamic and evolving medical situation. Examination of attitudes toward hysterectomy provides an ideal context for studying how physicians' and patients' explanatory models distinguish medically defined physical abnormalities or malfunctions and socioculturally defined perceptions of illness.

According to the ethnomedical perspective, popular explanatory models define illness as deviance from socially determined norms of health. Thus, a malfunctioning uterus may deviate from a valued state of femininity, menstruation, motherhood, and bodily integrity. The depression often experienced by women who have undergone hysterectomies may be a potent indicator of complex psychological changes experienced during illness. Young (1976) has applied Schutz's (1962) concept of everyday thinking to the way in which people make health care decisions. Women may be "occupied with the contingent and pragmatic" as they decide what to do. For example, a woman wants to know if her hysterectomy will affect her marital relations or cause premature loss of sexuality. Physicians, however, engage in systematized thinking. They are interested in discussing an illness episode in terms of a coherent model of scientific explanation, to define it as a "disease" in ethnomedical terms.

Since women are becoming more active in the choice for or against surgery, it is vital for social researchers to determine how women's perceptions of gynecologic disease integrate with medical definitions. Medical anthropologists have examined explanatory models and the distinction between illness and disease primarily in non-Western settings, with the focus usually on folk illnessess that do not fit biomedical categories (Good 1977; Kleinman 1981; Like and Ellison 1981). Some studies have begun to appear which apply these concepts to Western medical settings (Blaxter 1983; Blumhagen 1980; Friedl 1982; Helman 1978). Such descriptions of explanatory models of unique illnesses will contribute to comparability in cross-cultural data.

Application of such approaches to the study of women's perceptions of elective hysterectomy is needed, for it would contribute to more effective health care planning and policies concerning this costly surgery, would aid better communication between physicians and patients, and improve informed consent prior to elective surgery. It would additionally aid efforts to prevent unnecessary surgery, to investigate therapeutic alternatives used by women who avoid surgery, and to improve recovery of women who do undergo hysterectomies.

NOTE

1. See Eisenberg 1977; Fabrega 1974; Hahn and Kleinman 1983; Kleinman 1980; Kleinman, Eisenberg, and Good, 1978; and Young 1982.

PART II

THE EFFECTS OF CULTURE CHANGE ON WOMEN'S HEALTH

Few areas of the world are untouched by Westernization and urbanization, which influence women's health in a variety of ways. Westernization results in women needing to find new health care services after migrating to urban areas, increased stress as a result of the effects of culture change, and the syncretism of traditional and Western health care practices. Women are not passive receptors in these situations of culture change, but instead they take active measures to maintain their health. These measures include finding new sources of health care, extending traditional birthing practices to Western contexts, redefining concepts of appropriate sex-role behavior, and developing coping strategies for themselves and their families as a response to culture change.

Dana Raphael's chapter on the *doula* has positive, global implications for birthing practices. Viewing the first childbirth and the transition to parenting (matrescence and patrescence) as rites of passage, she discusses the importance of a support person during this time. In some non-Western societies, *doula* is the term given to the person who acts as a psychological and

69

social comfort to the mother during late pregnancy, birth, and early lactation. The role of the *doula* is spreading to Western societies in the form of the labor coach. The labor coach, frequently but not always the child's biological father, helps the parturient woman through labor and birth, and offers support while lactation is being established. The *doula* eases the social and psychological transition to motherhood. Clinically, there is evidence that women who have a *doula* or labor coach require less medication during labor, and have a chance to bond earlier with their offspring than women who lack this means of support. A positive birth experience is reported by women who have a *doula*.

Judith A. Marmor's chapter discusses how female Turkish migrants in Berlin locate new sources of health care. To do so, these women must face language barriers, discrimination from the larger German society, and traditional Moslem concepts of modesty and appropriate female behavior. Turkish women nonetheless succeed in finding gynecologic and general health care which meets their needs. They do so by using other females to support them in finding and visiting the doctors, and by manipulating traditional sex-role behaviors.

The switch from breastfeeding to bottlefeeding infants in many Third World countries is having tragic results for infant nutrition. Penny Van Esterik examines the phenomenon of insufficient milk syndrome (IMS), in which women produce too little milk to nourish their infants adequately. She perceives this problem to be culture bound. In her discussion of IMS, Van Esterik explores the effects of Westernization on the mothers' choice of feeding practices and the sociopsychological effects of IMS on the mothers. She offers suggestions regarding education of women and health care practitioners, and the provision of social support for lactating women to reduce the incidence of IMS in the face of Western-based pressures to bottle and formula-feed infants.

Barbara D. Miller and Robert N. Kearney discuss the rise of female suicide rates in urbanizing Sri Lanka. It is noted that not all areas of Sri Lanka which are undergoing urbanization are experiencing an increase in suicide. A comparison is made between those areas which are experiencing increased suicide among women and those which aren't. Factors contributing to suicide include economic and social pressures which result in feelings of anomie. Suggestions for preventing or reducing the incidence of suicide, including employment opportunities and supportive social networks, are discussed.

Using a case-study approach, Jane Szurek discusses how women living in a coal mining town in Northern England are adapting to the economic and contemporary social pressures created by urbanization. Women deal with these pressures by expanding their economic and educational bases and redefining male-female interactions. While modernization is initially disruptive to these women's lives and health, the net result is a reduction in stress, an improved psychological outlook, and expansion of their roles as women.

From these chapters it is seen that culture change due to Westernization and urbanization is influencing women's health care in a variety of ways. While the *doula* is a positive, non-Western practice adopted by Western countries, many of the changes involve Western behaviors being introduced into traditional societies. Frequently, these innovations initially pose problems for the health of many of the women. In an attempt to either alleviate or resolve these problems, women redefine appropriate behavior, adopt new roles, and actively seek sources of medical care through the use of female social networks. Women, faced with modernization, actively respond to meet their health care needs.

5

THE NEED FOR A SUPPORTIVE DOULA IN AN INCREASINGLY URBAN WORLD

Dana Raphael

Westernization and its accompanying culture change affect numerous areas of people's lives. In this chapter, Raphael discusses how the non-Western birthing custom of the *doula,* or supportive birth attendant, is being adapted to Western obstetrics. This aspect of culture change frequently takes the form of a labor coach, who is often the biological father of the baby. The use of a coach during labor and birth is increasing in Western countries, including the United States. Becoming a parent is discussed as a rite of passage. The *doula* helps everyone—mother, fetus/newborn, and father—through this liminal state and period of transition.

Supportive behavior is that part of human interaction which tends to enhance the quality of life for at least one of the participants. It is a form of behavior that is a differentiating characteristic of all mammals, and it would be hard to dispute that it has made a substantial contribution to the survival of the species. In human beings, it represents the best of what is our humanness.

The protection, pleasure, comfort, and security which supportiveness offers is a reward an individual receives for being part of the group. Those individuals who do not agree to live within a community will be less likely to receive support. They suffer most during times of crisis when they cannot fall back on the grace of others whom they have helped or who anticipate their help in the future. Many institutions, such as the family, religious groups, medical, and economic organizations, take care of these crises.

The behavior found in 278 cultures (Raphael 1966) and among ninety-seven species of mammals (Raphael, Hale and Breakstone 1976) was reviewed in the cross-cultural, mammalian, and primate literature, and hundreds of interviews were conducted by the author (Raphael 1966) for evidence of supportiveness. The nature, nuances, and value of that support are now being studied in many fields.

73

Van Gennep (1960) pointed out that all human cultures have arranged to care for the individual during his or her life crises in well-defined cultural patterns which he called *rites de passage*. Marriage and burial ceremonies, baptism and puberty rites are examples of these times of change. Specific individuals inherit or accept very structured activities (roles) which are performed during these special life crises. When a culture is well integrated, the supportive patterns which accompany these rites are clearly discernable. They fulfill the basic needs of the individuals within the community. When a group, however, is in a stage of sudden change or stress and tension due to economic or ecological disaster, the supportive patterns can break down, even disappear.

Supportive relationships which occur during the dramatic changes of pregnancy, childbirth, and lactation can be some of the most powerful and important in a woman's life. Most recorded societies have supportive interactions for this transitional period which are built into their social mores. These supportive behaviors occur during the time when a woman is experiencing her matrescence and a male his patrescence[1]: when she changes from a woman to a mother and he from a man to a father. Becoming a parent is a basic behavior for human beings; it is finally receiving due attention from the social sciences.

In traditional societies it is expected that a certain amount of visiting between the pregnant woman and her family will occur during her pregnancy. Food is shared, but this is not yet a time for feasting because of the dangers inherent in childbirth and child survival. There will be a time to celebrate once a child has survived the first few weeks or months. A minimal amount of infant clothing and other necessary items are presented to the mother during predelivery parties which often are attended exclusively by female guests. These women are usually relatives, unlike in the United States and in Japan, where, if the woman works outside the home, the party is often given by co-workers.

The type of gift is fairly well-patterned and generally predictable. The eldest sister-in-law in some areas of India is expected to give her pregnant sister-in-law a new sari, while her husband's mother is obliged to see she has special foods which are appropriate for enhancing the health of her daughter-in-law and future grandchild. In the United States, the typical pattern is to hold a shower for the future mother. If her mother-in-law is present, she is expected to give the most elaborate, often the most expensive present. If not, it is the woman's best friend who gives the most elaborate baby blanket or sleeping crib, and all the other friends and relatives give according to their relationship to the pregnant woman and her family.

Over a period of months her own mother will donate or help the young couple purchase whatever necessities are still needed. After the baby is born, close relatives and friends visit and give slightly more elaborate presents, depending again on their relationship to the family. Gifts from the new

mother's family are generally more plentiful, whereas in a traditional, pa-
trilineal society, gifts from the new father's family would be just as
numerous.

Women are not the sole recipients of support in traditional societies.
The father, too, is made to understand that his new role is of great importance
to the group. The male also makes a dramatic role change during patrescence, especially the first time his partner gives birth. In Melanesia, he is
offered a new spear in anticipation of his future fatherhood and his entrance
into the adult male group; in fact, in many communities adulthood is only
achieved when the man or woman becomes a parent. After the birth or after
a period of time when the group becomes confident that the child will indeed
survive, the parents are often officially welcomed into the clan with formal
rituals and feasts to commemorate the event.

In Western cultures, the focus of social concern is on the mother first,
and secondarily on her partner. In traditional societies, however, the family
plays a more prominent role. It is the family unit which is to accept the new
member into their group; the new child creates aunts, uncles, and grand-
parents. Thus the whole family contributes to the gifts of food which the
grandfather presents to the priests who will then intervene with the sacred
world in behalf of the safety of mother and child. On their part, the couple
commit themselves to abstain from intercourse as their sacrifice to placate
the spirits and assure a safe delivery. Once birth occurs, it is family members
who are assigned to carry on the new mother's work, tend her fields or take
over the responsibility for feeding her family.

If the acts just described were simply kindnesses offered now and again,
we could ignore them. But they are formal, culturally prescribed patterns
which are part of those activities we define as supportive behavior. They
function to keep the baby alive, to increase the well-being of the mother,
to maintain family continuity, and ultimately, to assure the survival of the
community. This chapter will later describe the changes and breakdowns in
those patterns in Western societies, and ways to rebuild a support system
for the new parents. In an attempt to emphasize the power and necessity
for supportive behavior, however, evidence of its evolutionary roots in non-
human social animals is presented.

There is much literature which indicates that in many species of mammals, females help each other during the perinatal period. These species
include elephants, dolphins, deer, elk, and some of the wild cats (Eloff 1973;
Lilly 1963; Prior 1968; Raphael 1969; Raphael, Hale and Breakstone 1976).
Many but not all of these animals who behave supportively towards parturient females are their uterine kin (Rowell, Hinde, and Spencer-Booth
1964).

Supportive mammalian behavior towards a parturient individual extends to primates, our closest relatives. Both monkeys and apes have been
observed to stay close to, groom, sniff, and observe birthing and postpartum

females and their young (Imanishi 1957; Itani 1954; Jay 1963; Lorenz 1959; Tinberg 1951). The attraction by adults of many species to newborns appears to be an evolutionarily old and widespread behavior (Lorenz 1959). Among many of these primates, the ties formed at birth between the mother and her young and supportive others exist primarily among uterine relatives intergenerationally (Dunbar 1983; Sade 1965; Lawick-Goodall 1967; Yamada 1963).

THE *DOULA* IN HUMAN SOCIETIES

The term I will use to describe a similar kind of emotional and social support for human matrescence and patrescence is the *doula*. In Greece, the woman who came to the home when there was a new baby, cared for the older child(ren), cooked the dinner, bounced the fretting baby, and generally helped the new mother through the early postpartum period was called *Doula* by the children (Raphael 1976). She was often a neighbor, sometimes a relative. I have suggested that this term would be appropriate to describe the behavior of other, mostly female helpers, towards the new mother.

Human males often are expected to perform specific actions when the woman is in labor. The *couvade* is an interesting example of a remarkable cultural practice. Among some South American Indian groups, for example, the man lies down and writhes in pain, calling out to the spirits that he is delivering the child. The expectation is that any evil intended by the supernatural will be directed towards him and not the woman in labor. She, on her part, must labor in silence and patience (Honigman 1959; Hunter and Whitten 1976; Oswalt 1986; Taylor 1973).

In human society, support by another woman during delivery is by far the most common pattern throughout the world (Mead and Newton 1967; Raphael 1966). The supportive person in France is called the *monitrice*, a nurse attached to an obstetrical team who works with the woman during her pregnancy and is with her during delivery (Vellay 1959). Usually the supportive relationship ends there. This person is now becoming known as the *doula* in the United States. She is the supportive person, nurse, or lay person who cares for the mother not only during her delivery, but often postpartum. Her presence tends to keep the mother calm during delivery and, as we shall see later, is instrumental in her success at breastfeeding.

In traditional societies the partner is sometimes present and assists his spouse at childbirth; in industrial countries, the mate was firmly removed from the birth scene for many decades of the twentieth century. In the United States, in Japan, and in many European countries, as more and more births took place in hospitals or under the care of medical professionals, and as social arrangements became less and less family oriented, this pattern of medicalized birth became well-established. In the United States during the early 1900s, women were separated from family members, doused with anesthesia, and delivered in an unconscious state. For the first time in history, the usual cluster of women attending the birth was replaced by a new class of unrelated professional men, mostly strangers—obstetricians and pediatricians—who took part in the intimate and heretofore private birth-lactation stage.

Since the 1960s, in many Western societies, the presence of the woman's partner during the delivery and feeding processes has become increasingly common. Now that "natural" childbirth has become the norm, the woman in labor finds herself in need of someone to be close by, preferably a husband or other trusted kin. But as people become more and more independent of extended kin, another consequence of urbanization, the person performing the role of *doula* or labor coach may be either her spouse, or a stranger.

In the United States, the struggle for the husband to enter the delivery room and to assume some of the *doula* roles began in the 1950s, but was not widely realized much before the middle of the 1970s. A change in the mores of the culture relative to appropriate male behavior and acceptable medical practices was necessary for this behavior to occur. Men had to be allowed to express a degree of tenderness which until the '70s had been equated with weakness. Men began to realize that it was acceptable to tenderly care for their children, to cry over the joy they experienced at childbirth, to acknowledge the woman's pleasure at breastfeeding. Research indicates that the presence of the father is beneficial to the well-being of the mother (Bradley 1965; Karmel 1965).

In addition, there has been a shift in attitude towards pregnancy and childbirth within the medical profession. Until recently, "modern" obstetrical practices in the United States moved away from the sociopsychological dimensions of supporting the woman during childbirth and towards the medical and physical aspects. Childbirth was considered to approximate a painful and dangerous illness, primarily a physical event that needed to be managed and controlled through technology and drugs.

Recent changes have incorporated the physical and sociopsychological dimensions of pregnancy and birth, including prepared forms of childbirth, family-centered childbirth, and little or no use of medication during labor. A major component of this "new" approach involves the use of labor coach or support person, generally the father of the baby, but sometimes a nurse-midwife, close friend, or relative. The labor coach takes on many of the behaviors and responsibilities of the *doula* during late pregnancy and through the early perinatal period. An additional component of prepared childbirth is a positive view and encouragement of breastfeeding, which will later be discussed briefly in terms of the birthing experience (Arms 1975; Boston Women's Health Collective [1973] 1976, 1984; Bradley 1965; Karmel 1965).

FINDINGS

A survey of 45,000 instances where the husband was present at the birth revealed many advantageous consequences of his presence. In fact, the results were so encouraging they were instrumental in changing hospital rules which had previously excluded other persons from attending the birth (Stender 1971). A Canadian survey reported similar results, leading to the use of consent forms and other materials helpful to the couple in arranging to be together (Ernst 1975).

In a pilot study conducted by Sosa et al. (1980) at the Social Security Hospital in Guatemala City, Guatemala, expectant mothers who were assigned an untrained, unfamiliar *doula* to provide reassurance and physical contact throughout labor and delivery had a shorter labor and a lower rate of cesarean section than did women who labored alone. Twenty women who had the support of a *doula* experienced 8.7 hours of labor compared with 19.3 hours for the control group. Further analysis showed that the incidence of cesarean section was 6.5 percent among 200 women assigned a *doula*, compared with 18 percent among controls. Mothers with *doulas* also required less medication and were more likely than controls to remain awake after delivery and to interact more often with their babies.

Unfortunately, this original and important work was interrupted by the tragic Guatemalan earthquake which occurred in the midst of the research and drastically limited hospital space. This may well have skewed the results. Other studies are under way to test these early assumptions with controlled samples and careful analysis.

The claims that husband participation can dramatically affect the future relationships between the infant and the parent, however, must be carefully assessed. Even more care should be shown before we can accept the suggestion that participation in the delivery room may affect the divorce rate (Allen 1983; Hommel 1971).

Such claims are often phrased in very romantic terms. The human being, however, is far too complex a creature to simplify behavior to one event, and to attribute a lifetime effect to that original experience. The reason to promote husband participation during childbirth is not that it will make some remarkable difference in the future, but because it is an enriching experience for both parents. This idea has some justification. Fathers who were present at the birth rated the birth experience more positively than fathers who were not present, and they had a more positive perception of themselves as an effective helper during labor. They also expressed greater feelings of closeness with their wives, though whether or not they were present, their feelings towards their babies were no different (Cronenwett and Newmark 1974).

The result of a survey of eighty-seven departments of anesthesiology showed that 97 percent of the fathers were allowed in the delivery room during vaginal births and 86 percent during cesarean births. These men were permitted to witness the event from the start of the anesthesia in 62 percent of the departments surveyed (Allen 1983). There is no doubt that the presence of the partner in the delivery room is becoming the accepted option.

The length of labor may not be affected by the presence of the partner; in thirty-eight cases, when a woman's husband was present, the length of first-and second-stage labor did not differ from the birth experiences of women without their spouse present. However, women whose husbands were present appeared to experience less pain during dilation and needed less pain medication during labor and birth. After birth, these women described themselves as highly pleased and enthusiastic far more often than did the women whose husbands were not present (Henneborn and Cogan 1975). Similarly, the presence of a partner during labor and delivery prompted women to reply more often that they had a "peak experience" in childbirth (Tanzer 1967).

In future research the obvious self-selection of these studies will have to be corrected. Nonetheless, it does appear that the presence of a *doula* can lead to easier and safer deliveries.

The *Doula* and Breastfeeding

The effect of a supportive person on the success of breastfeeding is a prime example of the critical need for a *doula*. In fact, as my own studies (1966) have revealed, without the presence of a supportive person lactation is usually inhibited, and breastfeeding often fails. There is a physiological basis for this reduced and inhibited lactation:

> The answer lies in the function of the critical ejection reflex that will or will not operate depending on the mother's physical reaction to her living situation. Here's how it works. The process begins when the infant sucks, triggering nerves in the nipple to send "messages" to the pituitary gland in the brain. As a result, the hormone, oxytocin, is released into the blood stream stimulating the cells in the mammary gland when the milk is being stored, causing them to contract and propel the milk out of thousands of tiny sinuses and into the central ducts leading to the nipple.
>
> If the ejection reflex is sufficiently strong, the milk becomes available to the nursling. Regardless of how long or how hard the baby sucks, or how much milk is stored in the breasts, it cannot be drawn out if this reflex is inhibited. And, when the mother is taken care of the ejection reflex is triggered. When she is left to care for herself and her baby all alone—despair and failure often can result. Then we hear the familiar complaint, e.g., "I don't have enough milk, my milk dried up." (Kato, Hirayama, and Kobayashi 1983).

A common time when breastfeeding failure tends to occur is ten days to two weeks after birth. If, however, a caring, helping person is introduced to play the role of *doula* towards that mother, the pattern is reversed and usually full lactation returns (Raphael 1966).

Theoretical Implications

With all these encouraging studies we can comfortably conclude that labor, delivery, and breastfeeding are immeasureably enriched by the presence of a *doula*: a friend, mother's mother, sister, or husband. There is another important issue which concerns the quality and quantity of that help in both the giver and the receiver of the support. All women are not the same, nor does each need the same amount of support. On the contrary, each needs a variety of different amounts of support at different times for each stage of reproduction. This is illustrated by the example of support from the woman's partner. A couple's interaction is not solely related to the experience of childbirth and breastfeeding. While in labor, the woman may expect a great deal of close contact or may be made miserable by such a display. She may have implicit trust in her partner, want him present but only at the head of her bed, as she may not want to appear too demanding, too dominant, or out of control in his presence.

Also at stake is the relationship of a woman to her obstetrical team. She may need a great deal of help, she may want to bear the child without advance preparation, or she may want to be in charge at all times. As for the interaction between herself and a *monitrice*, or *doula*, the woman in labor may cling to her in fear, or expect her to be present but silent, as the laboring mother herself gets on with the job.

The future father himself brings to the delivery experience many mixed feelings. He may be overly concerned about his wife and unconcerned about the child. He may be distracted because of his great wish that the baby be a boy. He may be fearful he will not be "strong" during the actual birth and embarrass himself.

It is clear that reactions in the parents are multiple and extensive. They should make us wary of accepting simple results based on single factors as causing major life changes unless the situation is most unusual or traumatic. How a father feels at the moment of birth, whether or not he is present, or whether or not the mother breastfeeds immediately will not normally have any long-term effect on the parents and child. A man may enjoy the birth experience as one of the great moments in his life and yet not be able to tolerate the daily noise of the baby. The woman may have a very difficult labor and delivery, not see her child for hours, and yet be an excellent mother. The presence of helpful persons during this sensitive perinatal period is important because the mother and father want it, they need it, and it enriches their present lives; but not because it insures some future hoped-for reaction in parent or child.

All those involved in responding to the need of new parents should be aware, concerned, and helpful in regard to their client's/patient's need for support, and the amount of help given and received. The emotional and practical needs of the helpers themselves are challenging issues for professionals today.

Contemporary Developments

Following are suggestions as to how to meet this challenge. Understanding the *doula* role in our own and other cultures, and what is actually done for the mother, are initial steps. By comparing various methods we can translate and adapt them to our needs. Study of supportive help focused on the pregnant woman and the new mother has revealed that the *doula* could, in fact, be one person or many persons (Raphael 1984). A single individual, such as the mother's mother, can assume full responsibility for the woman and her child. Or there could be two persons, one who works to make the mother comfortable, usually her own mother, and another who tends the newborn, a traditional role expected of the father's mother. The *doula* role could be played by many persons, each performing a specific, necessary task: the new infant's grandmothers could fill the roles just mentioned, her godmother (or *comadre* in many Latin American cultures) pinch-hits for her mother or mother-in-law in helping with her personal needs. The sister-in-law works the new mother's garden plot, while the grandfather provides special foods for the new mother to encourage lactation. The new father takes off from work and plays host to the visitors.

The role of *doula* can be filled by one or several people, and, as a rule, the more economic assets the family has the more persons are invited to participate in the process of helping mother and baby survive. In affluent societies, the father is expected to take care of the housing, to pay for all food requirements of the family, and the intimate parts of the infant's wardrobe, such as the diapers. In these cultures, friends help provide the external clothing for the baby, while relatives provide the equipment for the infant's nursery such as cribs and bassinets.

In most cultures a woman's mother is the "relative of choice," but if she cannot help, a "functionally equivalent" person such as a sister or grandmother is chosen. These human arrangements can be very complex. For example, one explicit function of the *comadre* role in Latin American cultures is the care of her godchild during this perinatal stage. The *comadre* will then perform many required services over the life span of her godchild, such as gifts at birthdays, at communion, and at marriage.

In our complex industrial societies it is often another woman in a similar stage of reproduction who provides this support for the new mother. A woman's "best friend" is seldom called upon for this role; she is usually too far away. The British say that the helper must be within "pram-pushing distance." Women who meet in the hospital during their delivery and live close by—in the same building or neighborhood, and within walking distance—are the best *doulas* to provide this support, which is almost always mutual. The *doula* and the mother work out patterns that are reciprocal and complementary, sharing babysitting, housework, and providing mutual emotional and social support.

Women in groups of three of four are now making compatible arrangements to meet each other's needs. In the United States, some of the culturally patterned competitiveness among women which was apparent from 1930 to 1950 has given way to a renewed commitment of women to women (Boston Women's Health Collective [1973] 1976, 1984). Today more women can appreciate and accept help from other women, and meet in groups with each other without being ridiculed as in the past.

A fourth type of *doula* arrangement is a professional lactation specialist, an expert in the normal management of breastfeeding, frequently a registered nurse. This professional worker is often a former leader of La Leche League, a support group for breastfeeding mothers. She is paid for her work and is often associated with a midwife or is attached to a pediatric group. The most effective method occurs when this *doula* can get to know the parents prior to delivery rather than to be contacted only when there is a crisis. Slowly, more and more physicians are becoming aware of how useful a lactation specialist can be, and how much time it can save them and their staff.

Physicians themselves play a large part of the complex *doula* role. They have found that if they make the initial call after a woman has returned home from the clinic or the hospital to inquire about how breastfeeding is going, they are not likely to be awakened by an exhausted father at dawn. One pediatrician in private practice in Connecticut tried to persuade a new colleague to accept this pattern of personal attention. The new partner refused, explaining that it just meant one more call in his very busy day. Within two weeks and after many night calls, he had changed his mind.

Still another supportive arrangement has been tried in Louisville, Kentucky, where a community advisor was employed for a breastfeeding program in a poor section of the city (Bryant 1984). One lay person was trained to be a breastfeeding support worker for women within several street blocks. Even though this *doula* was relatively near the mothers, phone availability was a major part of the program. As long as the telephone bills were paid by the organizers, the program was successful in helping women to breastfeed. When the telephone was no longer subsidized, however, the program ended.

It is apparent that there are many useful means of helping a woman care for her child, to give her support so she can breastfeed that child. It is the responsibility of the professional medical team to help her recognize these options and find the best one for her.

CONCLUSIONS

A rite of passage is a liminal status, a time when individuals are in transition—when they leave behind known, familiar behaviors and values and adopt new ones. As such, this period of limbo, the unknown, can be threatening and frightening to the participants. They need social and psychological support from their larger group in order to get through this period. Childbirth is such a transition for everyone involved—the fetus/newborn and the parents. A socially and psychologically supportive person such as the *doula* helps the parents through this liminal phase.

As part of our mammalian and primate heritage, the *doula* has deep roots. Common in traditional societies, it was lost for a time in Western culture as a result of technical advances in twentieth-century American obstetrics. Since the 1960s, however, the concept of the *doula* has been increasingly accepted in our birthing practices in the form of labor coach. The labor coach eases the way for the participants in this particular rite of passage (Boston Women's Health Collective [1973] 1976, 1984; Masters, Johnson, and Kolodny 1982).

Many claims have been made for the value of a happy, intimate, supportive first childbearing experience. A full first relationship gives the parents a richer experience. As family patterns change in response to urbanization and modernization, and as the supportive *doula* becomes more and more often a stranger, we are beginning to realize that a great deal of money can be saved by making the whole perinatal period a successful, creative experience. The health professional is in a position to help parents take a giant step towards what may be their most creative and most important experience. When a family gets started in a most enjoyable and loving way, it increases the chance that they will have a positive birth experience, and a happier and healthier newborn.

NOTE

1. Conrad Arensberg is credited with supplying these terms, which so adequately portray this dramatic change in people's lives (cited in Raphael 1976).

6

HEALTH AND HEALTH-SEEKING BEHAVIOR OF TURKISH WOMEN IN BERLIN

Judith A. Marmor

Moslem Turkish women migrating to Berlin in order to be with their husbands face problems in finding health care. In seeking it, they must surmount larger societal discrimination, language barriers, and deal with inherent ideal/real behavioral conflicts. This last problem stems from traditional Turkish definitions of female modesty and expectations of behavior patterns for wives and mothers. Turkish women's ability to meet their health care needs relative to reproductive and general concerns is a statement of their determination to resolve the ideal/real behavior conflict. They do this in part by utilizing woman-centered social support networks to locate and visit physicians.

Since the 1950s, millions of people from Southern and Eastern Europe and the Middle East have taken advantage of employment opportunities in the rapidly growing industrial sectors of northwestern Europe. As economic growth has slowed, and unemployment in the host nations has increased, government policies have begun to encourage labor migrants to return to their homelands.

West Berlin was particularly interested in attracting foreign labor. The postwar political situation, especially after the building of the Berlin Wall in 1961, was responsible for the decision of many people of working age to leave the city to work and raise their children in more secure environments. Worried about West Berlin's continued viability as a free city, officials at first welcomed immigrant workers. Turkish workers have been especially responsive to northern Europe's need for labor. After the signing of formal labor agreements by the West German and Turkish governments in 1961, Turks poured into West Germany. The Turkish population expanded rapidly from 225 in 1960 to nearly 80,000 in Berlin in 1973. By 1973, there were more than one million Turkish "guest workers" in the Federal Republic of Germany (Rist 1978:10). Despite efforts to slow and reverse this trend, the number of Turks in Berlin had grown to 119,000 by 1983, including 41,000 children and 34,000 women (Statistisches Landesamt Berlin 1983).

The effects of migration on the physical and mental health of migrants have been topics of discussion since the 1950s. The degree of voluntariness of migration, amount of shift along the rural-urban continuum, and the size of the "cultural gap" between homeland and destination are considered major indicators of postmigration health status (Hull 1979). It has been noted that voluntary migrations involving little cultural change or difference in urbanness, such as those of the American middle class, seem to be relatively trouble-free and not associated with any particular health problems (Gutman 1963; Landis and Stoetzer 1966). On the other hand, migrants who perceive their move as involuntary, or who are required to make large adjustments to new sociocultural environments, are more likely to have health problems. These often take the form of stress-associated diseases such as hypertension (Scotch 1963) or coronary heart disease (Syme, Hyman, and Enterline 1964).

The case of Turkish migrant women in West Berlin would seem to represent an extreme example of disruptive migration. Many of these women stem from small, traditional villages and are unused to the hectic lifestyle of an industrial Western European city. The kinds of health problems related to their migration experience, and the health-seeking strategies devised by some of these women, are the topics of this chapter.

Household interviews were conducted in the winter of 1983–84 with a group of twenty-five Turkish women about their health and their migration experiences. The informants were primarily self-selected from neighborhood Turkish women's centers where they attended literacy courses, German classes, or just met to talk and relax. Although this selection method tended to pick up the more outgoing, less tradition-bound women, a number of referrals allowed for the inclusion of unemployed, isolated women. The sample group included teenage girls, several university graduates, and young married women, as well as grandmothers. Some had been in Berlin for more than ten years, others less than a year. Their comprehension of German extended from rudimentary to fluent. Once potential interviewees had been identified, arrangements were made to meet with them individually in their homes. The interviews were conducted informally with the help of an interpreter around a core of questions. Often female friends and relatives were present. If possible, interviews were obtained from them as well. Although health-related issues were the main focus, the interviews included questions about life in Turkey, their migration experience, family history, and social networks in Germany. These interviews revealed a number of health problems which can best be grouped into two areas: stress-related illnesses and reproductive concerns. A third area, mental health, was not included in the study.

MIGRATION-RELATED STRESSORS

For many Turkish women, the migration experience began with a separation of several years from their husbands. Originally hired for a limited period of one to two years, many Turks came to Germany alone to "make their fortunes," leaving their wives and families at home in familiar surroundings. A recent West German study of migrant workers reported that in 1968 only 34 percent of married Turkish workers were accompanied by their wives (Mehrländer et al. 1981). As the length of stay in Germany became even longer, an increasing number of men brought their families to join them. By 1980, although the percentage of married Turks had changed negligibly (1968: 82 percent; 1972: 86 percent; 1980: 84 percent), the percentage who had brought their wives rose dramatically from 34 percent to 77 percent (Ibid. 1981).

It proved to be more difficult than expected to accumulate savings, and the probability of employment in Turkey remained low, so many Turks chose to renew their work contracts in Germany. Many women were left in an ambiguous position due to the prolonged absence of their husbands. Aside from the stress of extended separation, and their dependence on money from Germany, their status and role as married women became dubious. Traditional Islamic village society does not allow women status independent of men. Because a family's honor is dependent upon female sexual purity, women are under the protection of fathers, brothers, or husbands all of their lives. A man who seeks employment in Germany leaves his wife without this protection; unless she is divorced or widowed, she is not her father's or brother's responsibility. Without male protection and in a social limbo, her reputation is vulnerable to speculation. Consequently, joining their husbands in a foreign country is an attractive alternative. Of the women interviewed in Berlin, over half of those who had been married in Turkey experienced a period of separation from their husbands. The shortest time reported was one year; the longest was fourteen years.

A similar, though not as extreme, situation occurred in reverse. Turkish women were also recruited by the German employment offices. In 1968, 71 percent of the migrant women were married, but only 73 percent of these were accompanied by their husbands or families (Mehrländer et al. 1981). The situation of the married unaccompanied women was probably more difficult than that of the married women left behind in the Turkish villages. The problem of maintaining the family's honor took on new dimensions. Not only were they removed from the protection of their immediate male relatives, but they were also beyond the network of social control imposed by the village. These women had to behave even more circumspectly than the wives left behind in Turkey in order to retain virtuous reputations. By 1980, the percentage of married women had increased slightly to 74 percent. Of these, 95 percent were with their husbands. In both cases, the significant increase in the percentage of spouses joining husbands or wives in Germany is a reflection of the loneliness of extended separation and of the perception that unaccompanied women are vulnerable.

For some women, the loneliness and anxiety of separation were by no means alleviated after their arrival in Berlin. Two of the women interviewed arrived to find their husbands living with German women. In one case, the girlfriend had had one child and was expecting another. In the second case, the husband refused to give up his girlfriend and forced his wife to remain in the apartment as well. Unfortunately, divorce does not seem to be a viable option for these women, or for others in similar situations. Although women are allowed to file for divorce under Turkish civil law, until recently that divorce had to be filed in Turkey. This made divorce nearly impossible for women who did not have their own source of income. Even though Turkish divorces may now be filed in Germany, the women are subject to deportation unless they have lived in Germany continuously for five years and have obtained a work permit (Der Senator für Inneres 1982).

The lack of control over their situation, the difficulties inherent in any adaptation to a foreign climate, environment, and culture, as well as a number of other factors which hinder the adaptation process, can engender stress. Several of the women interviewed commented negatively about Berlin's climate: how cold it was, how often it rained, and how poor the quality of the air was. They missed the variety of fruits and vegetables available in Turkey. They missed their families and communities. Woman also mentioned that in Germany they felt under much closer scrutiny by Turkish neighbors who reported any "unacceptable," non-Turkish behavior—such as Western dress, or talking to strangers—to friends and neighbors in Turkey.

The majority of Turkish families (59.9 percent) intend to return to Turkey at some point (Mehrländer et al. 1981). There is little desire to adopt German lifestyles and become assimilated into German society. Although 40 percent do not plan to return to Turkey, only 6.2 percent of the Turks interviewed in the same study are interested in acquiring German citizenship. On the contrary, Turks may exaggerate their adherence to Turkish morals and customs in an attempt to retain their identity as Turks, especially in the eyes of the larger Turkish community. Women are particularly affected by this tendency. Because the world outside the family circle is perceived as hostile and dangerous to women, many Turks don't like to see their wives and daughters leave home unless accompanied by a male family member. This makes it difficult for women to go shopping, go to the doctor, or attend literacy or German language classes. Life in the Turkish village is communal, with women sharing their work. The transition to an urban industrial environment where each woman is isolated in a small apartment can be difficult (Bagana et al. 1982).

The dilemma posed by adherence to traditional Turkish dress, which includes headscarf, long sleeves, long skirt as required by Islamic rules of modesty, also becomes a factor in the daily stress experienced by migrant women. Turkish clothing styles set women apart as members of an unwelcome minority and target them for racist remarks and worse. One woman, for example, told me she was convinced that she had been mugged because she was wearing clothing that identified her as a Turk. On the other hand, dressing to blend in with the German majority invites criticism from family and community about lack of respect, doubtful morals, and a loss of Turkish values. Some, older women especially, "resolve" the issue by staying at home.

An important source of loneliness and worry for Turkish women is the separation from family and friends. Thirty five percent of the Turkish families questioned in a 1980 Berlin study reported that they still had young children between the ages of six and fifteen living in Turkey (Broeg et al. 1980). Nearly 60 percent of these families were not planning to bring their children to Berlin. Since children represent the fundamental reason for a woman's existence in Islamic culture and are the source of her power in the family, this separation is tremendously difficult. In an attempt to limit the number of Turks migrating to Berlin, the Berlin government is considering measures that would prohibit children over the age of sixteen from joining their parents. German rationale is since these children are too old to be incorporated successfully into the German school system, they would thus be unemployable and end up on welfare. Some officials would like to lower the age limit to six years (Der Senator für Gesundheit, Soziales und Familie 1982).

The differences in the rates of adaptation to German society experienced by the working husband and schoolchildren compared to the homebound wife are also important causes of marital and familial strain. The Turkish woman, with fewer opportunities to learn the German language or develop contacts with German society, trades in her role as advisor to her children in such matters as homework, peer group interactions, and all the normal dilemmas of growing up, for one of dependency. The children act as her translators at the doctor's office or government bureaus, and they are more familiar with the public transportation system. They are often asked to read letters from home or other documents their illiterate mothers are unable to decipher. The mother's position of authority is thus undermined, or lost, without being replaced by a substitute role.

Employment is perceived as an escape from the isolation of the home environment, as an attempt to find a role beyond that of the increasingly frustrating one as wife and mother. This opportunity to help save for the family's financial future can be an important factor in rebuilding self-esteem. However, as pointed out by Heckmann (1978), employment increases the probability that women will learn more independent behavior patterns. This deviation from expected or approved behavior could be interpreted negatively by husbands and again act as a source of psychological strain. Furthermore, the sociocultural background of the majority of Turkish migrant women which makes it difficult for them to fulfill their roles as mothers and wives also severely restricts the type of employment for which they qualify. For example, nearly 15 percent of those interviewed in a 1980 study had never gone to school, while 64 percent reported between one and five years of education (Broeg et al. 1980). Only 10 percent had attended school for more than nine years. The lack of German language skills is another barrier to employment. Although a variety of agencies offer German language courses, Turkish women are unlikely to go: their husbands won't let them, they are offered in the evening, they cost too much, or they don't have anyone to take care of the children. Illiteracy in the native tongue also makes it that much more difficult to learn German.

A barrier to employment imposed by the German government is the requirement that family dependents reside in Berlin for five years before they become eligible for work permits (Senator für Gesundheit, Soziales und Familie 1982). The only alternative is to seek employment "under the table," with the attendant problems: no job security, no benefits, and constant fear of discovery by the authorities. About 30 percent of the Turkish migrant women who find work in Berlin are employed in physically demanding and stressful jobs (Burmeister et al. 1981). Those who aren't employed as cleaning women work as unskilled labor in factories, often under adverse conditions. Research shows that factory-employed Turks have higher accident rates than their German counterparts because they tend to be forced into positions associated with greater health risks (noise, temperature extremes, piecework, etc.) (Deppe 1973). Working migrant women are expected to put in a full day of work at home as well as on the job. Their traditional role expectations are unchanged by the fact that they have taken on additional responsibilities. Physical exhaustion is thus not uncommon.

The housing situation of many Turkish families adds a final touch to the stresses of daily life. Because many Turks claim that their stay in Berlin is only temporary, a high proportion of monthly income goes to savings or to relatives in Turkey; not much money is allocated to daily necessities such as living quarters. According to a comprehensive study of the housing situation of Turks in Berlin, the average rent paid is between $38 and $63 per month (1984 exchange rates), regardless of income, size of household, or length of time in Berlin (Prognos 1980). Apartments in this price range tend to be small and situated in the oldest buildings in the least desirable parts of town. Nearly 75 percent of the Turkish families in Berlin live in three inner city districts adjacent to the Berlin Wall. Most of the apartments are woefully inadequate.

HEALTH STATUS

Although the pressures with which migrant women live are well-documented in the German literature, the connections between stress and illness have become the focus of research only recently (Burmeister et al. 1981; Grottian 1984). The combination of the factors explained above creates a vicious cycle for Turkish women from which it is difficult to escape. The stress and tensions with which these women attempt to cope daily is reflected in their illnesses.

Stress-related Illnesses

Five of the women had ulcers or preulcer conditions that had required treatment. Most women reported a postmigration onset of symptoms. One woman came to Berlin with gastritis, but said it had become much more severe since her arrival. Two other women had been diagnosed as hypertensive, and six women reported chronic headaches for which they had sought medical help. When asked about the causes of these illnesses, replies included, "the dirt of the city," "undernourishment," "worrying too much and not taking care of yourself," "troubles and problems," "nerves—tension and stress—and bacteria." Most of the quantitative research on peptic ulcers deals with the condition in men (Neukirchen and Haase 1978; Quaquish, Burchardt, and Heilmann 1979). Information about the prevalence of peptic ulcers in migrant women is unavailable but is likely to be elevated as well.

German research into the health problems of Turkish women has been heavily weighted in the direction of reproductive health. Thus, comparison of the rate of stress-related problems with epidemiological studies is not possible. However, recent qualitative studies accept elevated levels of these types of problems as matter of course (Grottian 1984; Theilen 1984).

Reproductive Health

Reproductive health has been the focus of more research. A 1984 study of a family planning agency in Berlin reported that Turkish women were, contrary to expectation, receptive to contraception information (Rohrmoser 1984). It is usually assumed that since children, especially sons, represent an Islamic woman's means of self-realization, birth control would not be well-received. Most of the women seeking assistance were married, reflecting the strict moral code of Turkish families. Two groups of women were represented. The first was women who had had all the children they wanted and wished to prevent further pregnancies. These women belonged to the first generation of migrants who had been married in Turkey and had borne at least one child before moving to Germany. The second group consisted of younger women of the second generation who had grown up in Germany with more exposure to German values and customs. These women were more interested in birth spacing and limiting their families to one or two children (Rohrmoser 1984). Though this study does not provide any figures on the percentage of Turkish women who practice family planning, it does suggest that what was previously thought to be resistance to the idea of birth control is now understood to have been ignorance of its availability.

Strobel (1975) investigated the participation of migrant workers and German women in prenatal care. The national health insurance system pays for ten prenatal visits as well as the delivery. Strobel found that 5.3 percent of the migrant women did not participate in the prenatal program, compared to 0.8 percent of the German women. Foreign women were also more likely to go to a general practitioner (34 percent) than German women (21.2 percent), who preferred specialists. Their first visit was more likely to occur later in pregnancy: 66.7 percent of the German women had seen a doctor by their fourth month, while only 47.1 percent of the migrant women had. Similarly, migrant women had fewer visits than German women: only 34 percent of them had six or more exams compared to 56.1 percent of the German women.

Reasons for the lack of prenatal care vary: ignorance of the importance or existence of programs, lack of time for visits to the doctor, lack of supervision for other children, a sense of modesty which discourages physical examinations, especially by men, and, always, language problems. Communication difficulties and the resulting frustration with treatment lead many women to change doctors frequently, a problematic solution. A recent examination of nearly 19,000 pregnancies in West Berlin shed additional light on the prenatal care issues outlined previously (Zink et al. 1982). Not only do Turkish women see their doctor less frequently, but they also receive fewer services per visit than German women do. Higher rates of infections and psychosomatic complaints were registered for Turkish women, but fewer medications and supplements were prescribed for them.

A second issue in reproductive health is whether or not foreign women have more frequent delivery complications than German women. For many Turkish women, previous births have taken place in the home, attended by a midwife and surrounded by female friends and family members. The sterile hospital atmosphere, filled with German-speaking strangers and male doctors, promotes fear and tension in the mother, which can negatively affect the birth process (Franger 1984). For the medical staff, the situation is difficult as well. The often missing and incomplete medical history, combined with language barriers, make it difficult to judge the level-of-risk of the delivery or provide the necessary emotional support (Wittlinger, Hohlweg-Majert, and Sievers 1977).

While some studies show a higher than average cesarean section rate for guest workers, other studies show the opposite. For example, a Berlin hospital showed lower cesarean section delivery levels for migrant workers than Germans (Wittlinger, Hohlweg-Majert, and Sievers 1977), but two West German hospitals showed higher surgical interventions for migrant women (Schliemann and Schliemann 1975; Schultze-Naumburg and Scholtes 1976). Similar contradictions abound in other childbirth-related topics: miscarriages, prematurity, infant mortality, and congenital defects (Hoffmann 1978). None of the women interviewed reported a cesarean section. However, five had had abortions, four had had miscarriages, and four reported serious infections resulting from birth complications, miscarriages, and intrauterine devices. Several had had babies die in infancy, both in Turkey and in Germany.

Another recent Berlin study investigated birth outcomes. Using comprehensive data from 1970 to 1980, the researchers found extremely low rates of illegitimacy among foreign births. They reported that German women had higher rates of premature and low-birthweight babies. Turkish women, however, had an elevated stillbirth rate of twelve per thousand compared with the German rate of eight per thousand (Burmeister et al. 1984). The researchers were surprised to find that pregnancy complications were responsible for a lower percentage of Turkish than German stillbirths. This is contrary to what was expected, given lower and later enrollment in prenatal care. The researchers speculate that communication difficulties during labor and "cultural differences" may lead to misunderstandings, and thus to more frequent complications. The infant mortality rate for West Berlin decreased from twenty-six per thousand in 1970 to fifteen per thousand in 1980. Turkish infant mortality averaged about twenty-five per thousand. Most of the Turkish infants died within the first week, a result the researchers link to the poorer utilization of prenatal care (Burmeister et al. 1984).

Nearly all the married women interviewed had had children. Five completed their reproductive experience before migration, three had delivered babies both in Turkey and Berlin, and seven had all their children in Berlin. All the Turkish births were home deliveries except one; all Berlin births took place in the hospital. Although the overall rate of home deliveries is very low in Berlin, for Turkish women it is in the single digits. Although one might expect that Turkish women might be more comfortable with a home delivery, surrounded by female relatives and a familiar environment, one woman had a simple explanation for the easy acceptance of hospitalized delivery: anyone who had ever gone through a complicated delivery in an East Anatolian village would jump at the chance of modern medical assistance.

HEALTH-SEEKING BEHAVIOR

The health-seeking behavior of Turkish migrant women can be analyzed using the ideal/presumed/real trichotomy described by Richards (1969). That is, ideal behavior constitutes what members of a society ought to do, presumed behavior is what they think other members are doing, and real behavior is what they are actually doing.

Given the emphasis on conformity to traditional Turkish norms in matters of dress, family roles, and social behavior, one would assume that health-seeking behavior would also be regulated by tradition. Thus one would expect Turkish women to seek out female physicians, preferably members of the Islamic faith. Women would go to their physician accompanied by their husband or other male relative. Reliance on home remedies would also be expected, especially on the part of women from rural villages.

As has been seen, departure from ideal behavior— adoption of Western dress, German patterns of relationship between the sexes—lead "neighbors" to presume immorality and abandonment of Turkish identity. Adaptation to German styles of health-seeking behavior might be expected to have a similar effect.

When asked about sources of health care (home remedies, advice from friends, or visiting the doctor), most women preferred going to the doctor. In fact several interviews were delayed or had to be rescheduled because the women had gone to the doctor. All the women had been to a doctor's office in the two months prior to the interview. Furthermore, the women reported regular prenatal care in Berlin, compared to little or none in Turkey. It seems that, for this group at least, adaptation to and utilization of the German health care system in the area of reproductive health are adequate.

When the women were asked how they located physicians, the most common response was that they started going to their husband's doctor. If they were dissatisfied, they asked friends or relatives for advice. Several stated that there was a doctor in the building or on the street, so that it was convenient to go to him or her.

The qualities nearly all Turkish women looked for in a physician were compassion and understanding, the willingness to listen to their problems. As long as their physicians made time for them, these women did not care whether they were German or Turkish, male or female, Muslim or not. They were very sensitive to discriminatory attitudes and had few qualms about changing doctors until they were satisfied.

Utilization of basic services such as the general practitioner is good because the German health care system makes it easy. Insurance payments are automatically deducted from paychecks, so that visiting the doctor is free. Most general practitioners have office hours during which patients walk in and wait their turn. Appointments are the exception. Most doctors' offices are located in apartments situated throughout the city, rather than concentrated in medical buildings, as they tend to be in the United States. The public transportation system is excellent. Thus, barriers to care such as cost and lack of access to doctors, both of which are common in the United States, are absent in Berlin.

More specialized services are utilized less often, although most Turks seem to be familiar with them. For example, while nearly three-quarters of those interviewed (3430) in a 1980 study showed familiarity with services such as marriage and family counseling or family planning, only 3 percent reported utilization. Similarly, nearly one-half were aware of the infant and child health program, yet only 10 percent made use of it. Schoening-Kalender

(1984) suggests that low utilization levels are due to the fact that these services are provided by city agencies, and that people trying to keep a low profile would tend to avoid them.

Despite their stated desire to retain their Turkish identity, traditional methods of healing were not well known. Several women could not name any cures, stating that they had always used aspirin. Several others knew that certain types of teas were useful and that rice soup was good when you had a cold. In Berlin they much preferred the doctor, and in Turkey they went to someone who knew more about health care than they did. In fact, when one woman was asked about the disparity between traditional behavior and the apparent willingness to seek help from German physicians, she replied with the Turkish equivalent to "When in Rome, do as the Romans do."

Familiarity with and utilization of the health care system are, however, no guarantee for quality of care. The language barrier is a good example of how care may be compromised. Although there are Turkish or Turkish-speaking physicians in the city, they are very busy and patients must wait hours to be seen. Many women therefore prefer to take a friend or a relative who speaks German and go to a German doctor. The quality of information transmitted through these interpreters is questionable. Does the doctor understand the woman's problem? Does she understand his explanations and instructions?

A second hindrance to some women is the lack of time to get to the doctor, either because no one is available to take care of the children, or because they can't get time off from work. Some women report that they are afraid of being fired if they ask for time off. Others are afraid that if they are declared sick officially and miss work, they will lose their jobs.

The "easy" acceptance of Western health care by traditional Turkish women would seem to be contrary to expectations. Their real behavior does not approach the ideal. Nor is the community's reaction negative, as it is when women's behavior in other spheres deviates from the traditional. One possible explanation is that the conception of the ideal has changed, and is, in fact, close to actual behavior. The value given to modern medicine in Turkey provides the motivation for this change. Although it is very unevenly distributed, modern health care is available in Turkey—for the right amount of money or influence. Several of the women, when asked about utilization of the Turkish health care system, replied that they knew about doctors and hospitals, but that they were either too far away, cost too much money, or that you had to know someone in order to get any kind of decent care. Dependence on home remedies or religious cures would seem to be more a result of having to fall back on something familiar, rather than a lack of belief in, or knowledge about, "modern" medicine. In fact, the practice of traditional medicine, including midwifery, is illegal in Turkey (Taylor, Dirican, and Deuschle 1968). Access to modern medical care can be described as a type of status symbol, thus the ready availability of such care in Germany is easily taken advantage of.

Another possible explanation for the gap between the ideal and real patterns of health-seeking behavior takes into account the bias assumed present in the study group. As stated previously, the majority of women interviewed were self-selected from Turkish women's centers. Their presence in the centers indicates a certain spirit of independence as well as a more pragmatic and forward-looking approach to life. These women would be more likely to follow the health-seeking behavior patterns described in this section, even at the risk of being perceived as nonconforming or immodest by traditional Turkish standards. Very traditional women, not seen at the centers, would be more likely to follow the behavior patterns described as ideal.

CONCLUSION

The health status and health-seeking behavior of Turkish migrant women can only be understood in the context of their migration, their sociocultural background, and the economic and political climate which surrounds them in Berlin. This paper attempts to illustrate that, for many of the women, migration and its aftermath have occurred under trying and stressful conditions. These include the exclusion from the decision-making process, long-term family separations, less than adequate living situations, and family problems brought about by life in an unfamiliar culture.

According to Hull (1979), health problems can be expected under these conditions. Indeed, the illnesses reported by the women interviewed include what seem to be a disproportionate number of stress-related syndromes. Unfortunately, too little epidemiological research focused on women migrants has been published to allow comparison. However, studies with male participants show much higher rates of stress-related problems in migrant workers than their German counterparts.

Since a majority of these women were self-selected from Turkish women's centers, one supposes that they already represent a more forward-looking, more flexible segment of the population. If they show an increased level of stress related problems, how high must the rate be in those truly isolated and lacking support networks? All the women interviewed have family doctors and are familiar with the health care system. Most value compassionate and caring qualities in their physicians over such characteristics as sex, religion, or nationality.

The second group of health problems reported is related to reproduction. Although such problems are less clearly related to the processes of migration, a large proportion of them illustrate the extremely difficult conditions in which these women live. They also help to explain the relative ease with which the German health care system seems to be accepted. Since pregnancy and childbirth are more common occurrences for Turkish women than for their German counterparts, visits to the doctor/hospital for prenatal and delivery care become routine events.

The almost eager acceptance of the German health care system is also explained on another level. Physicians are outside the normal realm of male-female relationships. Thus it is acceptable for Turkish women to go to their doctors without being overly worried about their reputations—a legitimate way of escaping from the confines of the apartment. Furthermore, the nature of the system—waiting rooms filled with patients, visits to other physicians to have tests done, return visits to pick up results—all provide a change from the daily routine, a chance to meet and chat with other Turkish women in a "safe" environment. Visits to the doctor may be important in facilitating adaptation to urban lifestyles.

Acceptance and utilization of health services occur to some extent. However, the health of Turkish migrant women cannot improve significantly until the underlying causes of illness—those related to the migration process—are addressed. Several courses of action are possible: (1) Most of the Turkish women's centers offer health courses— basic biology, first aid, infant care— as well as German language courses and other educational programs. City support for these efforts should be continued and expanded where possible. (2) A major contributor to migrant women's lack of self-worth is the law denying work permits to migrants' family members their first five years of residence. This law should be repealed or amended to require a shorter waiting period. (3) Many German physicians are woefully ignorant about their Turkish patients' customs and traditions. The development of educational materials directed at privately practicing physicians might begin to improve the relationship between doctor and patient and raise the quality of care.

7

THE INSUFFICIENT MILK SYNDROME: BIOLOGICAL EPIDEMIC OR CULTURAL CONSTRUCTION?

Penny Van Esterik

Insufficient Milk Syndrome (IMS), a condition where breast milk either "dries up" or is perceived to be produced in inadequate quantities to nourish an infant, is seen as a function of Westernization. Primarily affecting women and their infants in developing countries, and described as a culture-bound phenomenon, IMS is presented as the expression of conflict between differing cultural norms relative to lactation, nutrition, and healthy infants. Women who accept Western norms, as defined by physicians and infant formula companies on these topics, find themselves under stress and have problems nursing their children. A cycle of negative reinforcement for the women's psychological health and the infant's physical well-being can thus develop. Steps to alleviate this problem include education and provision of social support for lactating mothers, and a change in attitudes on the part of Western-trained physicians and formula-producing companies regarding breastfeeding relative to bottlefeeding.

Something has been happening to women all over the world since the 1960s and 1970s. A mysterious disease has transformed thousands upon thousands of women from physiologically normal mothers capable of breastfeeding their infants, to victims suffering from a recently identified and rapidly spreading disease—the insufficient milk syndrome (IMS). This strange condition has proved difficult for epidemiologists to explain.

The problems in measuring the prevalence of the disease are matched by problems in defining it. The disease is produced by a wide range of conditions rather than by a single biological cause. Some symptoms are considered a problem and used as evidence of the disease (e.g., "soft breasts"); others go unrecognized. Some symptoms identified as problems are culture-specific and not physiologically confirmed (e.g., "agitated milk"). Finally, the women who know how to "cure" the disease do not recognize it as a disease at all.

The insufficient milk syndrome is poorly understood, but it is highly unlikely that women throughout the world are becoming less capable of producing enough milk to feed their infants. The problem of insufficient milk is part of a wider trend in the worldwide decline in rates of initiation and duration of breastfeeding, and the increasing use of breast milk substitutes alone or in combination with breastfeeding. This pattern of combining breast- and bottlefeeding, or "triple nipple feeding" (Latham et al. 1986), is implicated in the increasing concern with the problem of insufficient milk.

These changing patterns of infant feeding would have been of interest primarily to health statisticians were it not for the publicity by advocacy groups such as Infant Formula Action Coalition (INFACT) and Interfaith Center for Corporate Responsibility (ICCR) concerning the promotion of infant formula in developing countries.

The advocacy position as defined by these groups is quite straightforward. It argues that the makers of infant formula should not be promoting infant formula and bottle feeding in developing countries where breastfeeding is prevalent and the technology for adequate use of infant formula is absent. Advocacy groups claim that multinational corporations like Nestlé, in their search for new markets, launched massive and unethical campaigns directed towards medical personnel and consumers which encouraged mothers in developing countries to abandon breastfeeding for a more expensive, inconvenient, technologically complex, and dangerous method of infant feeding—infant formula from bottles. For poor women who have insufficient cash for infant formula, bottles, sterilization equipment, fuel, or refrigerators, who have no regular access to safe, pure drinking water, and who may be unable to read and comprehend instructions for infant formula use, the results are tragic. Misuse of infant formula is a major cause of malnutrition and the cycles of gastroenteritis, diarrhea, and dehydration, which eventually lead to death. Advocacy groups place the blame for this "commerciogenic malnutrition" on the multinational companies selling infant formula (Jelliffe and Jelliffe 1978).

There is an assumption underlying research on women and health issues that as the status of women improves, so do the health, nutritional status, and general well-being of their children. Since the interactions between nutrition and health are mediated biologically through women (Winikoff and Brown 1980), the status of women should be important for understanding women's decisions concerning infant feeding. For successful breastfeeding, women need the opportunity to rest after childbirth and to have their basic needs met by others during the period of vulnerability. In addition, they are most likely to avoid problems such as insufficient milk if they have confidence in themselves and enough self-esteem to protect their right to breastfeed. Women with a positive self-image are less likely to assume that they do not have enough breast milk or that their breast milk is of poor quality. Brack (1978) argues that breastfeeding decreases when women's social power decreases relative to that of men in their own groups.

Insufficient milk is widely cited in the infant-feeding literature as a reason for the early cessation of breastfeeding (Cole 1977; West 1980). The WHO collaborative study on infant-feeding patterns in nine countries identified insufficient milk as the most common reason given for stopping breastfeeding and introducing breast milk substitutes (World Health Organization 1979). Expectations of insufficient milk or a faulty understanding of the process of establishing a milk supply after childbirth may also be implicated in the failure to initiate breastfeeding or to continue it for more than a few days.

In their review of the insufficient milk syndrome, Gussler and Briesemeister (1980) identified forty-four research studies conducted worldwide which indicated that as many as 95 percent of the interview sample complained of insufficient milk. They attributed insufficient milk to the stresses of urban life which required long periods of separation between mothers and infants. The suggestion is made that there is an inherent incompatibility between breastfeeding and some urban lifestyles. Gussler and Briesemeister argue that "insufficient milk" is by far the major cause of early termination of breastfeeding, at least in urban areas, that "insufficient milk" is a "real" phenomenon, not simply an excuse or rationalization given by mothers to cover up other reasons for termination of breastfeeding, and that "insufficient milk" is caused largely by a lack of constant contact between mother and infant.

LACTATION PROCESSES AND IMS

The physiological process of lactation is dependent on the release of two hormones, prolactin and oxytocin. While the former stimulates milk production, the latter controls the let-down reflex which ejects the stored milk. There have been a number of hypotheses regarding the pathways leading to insufficient milk. Researchers have attributed the phenomenon to the following causes:

1. Mother's low nutritional status (Abbott Laboratories 1978; Hamilton, Popkin, and Spicer 1984; Martinez and Chavez 1971; Whichelow 1979). This fails to account for the fact that insufficient milk is found in areas where malnutrition is least serious, e.g., United Kingdom, North America.
2. Mother's illness: certain diseases such as tuberculosis may prevent women from breastfeeding (Neifert 1985).
3. Contraceptive pills. Hull's (1981) review of recent research on hormonal contraception concluded that estrogen pills lead to a decrease in milk, and progesterone-only pills affect breast milk composition.
4. Stresses of modern urban society (Newton and Newton 1950). These theories fail to discuss the mechanism whereby modernization or urbanization affects maternal milk supply.
5. Mother's activities requiring separation from her infant. Women's work is commonly related to insufficient milk (Van Esterik and Greiner 1981).

In a response to Gussler and Briesemeister, my colleagues and I (Greiner, Van Esterik, and Latham 1981) argued that these explanations fail to explain the phenomenon of insufficient milk, and instead added subtle distortions to existing interpretations and understandings of the problem. We argued that the authors failed to discuss the introduction of supplementary bottlefeeding as a cause of insufficient milk, and that they overemphasized humans as a continuous contact species requiring almost constant sucking to maintain lactation. There are many societies where breastfeeding is managed successfully despite separations of mothers and infants. In addition, the researchers concluded too pessimistically that the insufficient milk syndrome points to the inevitability of mixed feeding, in which breastfeeding is combined with bottlefeeding in urbanizing areas of developing countries.

THEORETICAL ORIENTATION

Based on our critique of past research and recent experience in an interdisciplinary study of the determinants of infant feeding in developing countries, it is clear that biomedical models are inadequate for understanding IMS. Symptoms associated with insufficient milk cannot be understood simply as manifestations of an underlying biological dysfunction.

Insufficient milk is an excellent example of a "culture-bound syndrome," in which the cognitive categories that constitute and express these symptoms are culture specific (Kleinman 1980). Culture-bound syndromes are patterns of signs and symptoms of a particular somatic dysfunction which are bound to the sociocultural setting in which they occur. Building on the hermeneutic or interpretive model of clinical practice (Good and Good 1981; Kleinman 1980), we can suggest new questions about the meaning of the insufficient milk. The first question asks, What is there in the social and cultural setting that affects mothers' experience and expression of the symptoms associated with insufficient milk? Our first task is to discover how mothers interpret insufficient milk as a culturally constructed category. The Goods write:

> The meaning of illness for an individual is grounded in—though not reducible to—the network of meanings an illness has in a particular culture: the metaphors associated with a disease, the ethnomedical theories, the basic values and conceptual forms, and the care patterns that shape the experience of the illness and the social reactions to the sufferer in a given society (Good and Good 1981:176).

The second question concerns the construction and labelling of insufficient milk as a syndrome by health care providers. Kleinman differentiates disease, the malfunctioning of physiological processes, from illness, the psychosocial experience and meaning of perceived disease, and argues that "health care systems construct illness from disease" (1980:72). The clinical discovery, definition, and labelling of the illness "insufficient milk" can actually cause the disease. According to the biomedical model, the disease results from a malfunctioning of the let-down reflex which causes stored milk to be ejected. Since this process is controlled by the hormone oxytocin, the health professional may cure the disorder by increasing the mother's oxytocin supply by means of nasal spray (Jelliffe and Jelliffe 1978).

However, in the case of insufficient milk, the physiological process is directly affected by the illness experience. The circulation of oxytocin can be curtailed or enhanced by emotional, cognitive, and social factors. When a woman thinks that she has insufficient milk and is labelled as having insufficient milk by other family members or by a doctor, it can be a self-fulfilling prophesy. As Kleinman (1980) argues, this is not simply a classification issue; labelling actually affects the experience of symptoms which come to resemble the patient's expectation of how women with insufficient milk are supposed to feel and behave. Our second task, then, is to determine how social interaction between health care providers, the infant formula industry, and mothers affects identification and labelling of the insufficient milk syndrome.

METHODOLOGY

In 1981–82, an infant-feeding study was conducted in Thailand, Indonesia, Kenya, and Colombia. The study was designed to examine the determinants of infant-feeding practices among the urban poor, including the role of women's paid employment, modern health care systems, marketing practices, government programs and policies, and other important social, biological, economic, and cultural determinants.

There were three components to the field research. A cross-sectional survey in each city collected data on mother-child pairs. Marketing data, including retail audits and consumer behavior, provided an overview on the distribution of breast milk substitutes in each country. Finally, an ethnographic study, based on participant observation and informal interviewing carried out before the large surveys were conducted, provided an in-depth study of selected neighborhoods and households within each city. Although the ethnographic fieldwork period lasted only three months, it provided a complementary source of data and hypotheses. Most of these observations about insufficient milk come from the ethnographic component.

In each study country, insufficient milk fit into a distinctive infant-feeding style. "Infant-feeding style" refers to the manner of feeding an infant in a given community at a particular time. It includes the way the tasks are accomplished, shared images of the ideal way to feed an infant, and the values, attitudes, and beliefs associated with that behavior (Van Esterik 1985b).

Building on arguments about the meaning of insufficient milk to mothers, there are several questions that need to be answered. First, is it the mother herself, the grandmother, or the clinic doctor who identifies and labels the problem? Second, once the problem is labelled, how does this word or phrase fit into a broader cluster of meanings? Third, in order to identify the condition, do mothers and doctors use the same clues and construct the disease from the same symptoms? Fourth, what are the proposed causes leading up to the condition? Fifth, after the condition is identified and labelled, what are the treatment and means of problem management? Finally, what is the outcome as defined by the response to treatment?

Not all these questions were answered through this research. Nor can all available evidence be provided here. Instead, the following short descriptions are intended to demonstrate that the meaning and experience of insufficient milk differs in each community, and is discussed and thought about in different ways.

Thailand

Among the ethnographic case studies, most mothers complaining about insufficient milk were already using infant formula as a supplement. One mother, Nang Porn, introduced infant formula to her baby at two months, and by four months the baby refused to breastfeed. Another mother, Nang Soodjai, was told that since she had too much milk, she should only allow the baby to nurse on one side at each feed. But she also gave her child Lactogen infant formula. By four months she did not have enough milk to breastfeed. The staff of a large Bangkok hospital started Nang Malee's newborn on Meiji infant formula, saying that she did not have enough milk. After four months of breast- and bottlefeeding, she stopped breastfeeding.

Thai mothers talked about their babies' refusal to breastfeed anymore, thus explaining the decision to bottlefeed them. Breastfeeding problems, particularly in the first few days after birth, confirm that a woman is not a "good nurturer" or that the baby was born into the wrong family (Van Esterik 1985a). There is therefore no point in seeking advice. Since very few rural women complain of insufficient milk, there are few well-developed traditional explanations for occasional lactation failure. The treatment is simply to breastfeed more often. In the urban context, mothers use insufficient milk as a rationalization to stop breastfeeding. Since bottlefeeding is often already established, insufficient milk is an acceptable reason to stop nursing. It reduces the double work load of breastfeeding and bottlefeeding.

Expectations of breastfeeding problems are quite high in Bangkok. Mothers know about food prohibitions associated with breastfeeding, and believe that eating "mistakes" can cause nursing problems. If they are not able to breastfeed "correctly" and follow all traditional food rules, then for the sake of their own health and that of their babies, they believe they are better off bottlefeeding. Therefore, the motivation to persevere with breastfeeding is not high once bottlefeeding is initiated. When mothers respond to insufficient milk by increasing bottlefeeding, then breast milk production will indeed decrease, confirming their assumptions about insufficient milk.

Colombia

Women in Bogota complain not of insufficient milk, but of milk "going bad," "getting overheated," and "drying up." When this happens, some mothers know what to do to increase breast milk production—drink liquids, eat well, and take drinks made with sugar water. Others argue that if a mother did not take care of herself and produce breast milk for her first child, she would not be able to produce good milk for subsequent children.

The special postpartum diet for Colombian mothers, consisting of soups and herbal mixtures, is meant to restore their strength after childbirth and to increase their supply of breast milk. This is a traditional, rural pattern less common in cities such as Bogota, since the social support and appropriate foods are less available. However, the diet is more likely to be followed by women who are breastfeeding.

In Bogota, women who go to a doctor for advice when they think that their milk is drying up often receive confirmation of their diagnosis and tins of infant formula. When Estella had a fever, the gynecologist advised her to drain off her milk since it would be bad for the baby. Instead, she stopped breastfeeding and let the milk dry up by itself. Other mothers are given tins of infant formula by their doctors for use when their milk starts to dry up, even though conditions are inappropriate for its use.

In Bogota, both mothers and doctors believe that insufficient milk is common and almost inevitable, considering the complexities and stresses of modern life—unemployment, poor housing conditions, and family disputes. Women are ready to accept the blame for producing bad milk and fear continuing with breastfeeding if they suspect a problem with the quality of their milk. If a child cries, they assume it is hungry and not getting enough nourishment from them. It is tempting to suggest that some of the complex cultural rules surrounding breastfeeding are meant, in part, to keep women "in their place." From the case studies, it appears that in a culture dominated by machismo values, it is difficult for women to breastfeed and remain in control of their lives. Any efforts to promote breastfeeding must consider how to reaffirm the social value of women's reproductive roles among both men and women.

Kenya

Unlike Colombia and Thailand, breastfeeding problems, including insufficient milk, were rarely mentioned by the mothers in the ethnographic study in Kenya. More difficulties involved too much milk. In fact, copious milk supplies are so much the norm among these women, that the cue for insufficient milk is a lack of dripping and a feeling that breasts are not overly full. There is less cultural expectation of insufficient milk in Kenya than in the other three sites.

There are few folk remedies for insufficient milk, although the study did mention old tribal recipes for increasing a woman's milk supply. For example, Kikuyu mothers suggested soups and porridge made with legumes, and Luo mothers mentioned a special fermented porridge. Few herbal galactagogues, or medicines to increase breast milk, exist.

Kenyan mothers do not think of infant formula and cow's milk as a response to insufficient milk, but as a way to improve an infant's health. For example, Wambui introduced infant formula because she believed her baby would grow better and faster if she ceased breastfeeding and began infant formula. Fortunately she had enough money for infant formula for that child. Her third son stopped breastfeeding at six months because she had no milk. Her long hours working on a farm resulted in infrequent breastfeeding, insufficient milk, and eventually, no milk.

Kenyan mothers appear to be good judges of their milk production. Most insufficient milk was reported by poor mothers who worked long hours in plantations or factories and were unable to breastfeed their infants frequently. For example, when Mama Gichui returned to work on a coffee plantation, she reduced breastfeeding to morning and night. As a result of this schedule and her lack of sufficient food, she felt that her milk production declined substantially over a six-month period until her twins no longer received any breast milk.

More common among these women is the problem of abrupt weaning at subsequent pregnancy. For example, Jennifer's baby refused to breastfeed after five months, when Jennifer discovered she was pregnant. Jennifer argued that the breast milk was no longer to the baby's taste, although there was an adequate supply. Jennifer claimed that the breast milk was affected by her pregnancy. She had, however, started giving the child Lactogen at two months of age, at which time the breast milk began to diminish and the child became ill with diarrhea. In general, Kenyan women did not stress insufficient milk as either a reason to stop breastfeeding or a reason to start bottlefeeding.

Indonesia

Similarly, among Javanese mothers, insufficient milk was not a serious deterrent to breastfeeding. In these case studies, mothers who nursed primarily from the left breast reported insufficient milk. When mothers favored the left breast, they observed that only the left breast produced milk. While some women use that as an explanation as to why they use that breast, others knew that the right breast had no milk because the babies never nursed from that side. However, some mothers managed to continue breast-feeding from one breast in addition to feeding infant formula. For example, Ibu Upa fed her daughter from the left side only. Since no milk came out of the right breast, the baby did not like that side. The infant had also been receiving Morinaga infant formula since birth. Ibu Atin gave her son the left breast only, as he refused the right breast. The right breast was swollen but no milk came out, and so she considered that breast to be unhealthy. The baby received Lactona infant formula in addition to breast milk, and was still nursing at nine months of age. Early supplemental feeding of solid foods may also have contributed to the decrease in milk production.

The most common response to problems of temporary insufficient milk in Indonesia is to drink herbal medicines (*jamu*), massage the breasts, or take a special ritual bath. These traditional practices are expected to increase a mother's milk production. Poor mothers talk about taking *jamu* to increase their milk supply. Wealthier and better educated mothers also take *jamu* but emphasize its cosmetic and strength-giving properties. They discuss the importance of eating a better diet to increase milk supply. As in Kenya, insufficient milk is not a reason to stop breastfeeding. Only one mother claimed that she was unable to produce breast milk for any of her children in spite of the efforts of doctors who tried to help her.

While mothers of Semarang, a central Javanese city, express a concern over maintaining a good milk supply, they have adequate means for in-suring this. They therefore have confidence in their capacities to feed their infants adequately, and do not discuss "insufficient milk" as an obstacle to breastfeeding. It is not more common in mothers employed away from home. Of greater concern to these mothers is the production of weak or watery milk.

Insufficient milk is not a single, undifferentiated problem in Semarang. Rather, mothers emphasize the means for maintaining a sufficient milk supply. Javanese and other Indonesian languages distinguish several difficulties regarding milk supply that need to be attended to, rather than anything that could be regarded as *the* insufficient milk syndrome.

CONCLUSION

Observations from this four-country study confirm the complexity of the problem of insufficient milk, and argue strongly for the need to consider the cultural construction of the "disease" by medical personnel and mothers. Clearly, there is more than one person labelling, more than one label, and more than one etiology for it. The validation and labelling of the insufficient milk syndrome by health care professionals contributes to the problem. This is particularly distressing since the health professionals have no appropriate treatment or cure to offer for the illness. To understand some of these differences, it may be useful to refer back to the concept of breastfeeding style.

There are subtle differences in breastfeeding styles in the four countries. Thai and Colombian mothers place more emphasis on breast milk as a product, while Kenyan and Indonesian mothers appear to place more emphasis on breastfeeding as a process. The focus on breast milk as a product fits better with the biomedical model which emphasizes breast milk composition and specific nutrients. Thai mothers experimented freely with the many infant formulas available. With their strong commitment to independent economic activities, dependence on Western-style medical specialists, and concern with nursing correctly, they are most likely to interpret their breastfeeding problems by reference to the insufficient milk syndrome. Colombian women also have high expectations about problems with the quantity and quality of their milk. Women who get angry or lose control of their emotions expect their milk to dry up. Poor women in particular blame themselves and are blamed for lactation difficulties which are more related to poverty and anxiety than to the quality of their milk.

Kenyan and Indonesian mothers, on the other hand, place more emphasis on breastfeeding as a process. Both groups see certain problems as intrinsic to this process. While Kenyan women have few expectations about insufficient milk, they know that long hours of hard labor and poor food will affect their capacity to feed their infants. Similarly, Indonesian mothers who breastfeed most successfully do not think of nursing as being either simple or natural. Rather, they assume it is complex, but have available to them cultural mechanisms to manage the process successfully.

Thus, the insufficient milk syndrome is linked most directly to the product interpretation of breastfeeding. Derived from the biomedical model with its emphasis on breast milk composition and nutrient content, the labelling of the insufficient milk syndrome is further evidence for the medicalization of infant feeding.

It is important to consider who benefits and who loses by the construction and labelling of the insufficient milk syndrome as a new disease. The definition of this new syndrome is most destructive to women who are confident of their milk supply, but who also trust their doctors and their diagnoses implicitly, and mention symptoms which the doctor associates with insufficient milk. They are then medically labelled as having insufficient milk, accept the label, and behave accordingly.

Second, young women without social support to provide the knowledge of how to keep up a good milk supply may "catch" IMS. Particularly vulnerable are women who do not understand the "supply and demand" principle of breast milk production, or who do not have someone to provide support (cf. Raphael 1976).

Women who are very anxious about the state of their own and their infant's health—to the extent that they lose confidence in their capacity to produce adequate milk to nourish their children—are also susceptible to IMS. The infant-feeding study revealed that women in all four cities were

concerned about their breast milk supply, and were worried about maintaining a good supply of milk. For these women, the increasing demands
of a growing baby, and the fluctuations in her milk supply are evidence of
the dreaded insufficient milk syndrome. Since this anxiety can indeed reduce
milk supply, the labelling becomes part of a self-fulfilling prophecy.

There are several groups that benefit from the labelling of the insufficient milk syndrome. First are women who do not want to initiate or continue
breastfeeding. They have been given a socially acceptable reason for not
doing so. They are not blamed for their decision to discontinue nursing
because they have a medically validated excuse not to breastfeed. Second,
doctors who no longer need to monitor the background conditions influencing
their lactating patients benefit from the definition of IMS. Doctors regain
control over their patients by labelling their disease and providing them
with a treatment that removes the problem. In our study, the treatment was
often infant formula feeding. Western health professionals are taught to
prescribe cures, not reduce stress or give social support to patients. It is also
not uncommon for health professionals to encounter a situation in which a
mother who claims that she has no breast milk is found to have copious
amounts upon a brief examination. This may account for the tendency among
some medical practitioners to consider "insufficient milk" primarily as a
psychosomatic problem. The third group of beneficiaries are the infant formula companies who can influence a mother's concern about the quality
and quantity of her milk supply through advertisements to health professionals. The identification of insufficient milk is a "legitimate" reason for
promoting their products. By labelling the syndrome, they can present themselves as providing the "cure." It is not in their interests to be concerned that
their products are in fact part of the cause of the syndrome.

One implication of the assumption that many women cannot produce
sufficient breast milk is that a substitute for human milk, even in early
infancy, is a widespread necessity. This view is attractive to the infant
formula companies who have stressed the importance of insufficient milk
in their writings. One such company, Ross Laboratories, has been especially
active in this regard, both in published papers (Benton 1975; Cox 1972 and
1980) and in their film, "Mothers in Conflict, Children in Need."

Promotion of breast milk substitutes can influence insufficient milk in
three ways. First, "insufficient milk" can result from infant food company
promotional activities that undermine a mother's confidence in the quality
or quantity of her own milk, especially when these promotional efforts are
channeled via trusted health professionals. Second, promotional activities
can help create and extend socially held beliefs about the likelihood of a
woman suffering from "insufficient milk." Again, this can be especially
powerful if health professionals as well as mothers are anxiously waiting
for the slightest sign of "insufficient milk." Third, infant food companies can
extend the availability and awareness of their products to ever wider mar-

kets. This is often combined with promotional activities to ensure that the response to "insufficient milk," when perceived, is to supplement rather than attempt to increase the volume of breast milk.

Policy Implications

There are several measures which can or have been taken to diminish concerns about IMS. These include a greater emphasis on breastfeeding as a *process* rather than breast milk as a *product* in the training of health professionals. Mothers seeking help for insufficient milk might then be encouraged to rest, drink more liquids, and breastfeed more frequently, rather than to supplement with bottlefeeding. WHO/United Nations International Children's Emergency Fund (UNICEF) are developing legislation to restrict the donation of supplies of infant formula for infants who are thought to need breast-milk substitutes. In emergency situations, charitable donations should be made through governments rather than directly to hospitals. WHO/UNICEF consultants can produce reports and recommendations emphasizing that most mothers can breastfeed successfully. More attention must be given to the needs of working women, including longer maternity leaves. Recognition of the needs of working mothers who are lactating might result in more innovative strategies for combining work schedules with breastfeeding. We must also develop research designs for infant-feeding studies which do not plant the idea of breastfeeding problems in the minds of the respondents, as if it is expected that they will have one or more difficulties. Instead of the wide range of subtle observations about milk quantity and quality, "insufficient milk" is becoming a widely accepted excuse to cover a number of conditions.

Finally, we must explore ways of transmitting information about the subtleties of breastfeeding without the medical labelling of conditions such as the insufficient milk syndrome. Mothers' support groups and traditional midwives both appear to be able to transmit the knowledge of how to maintain a good milk supply without undermining a mother's self-confidence, or communicating a facile romanticized notion about breastfeeding. A key policy question, then, is how to transmit information about the subtleties of this process, while bypassing the medical labelling of conditions such as the insufficient milk syndrome. By viewing IMS as a culture-bound syndrome, we can examine and perhaps improve the specific conditions that make it difficult for mothers to raise healthy infants.

NOTE

1. This study was conducted in collaboration with the Population Council, Columbia University, and Cornell University, with funding from the U.S.

Agency for International Development under contract number AID/DSAN-C-0211. Research consortium staff included Michael Latham, Virginia Laukaran, James Post, Giorgio Soliamano, and Beverly Winikoff, and local teams in the four countries.

8

WOMEN'S SUICIDE IN SRI LANKA

Barbara D. Miller and Robert N. Kearney

The incidence of female suicide is increasing in some parts of urbanizing Sri Lanka. Variables such as age, the lack of viable social support systems, and economic changes appear to influence the suicide rates. Women at high risk seem to experience anomie as a result of changes associated with urbanization. Traditional beliefs about suicide and death, and the relative absence of suicide in some urbanizing areas, are examined in order to both explain the phenomenon and offer suggestions for reducing the incidence of this behavior.

In 1897, the first edition of Emile Durkheim's classic book, *Suicide*, was published in France. Durkheim categorized suicide into three major types: egoistic, altruistic, and anomic:

> Egoistic suicide results from man's no longer finding a basis for existence in life; altruistic suicide because this basis for life appears to be situated beyond life itself. The third sort . . . [anomic suicide] results from man's activity's lacking regulation and his consequent sufferings (1966:259).

Durkheim's typology was derived from data on "modern" European nations and was meant to apply to "modern" societies. "Modern" refers to a conglomeration of traits associated with industrialized societies, such as a high degree of specialization of labor, the extensive application of technology, and the replacement of subsistence agriculture by wage labor or production for a cash market.

In Durkheim's scheme, considerable emphasis is placed on the individual's integration, or lack of integration, into the social collectivity. The term "anomie" is used by Durkheim to refer to a condition resulting from the destruction or confusion of the norms and values that regulate behavior,

110

that give a sense of direction and purpose to the individual within a social setting, thus helping to maintain one's integration within the society. Anomie is viewed as a consequence of rapid and disorienting social change.

Although Durkheim is aware of gender differences in the rate of suicide, he largely brushes aside questions about female suicide by saying that "if women kill themselves much less often than men, it is because they are much less involved than men in collective existence; thus they feel its influence—good or evil—less strongly" (1966:299). Durkheim's purpose was to expose the effects of "collective existence" on suicide, and, since European women had far lower suicide rates than men, he reasoned in reverse that therefore women were much less affected by societal disruption than men. Nearly a century has passed since Durkheim's groundbreaking work on the social causes of suicide. Modernization and social change are occurring everywhere and affect both men and women, though perhaps in different ways. Yet, little attention is given to the disruptions of modernization and their possible effects on suicide rates in developing countries, and especially on women's suicide rates.

Sri Lanka, an Indian Ocean island nation located near the southern tip of India, was formerly known as Ceylon. The nation is populated by slightly more than fifteen million persons. Sri Lanka underwent a period of rapid population growth after the 1940s, contributing to internal movements of population from the densely populated "Wet Zone" of the Southwest to the more sparsely populated "Dry Zone" areas of the north-central and eastern parts of the island (Figure 1). Over recent decades the nation also experienced a major expansion of education and increase in literacy, accompanied by high rates of unemployment among educated young persons seeking their first jobs. Despite many currents of social change, Sri Lanka has not experienced a marked degree of urbanization, and less than 22 percent of the population is classified as urban (Department of Census and Statistics 1981). Although some migration to urban areas has occurred, internal migration has been largely rural to rural.

Durkheim's concept of anomie seems to apply well to modern Sri Lanka, as does his concept of anomic suicide. Between 1950 and 1980, the number of suicides in the nation increased by 860 percent, changing the aggregate rate of suicide from 6.5 to 29.0/100,000 population. Sri Lanka now has one of the highest rates of suicide in Asia (Headley 1983), and perhaps in the world. Another unusual feature of suicide in Sri Lanka is the very high rate of female suicide, which rose from a 1950 rate of 4.4/100,00 to a 1980 rate of 19.7/100,000 population, an increase of 348 percent. Overall, the female suicide rate in Sri Lanka is lower than the male rate (Figure 2), but the difference between the two rates is less than in many countries.

In this article we first explore traditional attitudes toward death and suicide in Sri Lanka, and then we briefly discuss our data on suicide. We next examine regional and age patterns of female suicide, and finally we

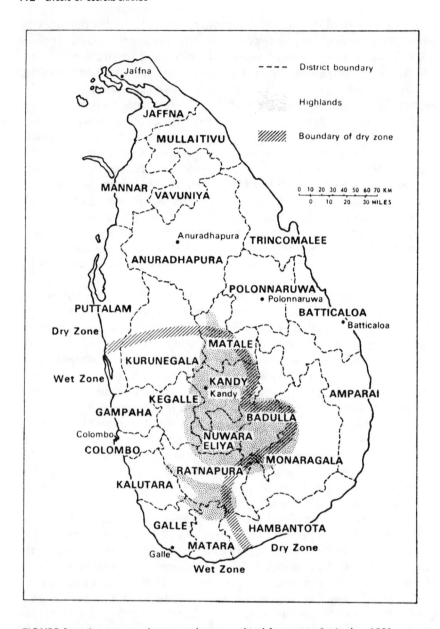

FIGURE 1. Administrative districts and topographical features in Sri Lanka, 1981

discuss female suicide in relation to various aspects of recent rapid social change in Sri Lanka. In particular we focus on the possible effects of literacy, employment, urbanization, marriage age, and internal migration.

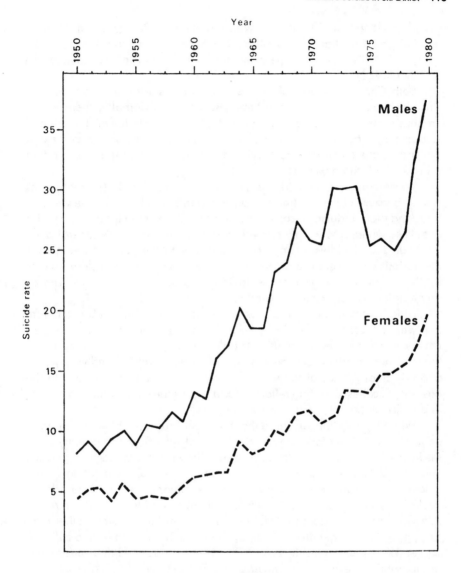

FIGURE 2. Suicides per 100,000, by sex, 1950–1980, in Sri Lanka (Registrar General, *Annual Reports*)

TRADITIONAL AND CONTEMPORARY ATTITUDES TOWARD SUICIDE

It is important to include a brief note on traditional attitudes toward suicide in Sri Lanka as they are expressed in the various religions practiced on the island: Buddhism and Hinduism, which account for 85 percent of the population, and Christianity and Islam, which account for the remaining 15 percent. This discussion is largely derived from a review in Dissanayake and de Silva (1983).

Both Christianity and Islam explicitly forbid suicide and consider it a sin which prevents one from reaching salvation. Doctrinally, there is less emphasis on suicide as a "sin" in Buddhism and Hinduism, but instead suicide might be viewed as a "mistake" which prevents one from making full use of one's life, and from trying to improve in this life so as to attain a higher birth the next time.

Westerners have gained a mistaken notion that Buddhism encourages suicide because of the self-immolation of Buddhist monks during the Vietnam War, and that Hinduism encourages suicide because of the infamous practice of *suttee*, whereby a widow burned herself on her husband's funeral pyre. It is true that Buddhism supports self-sacrifice to the point of death as a meritorious act if there is a cause, but this support would not include suicide for Durkheimian, anomic reasons. In Sri Lanka, *suttee* was not practiced by any religious group including Hindus.

Little is known about the causes and extent of suicide in Sri Lanka before the twentieth century. Clearly, however, religious traditions in Sri Lanka do not encourage suicide as a solution to an individual's problems. Furthermore, the religious identifications, beliefs, and practices have changed very slowly and marginally. The suicide rate, in contrast, has risen dramatically in the past few decades. Enduring religious factors, consequently, cannot contribute to an explanation of the rise in suicide rates.

While there is little evidence that traditional cultural values encouraged or condoned suicide, one theme of traditional literature has recently been resurrected in which suicide appears as a solution for thwarted young lovers. This theme has become popular in the pulp literature circulating in the villages. An example of the contemporary romanticization of suicide by young lovers also appeared in a major Colombo newspaper in 1980. A folk tale was recounted about the plight of two youthful lovers who, rather than face separation, committed suicide by throwing themselves from a cliff into a river (*Weekend*, August 3, 1980:15). This story suggested that suicide was an appropriate response to problems of youthful love.

A common contemporary belief regarding suicide among adolescents and youths is that it is impulsive, triggered by trivial circumstances, and easy because of an abundance of readily available pesticides, the ingestion of which is a common means of suicide. Partly because of this belief, in 1980 the government introduced in Parliament a bill to regulate the distribution and sale of pesticides. In the course of debate on the bill, one member of Parliament, a medical doctor, noted: "One of the problems we face in the villages with this pesticide is that, because of easy accessibility, young girls tend to commit suicide. As a medical officer I have had the misfortune of conducting several post-mortems on such cases" (Sri Lanka 1980, col. 21). The cabinet minister introducing the bill argued: "This Bill has become very necessary because every day when you open the newspapers—even today— you read about suicides. Owing to some little thing, a person gets angry with the wife or husband or mother, rushes to a boutique, buys some insecticide and swallows it" (Ibid., col. 25).

The tendency to romanticize suicide and the facilitation of impulsive suicides by the availability of pesticides are important ideological and instrumental aspects of both male and female suicides, but are not themselves causal. Since romanticism and impulsiveness presumably have the greatest weight among adolescents and young adults, the large proportion of female suicides concentrated in the years of adolescence and young adulthood suggest that these factors may be particularly relevant in precipitating female suicides.

THE DATA ON SUICIDE

Official data on suicides are invariably subject to some degree of skepticism. Almost certainly, in Sri Lanka as in other nations, some suicides go unreported and some deaths from other causes may be reported as suicide. Nonetheless, suicide data, together with other demographic data from Sri Lanka, are nearly as reliable as those from most developed nations, and probably considerably more reliable than data from most other developing nations (see Kearney and Miller 1985; Langford 1984; Nadarajah 1983; Straus and Straus 1953). There is no reason to believe that changes in reporting have had a significant impact on the number of suicides recorded over the period since 1950.

Figures on the numbers of suicides were obtained from the Registrar General's Department in Colombo during field trips by Kearney in 1980, 1981, and 1985. The figures for 1950–1966 are from the published annual reports (Registrar General); those for subsequent years are from unpublished data compiled and maintained by the statistical branch of the department. Unless otherwise indicated, the rates of suicide per 100,000 population were calculated using estimated midyear population figures from the annual *Statistical Abstracts* (Department of Census and Statistics).

All of our discussion in this chapter is based on an analysis of published and unpublished statistical data, an unusual approach from the point of view of traditional anthropology, but not at all unusual for epidemiological studies. In this way we hope to describe the wider social determinants affecting women's health, as viewed through one aspect of it (suicide), and to reveal the seriousness of a previously unrecognized problem.

CHARACTERISTICS OF FEMALE SUICIDE

In virtually all populations, male suicides are several times as numerous as female suicides in every age group (Dublin 1963; Resnik 1980). In the past, suicide in Sri Lanka has conformed to this pattern; male suicides have out-numbered female suicides annually by about 2.4 or 2.5 to one. In the late 1970s, however, the ratio dipped to slightly below 2.0 male suicides for every female suicide, reflecting the rising incidence of suicide among females in those years. More remarkable is the fact that in the 15–19 year age range female suicides have consistently equalled or exceeded male suicides an-nually since the 1950s.

In this section we examine two major characteristics of female suicide in Sri Lanka in order to identify particular segments of the female population that are at the highest risk of committing suicide. The factors we discuss are regional differences in female suicide rates and the age distribution of female suicide.

Regional Patterns

The spatial distribution of suicide on the island of Sri Lanka is markedly uneven (Kearney and Miller 1985). The highest suicide rates are found in the north-central Dry Zone districts of Vavuniya, Polonnaruwa, and Anu-radhapura. Southwestern Wet Zone districts of Colombo, Kalutara, Galle, Matara, and Kegalle consistently register the lowest rates of suicide in the nation. However, all districts have experienced rising suicide rates since the 1950s, although to varying degrees.

District suicide rates show a marked parallel between male and female suicide rates: wherever male rates are high, female rates are also high, and wherever male rates are low, so are female rates. Male and female suicide rates by district are highly and positively correlated (Kearney and Miller 1985). The range of suicide rates among districts, however, is much greater for females than that for males. The highest district suicide rate for females in 1980 was nearly twenty times higher than the lowest female rate, while the highest male rate was only six times higher than the lowest male rate. Hence, the incidence of female suicide, displays a more marked regional variation than that of males.

Age Patterns

Suicide in Sri Lanka is predominantly a phenomenon of adolescents and young adults, with rates peaking in the age range of 15–29 years. Since the 1960s, the increase in suicide rates for both sexes has been most marked in the late teens and twenties. Consistently, female rates in the age range of 15–19 years are higher than male rates in that age range, and in most years this age group has accounted for the highest percentage of female suicides. Thus, teenage female suicide is more prevalent than for males, though male teen suicide rates are also high in cross-national perspective. Suicide rates decline after the 20–29 year age groups, sharply for females and more gradually for males, until a second rise occurs in the late years of life for those persons 65 years and older.

The proportion of all female suicides concentrated in the younger age groups has been rising. Of all female suicides in 1980, the 15–19 year age group accounted for 30 percent, and the 15–24 year age group accounted for nearly 60 percent.

The above brief description of regional and age patterns of female suicide raises important questions. First, why is female suicide in Sri Lanka distributed unevenly over the island in roughly, but not exactly, the same way as male suicide? Second, why are the teen years an especially suicide-prone time of life for females?

In order to investigate these questions and to ascertain the extent to which aspects of rapid social change affect female suicide, we have chosen ten districts: five with the highest female suicide rates and five with the lowest female suicide rates in 1980. For these ten districts we examine a group of variables related to the rapid social change which the island of Sri Lanka has been experiencing in the past few decades.

SELECTED DISTRICTS

The five districts with the highest female suicide rates are Mullaitivu, Vavuniya, Anuradhapura, Polonnaruwa, and Batticaloa (Table 8.1). The five districts with the lowest female suicide rates are Galle, Colombo, Kegalle, Kalutara, and Gampaha. These selected districts form an interesting regional pattern. The five districts with highest female suicide rates are all in the Dry Zone in the northern and eastern parts of the island, while the five districts with the lowest female suicide rates are all clustered in the Wet Zone, in the southwestern region.

The districts, both those with high female suicide rates and those with low rates, display similar patterns of distribution of suicide rates among age groups, with an early peak followed by a decline through the middle years until a second rise occurs in the late years of the life cycle. Despite the overall similarity of the pattern, the absolute levels of suicide rates show striking contrasts between the two groups of districts.

Literacy Rate

The high level of literacy and expansion of education among Sri Lankans is well-known and often cited as an integral part of social change that has been occurring on the island. Although one might assume that a high level of literacy would promote enhanced mental health, increasing levels of education and literacy in fact may instead be a cause of social disruption by creating heightened aspirations among youths (Kearney 1975).

Female literacy has risen substantially over the past four or five decades.

TABLE 8.1 FEMALE SUICIDE RATES AND SOCIAL CHANGE MEASURES IN SELECTED DISTRICTS[a]

Districts With Highest Female Suicide Rates

	Mullaitivu[b]	Vavuniya	Anura-dhapura	Polon-naruna	Batticaloa
Suicide Rate (1980)	87.3	69.4	42.2	40.0	38.8
Literacy Rate (1981)	83.5	72.2	79.7	82.1	59.4
Activity Rate (1981)	16.4	16.5	21.2	15.7	8.0
% of Population Living in Urban Areas (1982)	9.3	19.3	7.1	7.9	24.0
Age at Marriage[c] (1971)	—	20.3	21.4	21.0	20.1
% of Residents Born in Other Districts (1981)	42.8	38.8	25.9	48.4	4.9
Sex Ratio (1981)[d]	122.8	113.6	127.0	129.8	102.4

Districts with Lowest Female Suicide Rates

	Galle	Colombo	Kegalle	Kalutara	Gampaha[b]	National Mean
Suicide Rate (1980)	11.5	11.3	8.7	8.2	4.6	29.2
Literacy Rate (1981)	86.5	91.7	82.4	86.4	92.2	82.4
Activity Rate (1981)	24.7	25.5	23.9	24.7	21.4	22.5
% of Population Living in Urban Areas (1982)	20.6	74.3	7.8	21.4	27.8	21.5
Age at Marriage[c] (1971)	25.8	24.4	24.4	25.2	—	23.5
% of Residents Born in Other Districts (1981)	5.7	19.6	7.0	10.1	15.0	13.3
Sex Ratio (1981)[d]	93.9	110.6	97.8	98.2	101.1	103.1

[a]Variables are explained in text
[b]Mullaitivu and Gampaha districts were not created until late 1970s. Previously, Mullaitivu was part of Vavuniya district and Gampaha was part of Colombo district.
[c]Since data are not currently available from the 1981 Census on marriage age, we relied on the most recently available data from the 1971 Census. In general, age at marriage has been rising in Sri Lanka; therefore, the 1971 data are somewhat low. Nevertheless, the regional pattern of change is nearly even, thus these data are consistently low for all districts examined in this chapter.
[d]Number of males per one hundred females.
SOURCES: Department of Census and Statistics (1974, 1981, 1982, 1983). Registrar General (1950–1966).

In 1981, 82.4 percent of all females (and 90.5 percent of all males) aged 10 years and older were literate. For census purposes, literacy is defined as the ability to read and write in at least one language. As is evident from Table 8.1, female literacy rates by district do not reveal any clear association with female suicide rates. Among the districts with low female suicide rates, Colombo and Gampaha have high rates of female literacy. These two districts are, however, the most highly urbanized districts on the island and literacy rates for both sexes tend to be higher in urban than in rural areas.

Among the districts with high female suicide rates, Batticaloa's female literacy rate is considerably lower than the national average. The low female literacy level presumably can be explained by the fact that literacy within the nation's Muslim minority continues to lag behind the aggregate national figure, and Batticaloa has a substantial Muslim population. Of the other districts with high female suicide rates, Mullaitivu, Anuradhapura, and Polonnaruwa all have female literacy rates at or near the national average. Hence, no evident pattern of association between suicide rates and literacy rates for females emerges from the data presented in Table 8.1.

Employment

It is frequently assumed that high suicide rates, considered without regard to gender, have been closely related to the growing incidence of unemployment. At the level of aggregation of the nation, suicide and unemployment both fall most heavily on the same young age groups. The activity rate is the proportion of the population 10 years of age and older who are classified as being in the labor force, that is, people who are employed or are unemployed but seeking employment. As shown in Table 8.1, female activity rates in the districts with the highest female suicide rates are consistently below the national mean. In the five districts with lowest female suicide rates, activity rates for females are all above or close to the national mean. This result clearly points to a negative relationship between women's activity rates and suicide rates: more employment for women is associated with lower rates of suicide, perhaps because employment raises the financial status of a woman and her household, while also contributing to her self-esteem.

Because of the complex interrelationships among activity rates, educational levels attained, and age at marriage for females, however, we are not able to specify activity rate as an independent factor in suicidal behavior, but can only point to the apparent association by district of relatively high female suicide rates and low rates of female labor force participation. Much more research and analysis should be done in this area. If it could be proved that more employment opportunities for women clearly lower the suicide rate, then important measures could be considered to bring women into the labor force.

Age at Marriage

Within South Asia, Sri Lanka stands out as having a late age at marriage for females (Dixon 1971; Fernando 1975), and the age at marriage for females has been rising steadily in recent decades. As implied above, there is a prevalent notion that female suicide may be linked to thwarted aspirations regarding marriage. One may then expect to see an association between those districts where female marriage age and suicide rate are both high.

The results, from examining the districts, are opposite to what such a simple hypothesis would suggest. In the districts with highest female suicide rates, average age at marriage for women is lowest. In the districts where suicide is less common, marriage age is consistently high. This finding is surprising, and we cannot at this time suggest what might be its full implications for the possible connections between women's marriage age and suicide.

Internal Migration

Sanday (1981) has discussed the possible effects of migration on women's status. The cross-cultural evidence, according to Sanday, demonstrates that migration can lead to stress for women, especially when the migration stream is heavily male-dominated.

We consider two measures of internal (district-to-district) migration: the percent of residents born in districts other than the one in which they lived at the time of the census, and the sex ratio, which is the number of males per one hundred females. The first migration measure indicates the proportion of migrants in the population. As displayed in Table 8.1, the high-suicide districts are associated with heavy migration in all cases except for Batticaloa. In the low-suicide districts, three districts are below the national mean for percentage of migrants while the remaining two are somewhat above.

The districts with highest female suicide rates all have extremely male-preponderant sex ratios, except for Batticaloa which is near the national mean. This higher proportion of men to women is largely caused by a preponderance of male in-migrants. The low-suicide districts, except for Colombo, all have sex ratios below the national mean. Galle is particularly noteworthy for its high proportion of women relative to men. Although the patterns are not perfectly consistent, in general it appears that a preponderance of males in the population, among other factors, is associated with high rates of both male and female suicide.

Clearly, the stress caused by the disruption of traditional family and village ties and ways of living can affect both migrant men and women. It is interesting, however, that in the southern coastal districts, in which the rural migration stream is predominantly female, whatever disruptions occur do not manifest themselves in high suicide rates for either women or men.

Internal migration, both in sheer numbers of displaced persons in the high-suicide districts and in the extreme masculinity of the population created by male-dominant migration streams, seems strongly related to female suicide rates. The loneliness and desolation of women in a dry zone settlement area are poignantly expressed in the following quotation provided by an anthropologist who did long-term fieldwork in the area:

> "We get crazy here," some said; "There is nobody here" (i.e., no relatives); "We do not live here as human beings but as wild animals." They could not cope with the problems of loneliness and poverty; and even less with the feelings of shame and loss of dignity. (Schrijvers 1985)

Internal migration, no doubt, interacts with other social change variables such as rising literacy, unemployment, and career expectations, and unmeasurable phenomena like attachment to home, which together create a situation of spiraling suicide by women in Sri Lanka.

CONCLUSION

Our analysis of several of the variables possibly related to women's suicide in Sri Lanka revealed that in the low suicide districts, women tend to have a somewhat higher literacy rate, a higher activity rate, and higher age at marriage than women in high-suicide districts. Additionally, in low-suicide districts, urbanization is somewhat greater, the proportions of in-migrants lower, and sex ratios more balanced than in high-suicide districts. On the basis of this analysis one could construct a very general model of the woman at highest risk of suicide in Sri Lanka: she is in her late teens or early twenties, somewhat less literate than the national average, probably not employed or fully so, married, and living in a district in the Dry Zone where urbanization is not prominent, there is a large proportion of migrants in the village, and males greatly outnumber females. These conditions, while not ever considered directly by Durkheim in his analysis of suicide in Europe, could well combine to create a difficult life situation for women in Sri Lanka that is similar to the anomie which Durkheim claimed prompted much of the suicidal behavior in Europe.

Policy Implications

The dramatically rising suicide rates of females in Sri Lanka are clear evidence that women are experiencing increased stress and are responding to that stress, in many cases, by taking their own lives. To phrase the situation in Durkheimian terms, it is apparent that women in Sri Lanka are seriously affected by social disruptions creating anomie and leading to suicide as one solution. Although women in Sri Lanka still have lower rates of suicide than men, the age and regional distribution of female and male suicide is quite similar, thus similar policy options might be considered for both males and females. Solutions for alleviating male suicide in developed countries often focus on problems related to employment, and evidence suggests that the same should hold true for women as well (Archer and Lloyd 1985:180).

One policy implication arises from our pinpointing a formerly unrecognized category of people at great risk of committing suicide. Our examination of the regional and age distribution of female suicide in Sri Lanka indicates that districts in the Dry Zone have much higher rates of female suicide than other parts of the island, and that the teen years are particularly hazardous for females. This kind of epidemiological analysis can help inform public health policy by providing "targeting" information. Thus, special efforts at suicide prevention should be geared toward the Dry Zone districts, toward teenagers, and toward women as well as men.

Our examination of social change variables as the possible causes of rising suicide among young women in Sri Lanka points to two major policy considerations concerning the nature of planned internal migration. First, every attempt should be made to encourage migration of entire families, not just males, to alleviate the sex ratio imbalance. Second, every settlement scheme should include employment options for women, not only for men. Women who migrate into the Dry Zone are confronted with restricted employment opportunities, which not only lower their earning capacities but also their self-esteem.

A related factor in enhancing mental health is the creation of social networks for migrant women, which would most easily be accomplished around common work activities (Dixon 1978). Research increasingly points to the positive effects of women's solidarity groups and organizations on women's mental health and welfare in developing as well as developed countries (Walsh and Simonelli 1986). Clearly, young migrant women in the Sri Lankan Dry Zone must suffer the psychological effects of broken kin and friendship networks, and steps could be taken to help women construct new associations.

There is no single policy measure powerful enough to repair a seriously ruptured society that has moved rapidly from an integrated, village-based, agrarian culture to one characterized by increased personal aspirations in the face of declining opportunities. Sri Lanka, a beautiful island nation, is an important example of how rapid social change often has deleterious consequences for women. Perhaps in future decades there will be a move toward reintegration of society and a strengthening of women's mental health. This research has provided a first important step toward reducing female suicide by illuminating the serious degree of the problem, locating the groups of women at highest risk, and pointing to the underlying social determinants.

NOTE

1. The authors are grateful to many persons for their help in gaining access to published and unpublished census and suicide data, in providing assistance with the statistical analysis, and in preparing this manuscript and the graphics for publication. Space limitations prevent us from listing the names of all these individuals. Institutional assistance from the Metropolitan Studies Program at Syracuse University is acknowledged.

9

WOMEN IN CONFLICT: STRESS AND URBANIZATION IN A BRITISH MINING TOWN

Jane Szurek

Szurek's chapter is unique in that she analyzes a group living in a Western society which is undergoing rapid modernization. A previously rural coal-mining town in northern England is being urbanized. Urbanization results in economic and social change and exposure to new ideas, material goods, and behaviors. One result is that the women experiencing sex-role changes are reaching out in new directions educationally, economically, and socially. Through a case study approach, Szurek discusses the stresses engendered by these changes and the coping mechanisms the women develop to positively deal with them. Awareness that role strain and redefinition of appropriate behavior are a function of culture change is important for those women immediately affected by the changes, as well as their larger social group and the medical personnel involved.

> During all periods of rapid social transformation especially those involving the restructuring of the social relations of production, new social roles and accompanying role demands are created, while traditional institutions, support networks and social bonds are disrupted or destroyed.
> (Singer et al. 1984: 28)

Colpitts, founded in the nineteenth century, is a coal mining town near Newcastle in the north of England. Larger social and economic changes here have occurred recently and rapidly, inducing role conflict and a questioning of self identity for nearly everyone in the town, particularly for young women. Female role models represented by the older generation of women are no longer appropriate for the younger women. Because the role models in the parental generation are inadequate for dealing with the demands of new social and economic circumstances, younger women are left to the confusion of trial and error in initiating new kinds of behavior to validate their status as women. Their experimentation, however, disrupts the social control processes in families and the community. Thus, in contemporary Colpitts, becoming an adult female means expressing behavior that confronts values and patterns which are part of the parental generation. The strain and role conflict women undergo can precipitate illness episodes that represent a call for social support from family and community, despite the dissonance the women's behavior causes. Illness episodes enlist family concern and authenticate a "time out" period during which women work out adjustments to new roles and gain attention, if not legitimation, for social mobility.

This chapter deals with the interrelationship of illness and the social organization of behavior. It looks at disease as a "socially created entity" (Fabrega 1974) to be seen in behavioral terms. Within this domain, it focuses on changes in role behavior and on the social context in which individuals experience forms of role conflict that lead to episodes of illness. The illness represents response and adjustment to new social circumstances that demand new role behaviors. There are two purposes to this chapter. One is to look at the impact of change in the social relations of production—the relations between mine officials and miners in the coal pits—on social roles. The second is to examine how social support is evoked through illness behavior to lend help and reassurance while new roles are created, and while individuals elicit acceptance and validation for new behaviors. Coping and adaptation to a new social environment "means manipulation of the environment in the service of self and adaptation means change in the self in an attempt to improve person environment fit" (Cobb 1976:311).

Evidence that stress-related illness is involved in creating new role definitions is found in the incidence of physical and psychological disease and social discomfort among young women. Hereafter, I will use the term "illness" to indicate a sociocultural category as distinct from "disease," a diagnostic category (cf. Fabrega 1974). Although many of the women with whom I became acquainted during my fieldwork were experiencing conflict and adjustment to new roles, I have chosen five who reacted most strongly to social and economic change, and whose circumstances rendered a clearer definition of factors focusing on social mobility.

A variety of symptoms emerged among the women during this study, rather than a specific syndrome or illness. What is important is that a socially recognized illness of some sort is part of a transition period when many women can reflect upon the adoption of alternative sets of roles in adjustment to new social demands. Constituting part of this adjustment for some women is the movement away from traditional mining life and values associated with rigidly prescribed roles, as well as adjustment to changed circumstances within the town. Younger women are marrying men who are not miners and are producing fewer children than their mothers; they have learned to become prime consumers for the family, and they have become more valued for maintaining sexual attractiveness than for working hard and long years as housewives and mothers of large families.

The data for this chapter come from fieldnotes I recorded in the course of conducting dissertation research during 1980–81 in Colpitts, a pseudonym. During the fieldwork period I lived with five different coal-mining families. I attended weekly dart matches played by a particular ladies' dart team in workingmen's drinking clubs and also worked as a barmaid in one of the clubs. I visited and socialized with women in their homes during the day and took part in their social life in public places in the evening. I went into half-mile deep coal mines where I observed coal production and working conditions. In more comfortable surroundings outside the pits, in their homes or in pubs, I discussed recent changes in pitwork with the men. In this way, I acquired a set of network relationships with the women, the men, and their families, and collected data through participant observation and informal interviews. The meaning and interpretation of the material collected in the case studies found in this paper is linked to the context of everyday life in Colpitts.

First, I will briefly describe the social and economic factors that precipitated change in the town. Second, I will discuss status and role, and the consequences of social change for the roles of young women. Third, I will provide five case studies of women who underwent illness episodes as a response to stress. I view these women as seeking recognition for the acuteness of their stress, as well as reassurance and acceptance during the period of their adjustment to new social demands and social mobility. Illness signaled the difficulties women experienced in adapting to an unfamiliar status.

BACKGROUND

Until the early 1960s, miners' wages were low compared to other occupational groups in Britain. There was little differentiation in pitmen's (i.e., miners') wages, and therefore in family incomes. There was minimal job differentiation in the pit for most miners. Nearly all families in the town were mining families. Few cars were owned by mining families, and travel beyond the town was difficult and infrequent. In this sense, the people of Colpitts were to a great degree socially isolated. Mining families continued to live in small, unrenovated, damp houses built by a Dickensian coal master in the nineteenth century. Sanitary facilities were out-of-doors in a backyard, separated from the house. Bathing took place in a tin tub that was filled with water heated on the fire and placed in front of the sitting room fireplace. Women washed laundry by hand for large families, including the coal dust embedded clothes worn by miners in the pit. As housewives, women were called "homely" because their roles required them to stay at home to care for their large families. The three most important values adhering to women's roles at that time were arduous domestic labor, consistent work, thrift, and self-sacrifice for the family.

Prior to modernization in Colpitts, men and women did not have many choices as to the kinds of roles they could adopt. In addition, the British class system did not grant coal miners or their wives high status. With modernization, however, more choices developed, local upward economic and social mobility became a reality, and the old ways, while not abandoned entirely, were critically scrutinized by the residents of Colpitts. The consequences of adopting new roles were not known either, so that the state of transition which accompanied mechanization produced ambiguity and stress.

In the 1960s, British coal mines were mechanized, bringing a more finely differentiated work hierarchy and, for some miners, substantial increases in wages. Marked economic and social inequalities developed among people in the town, nearly all of whom only a generation ago had experienced almost the same standard of living and life experiences. At the same time, machines replaced many pitmen who were discharged from the workforce. To support their families, they resorted to Britain's national welfare system, commonly known as "the dole." On the other hand, families whose incomes increased changed their standard of living. They purchased and installed indoor bathroom facilities and labor-saving devices that provided greater household comfort and reduced women's home labors in household maintenance. Larger family incomes and a decrease in family size opened the way for learning and adopting consumer roles. This was a significant departure from the necessity of thrift and sacrifice on the part of women in the pre-1960s period. The generations-old pattern of well defined roles, based on nearly unremitting work and wear and-tear of women, was broken.

As more money became available to spend on leisure, the range of social activities increased for young women in coal-mining families. Families purchased cars and women took driving lessons, called "hobbies," to earn licenses which allowed them greater geographic mobility. Via television soap operas and sitcoms they were exposed to social and commercial aspects of the larger British culture. Women focused their energies on acquisition of home and personal commodities found in large department stores recently established outside Colpitts. They expanded their wardrobes to include a great variety of fashionable clothing through which they could project new female images. They traveled to Newcastle, a large, nearby town, and participated in night-life activities, such as rock concerts featuring internationally acclaimed rock stars, and danced and drank at fashionable discos. Women, in pairs or groups, spent two-week holidays in Mediterranean resort complexes. As viewed by many women and men of the older generation, female adult leisure time was characterized by seemingly superfluous and random behavior. Some women were sent from Colpitts to become first-generation college students. In these places, far-flung from Colpitts, women met potential marriage mates who were not miners.

These new experiences and activities, based on economic change and mechanization of mining, characterized the transition period from an adolescent role to new kinds of adult roles. What the new female adult roles would be was an open question for young women of Colpitts. Until that question was answered or resolved in a specific way for individuals, it persisted as a source of stressful anxiety for many women. The younger women found little value in the role models of their mothers' generation for coping with the new social conditions to which their generation was exposed. Young women wanted small families of one or two children. They now could have labor-saving machines and conveniences in their homes. They had new-found leisure time either for social life or paid work outside the household. For many, material aspirations were raised; for others, aspirations could only be met by leaving altogether the lifeways and demands of a town dominated by the coal industry. Changes in the economic and social relations of production in the coal industry imposed changes upon the personal and social lives not only of the men, but of the women whose lives were intimately bound to them. These women were caught between a traditional socioeconomic structure that allowed, on the one hand, little choice and low, but recognized, social status from the larger society and on the other, the possibility of upward socioeconomic mobility without knowledge of what these changes would entail.

Precisely what could be defined as having meaning and worth in traditional terms was elusive. Values and roles that supported communalistic sharing when people lived at the same low level of subsistence were turned upside down; under the new socioeconomic conditions, people became competitive. What would individual women's status and role in the town become if not controlled and represented by the common factor of marriage to a miner and all that it entailed?

At the same time, many older women who saw their daughters assume quite different roles and lifestyles, with all the seeming advantages and potential social mobility associated with them, came to question the freedom of the young. They reflected on the meaning of the way they had spent their own lives, some regarding it with satisfaction, others with bitterness and envy of the next generation.

STATUS AND ROLE

In Ralph Linton's definition, status and role are inseparable. Role is the way in which an individual behaves in carrying into effect the duties and rights recognized and enforced by the members of the kinship and larger social group. Status and role are "models for organizing the attitudes and behavior of the individual so that these will be congruous with those of the other individuals participating in the expression of the pattern" (1973:188). If roles change in unexpected ways for some individuals and not others, incongruous and contradictory behavior among family or group members can result in stress until a new behavior pattern is established and accepted. According to Linton, a series of roles can be summed up as "a role general," which determines what individuals contribute to their society and what they can expect to receive in return (1973). If this role falls outside the normative pattern of a social group, what an individual can be expected to give or get from the group is uncertain, and therefore unpredictable. If trial-and-error behavior occurs as an individual casts about for satisfactory new roles, stressed relationships may ensue for the individual and those around her or him. What then can be expected of individual relationships between parents and children in terms of long term reciprocity becomes unpredictable, and threatens the continuity of expectations between generations.

In Colpitts, as in other British mining towns and villages that were established in the nineteenth century, work in coal mines was labor intensive up until the 1960s. Mining was the most hazardous occupation in Britain, except for deep-sea fishing. Fathers and sons were frequently killed or permanently maimed in the course of mining. This perpetual hazard resulted in precarious livelihoods for mining families. The expected role of offspring who attained adulthood was to support living parents. A reflection of this norm and value is the loyalty adult children manifest to this day, especially toward their mothers, as in the ritual attendance at a mother's or maternal grandmother's table for Sunday dinner. The daily visitation of mothers and adult daughters is an entrenched pattern. Mothers in mining towns have come generally to expect as their right some care-giving, labor, and material reciprocity from adult children. Recent role redefinitions influenced by economic changes threaten this longstanding supportive relationship between generations. As recent as this shift in reciprocity between generations is in Colpitts, compared to its acceptance in most sectors of contemporary industrialized societies, it does "display a trend toward a lifetime exchange balance that is favorable to the younger generation" (Harris 1983:64).

When the status and role structure begins to lose its relevance because of social change produced by external forces, individuals in the younger generation face an amorphous situation and are left to experiment with role alternatives. Trial-and-error efforts result in new role behaviors that may conflict with the older generation's. The result can be disapproval from the latter, which still holds authority and control over material and social resources.

Inconsistencies and contradictions involved in moving from one role to another can generate stress which contributes to occurrences of illness for individuals, even when the transitional period and the succeeding roles are known and expected by members of a group. During periods of socioeconomic change, when traditional roles are inadequate to meet new social demands and expectations, difficulties in making these transitions may be greater, resulting in illness. Under new circumstances, stress can come from the self and/or others in the community. The young woman presented with inadequate role models must experiment with, create, or find behavior models through which she can satisfactorily cope with social contradictions and achieve both social and self-validation. As young women move out of socially defined behavior patterns linked to the life cycle and assume different roles, they constitute a threat to the continuity of lifeways expected and experienced by older generations. Thus, the psychosocial stimuli producing stress can also come from the parental generation. Failure of young women to follow the accepted set of role patterns can incur signs of rejection, either real or perceived.

The onset of a recognizable state of illness is one effective way to call upon focused support and reassurance from the community. Illness absolves one of the responsibilities of daily routine and expected behavior. Illness buys time to sort through the conflicts and confusion created by larger socioeconomic change. As Polunin points out, "Physical signs are more likely to be noticed if they are obvious. If they are not noticed, they will not influence the assessments of others" (1977:88). What constitutes a valid female adult role assessment by the parental generation may demand negotiation. Calling forth the involvement of the parental generation in the negotiations may require a forceful invitation to identify the difficulties and deal with them. Hence, a young woman must create a situation wherein her struggle for a potentially new set of role behaviors will receive some support and acceptance rather than opposition. The sick role helps deflect or set aside direct criticisms and negative reactions toward an individual whose behavior is seen as willful, unconventional, or simply selfish. Indeed, where circumstances are so changed and forthcoming responses so ambiguous, the occurrence of illness is a clear communication of concrete distress requiring the attention of others. It allows the ill person to receive support, attention, and tolerance from friends, family, and co workers during the period of transition. It has survival value in the social context in the sense that "social support facilitates coping with crisis and adaptation to change" (Cobb 1976:302).

Thus, mechanization of the coal-mining industry and related economic restructuring directly affected people's lives in a variety of ways. Culture change is not unilateral in its effects on the group or individual. With opportunities for intellectual growth, economic security, comfort, and travel, came new ideas, options, and the flexibility to challenge the old way of life. The changes created stress as people moved through a transitional stage, sifting through familiar values and behaviors, discarding some, retaining others, and adopting new ones. Illness became part of the unconscious adaptive strategy for some women during this period of change because it reduced stress and provided some of these women in transition with support and attention from kin and friends.

WOMEN IN CONFLICT

Many of the women I interviewed manifested conflict and strain as they moved into new statuses and roles. The five women described in the following case studies represent some of the more extreme manifestations of illness in response to anxiety over new role testing. Nevertheless, through the clarity of their manifestations, they represent the more muted and controlled distress experienced by other women. I knew these women in their social and familial contexts rather than in a clinical one. Four common factors characterized their circumstances: their families were actively concerned and involved in fostering the well-being of the women, although they disagreed with the women's behavior; the women were taking medication or drugs to help them cope with "nerves"; they led social lives in the community, where a main focus of conversation was their state of health (most facets of coping with illnesses were common knowledge among women); and the women came from, or were part of, mining families.

Molly, 27, is the daughter of a miner, the leading union official at his pit. His higher earnings after mine mechanization, and his exposure to foreign cultures and ideas due to his particpation in the union conferences, held in various countries, combined to provide him with more cosmopolitan views and rising expectations for his family. This included a positive value placed on education for women. These new values contributed to the decision to send Molly to college, a rare occurrence among coal-mining families. Molly spent two years at a London college, during which time she became increasingly depressed, enough so that she could no longer function as a student there. She was placed on medication in London and sent back to her family to recover. For one year she continued on the medication, unable and unwilling to return to London to college. The second year her father found her a secretarial job at one of the local coal pits. Still on medication and occasionally slipping into the depths of depression, she succeeded, nevertheless, in holding her job. In the third year, by living in the supportive surroundings of her natal home and community, and by continuing the medication, she had regained much of her equilibrium and self-esteem. She began taking one course at a time at the University of Newcastle, a two-hour commute by train.

Despite having experienced the contradictions in the culture clash between the values and behaviors of a relatively isolated mining town and London, Molly's aspirations had been raised. During her recovery, using her home and family as a base for rebuilding her self-confidence, she attended the opera, concerts, and stage plays in Newcastle. At Newcastle University she succeeded in her courses. She also met a male student from London who was studying computer science. While occasionally living with this man, attending classes, and taking the medication, she experienced no depression. When at home with her family, however, she frequently was depressed.

The courtship continued, and the suitor was invited home. Molly's mother and grandmother made elaborate preparations for the visit, which was successfully managed. Subsequent visits took place, and the courtship finally led to marriage. Molly moved out of Colpitts to the south of England,

and terminated the medication since it was no longer needed. Illness behavior had elicited social support responses from the family, while Molly made a role adjustment that eventuated in her leaving mining town life altogether.

Joan, 37, was married to a former miner. During the period of mechanization of deep-seam coal mining, her husband left his work at the pit. He assessed for himself that the work had become too routine and boring because pitmen were reduced to doing only one task on a machine every day, every week, every year: "We've become human machines." Joan's depression and subsequent medication began when her husband left the pit and entered college to become a mathematics teacher. While she continued the medication, she was able to maintain the household and work short-term, part-time jobs in the town. At the same time, she expressed her unhappiness at her husband's change of jobs by telling her "former" friends, when she met them on the streets and in the shops, how unhappy and isolated she was now that her husband was no longer a miner. Her repetitive story focused on how different her and her husband's life together was. She explained that since her husband left pitwork, they no longer had friends who were pitmen whose ways she knew the best. Coming from a mining background, she no longer had any conversations with her husband because she knew nothing about teaching or mathematics.

The content of her role as a miner's wife had dissipated. No longer sharing a common role definition of pitman's wife, she was "sent to Coventry" (i.e., was socially isolated) by those who were once part of her support group. In an attempt to elicit support from other women, she made a litany out of the symptoms of her distress, interweaving them with expressions of desire to return to the role of a pitman's wife. The role conflict she experienced arose out of the fact that she no longer shared the daily routine of a pitman's wife and the solidarity with other such women. It was evident that she had undergone upward social mobility through the change in her husband's occupation, and although her lifestyle had not changed totally from what it was before, she was now required to establish other forms of commonality with town women. Her sick role behavior partially served this purpose.

Lillian, 29, was raised in Colpitts according to mining-town codes of behavior. Her mother was a miner's daughter. Lillian's father was an architect. She was sent to college in London where the social milieu was defined by people from radically different cultural backgrounds. Appearing different from the others, she was mocked for her northern mining-town speech, attitudes, and behaviors. She described how female students from other parts of England and from different social classes mimicked her ways, and although she learned to laugh at herself with them and began to change herself and her ways of looking at the world, she was never comfortable there. Nonetheless, she endured the distress and state of "nerves" and after finishing her degree returned home to teach in a local school. Soon afterwards she married a schoolteacher whom she had met at the college. He was a miner's son from the north who had also gone to college in the south of England to be educated.

After three years of marriage spent in a mining town, during which time she became a mother, she decided to separate from her husband and live on her own with her daughter. She described the lack of freedom of being a person and a mother in a mining community. "Everyone watches what you do and gossips about you if you do something different. You lead a dull life if you do what they do and think." Lillian rented an old colliery house[1] in another town. She refurbished an upstairs room which included covering the ceiling with reflective tin foil, and created an overall environment congenial to wild parties. Her discomfort with her married role in the context of the northern coalfield social environment was expressed in taking street drugs, purchasing a large red motorcycle, throwing parties, and experimenting with a series of lovers.

While she was living out, in a nonconventional way, the year-and-a-half of separation from her husband, she adeptly concealed most of her behavior from her parents. Nevertheless, she maintained ties with her family, who showed direct concern with her behavior. Her mother frequently visited to care for the house, carrying out such tasks as polishing the brass door knocker, cutting the hedge, and painting the house interior. She also played the customary role of baby sitter, taking her granddaughter home with her for several days at a time. In addition, the parents also insisted that Lillian have dinner with them every Sunday. Lillian accepted the social visits with her parents, despite having to endure their reprimands during these times for her behavior, symbolized by the possession of the motorcycle. When free-wheeling life became too hectic or unmanageable, Lillian sought the order and support of her family, taking time to recuperate for two or three days at their house, which was several miles away from her own. Finally, after persuasion from her parents and husband, and having herself grown tired of maintaining a lifestyle that emphasized the role of freedom largely unshared by any other women she knew, her transitional state between roles ended. Lillian reconciled with her husband and moved out of town with him to a large urban area. She discontinued taking recreational drugs and became pregnant.

Myra, 20, is the daughter of a miner who was promoted to the level of a mine supervisor during the period of pit mechanization and wage increases. Her discomfort with traditional mining-town female role models was manifested in a long-term recovery from a physical, rather than solely emotional distress. An accident, linked to a visit by a gypsy who appeared at the colliery house door one rainy afternoon, marked the beginning of this episode. Standing at the doorway, Myra's mother talked with the gypsy who tried to cajole her into having her fortune told for a fee.[2] Upon refusal of a consultation, the gypsy declared to the mother that a curse was cast upon her daughter. The curse consisted of the pronouncement that something "bad" would happen to her only daughter at that precise moment. When Myra's mother returned to the sitting room, she found Myra on the floor unable to get up and walk. Myra had suddenly lost the use of the muscles of one leg.

The circumstances preceeding this event are varied. Myra's precociousness in wanting to step outside the boundaries of sanctioned female behavior was visible. Upon dropping out of the comprehensive high school, she applied for two training programs, both of which were beyond the usual aspirations of most mining-town women. One was a training program for policewomen, the other for physical education assistants. Both programs required peak physical condition and stamina. Myra was rejected by both programs. Another sign of her precocious social behavior was her expertise in playing pool, largely a man's game, at her father's workingmen's club. In addition, Myra was exposed to London life on several visits with her cousins in the city. While at home in Colpitts, she spent hours each day passively watching television soap operas. Although both parents were tolerant of her behavior, parental control and authority manifested themselves in the form of statements about when Myra would get married, presumably to a miner, and leave home. Her behavior of sitting idly in front of the "telly" day after day was aggravating to her parents. Perhaps more importantly, Myra's limited education curtailed her eligibility for the training programs to which she applied, and the independent, relatively unconventional roles to which she aspired.

Myra's testing behavior was limited after the accident. She was taken to a hospital, but the cause of the accident and the nature of the injury to her leg could not be determined. She returned home and a few weeks later collapsed to the floor again unable to get up and walk. She had become the center of concern and activity for the family. Her mother explained tirelessly of how many days and weeks were spent consulting various medical practitioners and consultants, until one decided upon an operation to open up her knee. The knee was diagnosed as having deteriorated cartilage which affected the strength of the shin. A metal plate was inserted into Myra's leg, and the stitches left a purple kite-tail scar a foot long. Myra repeatedly showed it to me and others regardless of the social situation.

Subsequent to the operation, Myra fell several more times, causing the surgical wound to break open each time. This meant periodic residence in the hospital and sedentary convalescence at home. To compound the complications, Myra also broke the ankle on the same leg and wore a cast for one and one-half months. In between medical crises, Myra was active, walking about the town, playing pool, and even dancing at the local workingmen's club hall with her family and friends.

She met a young miner at one of the dances and began a courtship. Her father began to instruct her on the proper behavior of a wife. He explained that when she was married she would have to give up her social activities. She would be expected to be at home with dinner prepared when her miner husband, exhausted and hungry, came home from the pit. The courtship appeared promising. The young miner was the son of a friend from the mother's dart team, and Myra's mother did everything she could to encourage its progress.

During the two-year courtship, Myra experienced less and less trouble with her leg, and no longer showed off her long purple scar in social situations. Finally, Myra married and settled into the role and status of a miner's wife, compromising some of her aspirations by filling a more traditional role than the other women previously described. Presumably her sickness role had indicated a refusal to obey and capitulate to the roles prescribed by the social community. "Indignation at the way everyday life is ordered" had turned to marked frustration (Hopper 1979:12). Illness behavior called forth a clearly solicitous response from the family, while Myra reflected upon and readjusted her role choices, eventually acquiescing to becoming a miner's wife.

Brenda, 29, was already married to a miner and had three children when I met her. Her role stress was less visible in terms of a clearly identifiable syndrome of illness. Nevertheless, there were sporadic manifestations of stress-related episodes and complaints of "nerves," for which she took prescribed medication. Her husband was one of the lowest-paid workers in the recently developed work hierarchy at the pit; in addition, he spent much of his wages on alcohol. Consequently, Brenda was less affluent than her female cohorts, even than her mother, who boasted of a newly carpeted house and recently purchased home furnishings. Rising material expectations were not easily met for Brenda. She held five part-time cleaning jobs in trying to make financial ends meet. For recreation, one of her favorite activities was to take a bus to the large town nearby and visit a department store. There she would sit on the display furniture and lie on the beds on exhibit.

When she became pregnant with a fourth child, she was determined not to bring the fetus to term. She intentionally lost weight and became weak. After four months of pregnancy, she experienced a miscarriage. In the rainy and biting weather common to the northeast England coast, she boarded a bus, not telling anyone where she was going, and entered the nearest hospital five miles away from town. When she arrived, she was in great pain, and stated that while in the hospital she did not care if she had died. Indeed, she wished it. She demanded to be sterilized, not wanting to risk having any more children. After spending two weeks recovering in the hospital, she returned home to Colpitts to resume immediately her family role and work duties which had been temporarily taken over by her mother. As a manifestation of her continuing stress, she complained of continued incontinence, weakness, and tiredness.

Eventually Brenda met a man from another town who was planning to emigrate to New Zealand. She had been thinking about leaving her husband for two years. This was her opportunity to carry out her fantasies, with less risk involved than being left alone with her children to support. The opportunity for mobility out of town was also present. Given these options, she left her husband, who threatened suicide at the prospect of her leaving him, and married this man. Shortly thereafter, she and her new spouse left for New Zealand, taking her three children with them. There, one can speculate, she could experiment and adopt a new set of roles, albeit under different kinds of stress in a foreign country. The important aspect of Brenda's migration is that she had released herself from the stress-producing confrontation which traditional mining-town constraints placed on female behavior.

CONCLUSION

Each of the women in these case studies coped with the social transformation with which she was confronted by finding her own solution in a restructured set of social relationships. The women were faced with new socioeconomic circumstances, imposed upon them by the larger socioeconomic changes in the coal industry. As a result of these changed economic conditions and new social demands, they experienced role conflict, stress, and anxiety. These developed into illnesses, marking a transition period between old and new role behavior and statuses, and in several instances physical and social mobility. To a large extent, during their illnesses they gained social support from those in their social networks. They were able to contemplate new role options while others' concerns about them were deflected away from their nonconforming behavior onto their illnesses. We have seen that generally, once the women were able to free themselves from the conception of more traditional female role models, their illnesses began to ebb or disappear.

These five case studies exemplify the effects which larger economic change has on the health of individuals and traditional social roles. Ostensibly, the chance for upward economic and social mobility is considered positively in Western society. However, as discussed, economic opportunity and social change have had mixed consequences for these women who have experienced a range of health problems as part of their adaptation to changing relations with their families, friends, men, and the larger society.

The women mentioned in this chapter represent other women in Colpitts who have been confronted with new choices, or who have become uncomfortable enough, under changed circumstances, to be moved to seek out or redefine their roles in concrete terms. While not all women in Colpitts became ill while struggling through role adjustments, those who did highlight the difficulties women have when they are presented with a new set of social and economic conditions requiring different role behavior. At the same time the whole community, or more precisely smaller social groups and families in the town, directly reckoned with the processes of socioeconomic change through the gradual acceptance of the new behavior and new choices of these women.

Illness, as shown in the case studies, is best understood in a social context. It is important to frame it as a sociocultural category, in this case as a social transition, rather than treat it as a disease within a medical model. Thus, the disruption or destruction of traditional institutions, support networks, and social bonds brought about by social change has implications for women's health and the establishment of new social roles.

Concentrating on the links between illness and the transitional state of women proceeding from one social role to another has been useful in understanding some of the impact of social change on women. Interpretation of pronounced illness episodes as a call for "time out," or withdrawal from the social circumstances that produce social or psychological dissonance, leads to a more comprehensive understanding of individuals and more relevant responses during periods of distress and illness. By definition, illness places an individual in a marginal, vulnerable state. In this state, individuals experience suspension of social rules and demands, thereby reducing the expectations from their parents to behave differently. Indeed, in the case of each woman discussed, illness deflected parental attention from nonconforming role behavior. While one cannot assume knowledge of individual motivation, psychological space was created in which the women could reflect and strategize toward new role options within broader limits than was once considered possible or proper.

Further research into the effects of social change and reorientation in role behavior, and their correlates in health and the appearance of individual illness in urban industrial societies, is important. The rationale is to identify and interpret the meaning of socioeconomic and sociocultural factors affecting the health status of members in a community. This could lead to better-informed decisions regarding treatment. In addition, promulgation in urban-industrial societies of a wider perspective on illness as a socially created entity, as opposed to a medical problem, can serve to dispel or counteract some aspects of individual and community demoralization. Treating individuals as solely medical problems outside of the social context is to disenfranchise them from crucial personal and social resources, the very means through which individuals may be able to manage social alternatives that form the basis for reversing illness or distress.

Health care providers need to clearly understand the differences between illness and disease, and the stressful effects that any culture change, even when positively intended and perceived, can have on those experiencing it. Sensitivity to the stress inherent in culture change requires a sociopsychological as well as a medical approach to the problem. This could include courses or lectures in medical and nursing schools on the effects of stress and culture change on an individual's health. In clinical practice, the medical team could include anthropological consultation when culture change appears to be a variable in either a patient's symptoms or prognosis. To fail to pursue an understanding of the interrelationship of socioeconomic and sociocultural factors with illness is to foster or sanction dependency of individuals on long-term medication.

As the old structure collapses, changes provoke conflict for young women. As we have seen, women generally emerge from their illnesses as healthy beings once they have been able to make choices that are accepted resolutions of conflict. These choices both mirror and are a response to social change.

NOTES

1. Colliery houses were small houses built by nineteenth-century coal masters who rented them out to miners and their families. They were located next to the colliery, or coal mine.
2. It is common for many people in the Northeast region of England to consult gypsies.

PART III

HEALTH CARE CONCERNS RELATED TO STRESS

Women's sex roles are changing as a result of shifting worldwide and culture-specific economic, political, and social conditions. As traditional societies become increasingly industrialized and Westernized, they are more influenced by fluctuations in world oil prices and supplies, and international food resources and their patterns of distribution. Such global, societal, economic and political developments affect the individual's health and lifestyle.

These changing conditions result in an increase in the number of both employed and unemployed women who either are single parents or part of two parent households. In addition, as economic contributors to either two or single income households, many women both in the United States and Third World societies currently work outside the home. Characteristically, these women have two underpaid and unpaid full-time positions—one in the workplace and one at home.

Economic pressures, combined with expectations to fulfill culturally defined reproductive and sex-role behaviors which may also be in a state of flux, create stress for many of these women. The stressors and conflicts created

139

by trying to balance potentially conflicting responsibilities, as well as those involved in redefining appropriate sex-role boundaries, affect both physical and psychological health. In this section, the kinds of health problems produced by conflicts in the larger economic, political, and social spheres, as well as stress-reduction mechanisms, are discussed. These mechanisms include fictive kin relations, use of power strategies, assertiveness, the redefinition of acceptable male-female interactions, and adoption of the sick role.

Poverty-level single mothers are a population known to be at high risk for clinical depression. Anna Baziak Dugan's chapter examines such a group of Mexican-Americans living in Detroit. Her research indicates that these women show few signs or symptoms of clinical depression. Despite their high risk potential, they manifest the lowest rates of these symptoms for any comparable group. Their effective depression-reducing mechanism is *compadrazgo*, a traditional Latino fictive kin relationship which provides them with emotional support, nonsexual adult male and female company, and help with child care. Most of these women consciously seek out and maintain this relationship, a behavior which supports Dugan's hypothesis that effective social support counteracts depression.

In contrast to Dugan's work, Ruthbeth D. Finerman examines how a group of Ecuadorian women respond to stress by developing *nervios*, a culture-bound syndrome which simulates depression. The appearance of *nervios* is a psychocultural phenomenon related to changing economic conditions and sex-role expectations. *Nervios* allows these women an outlet from demanding sex-role obligations and conflicts, and provides them with culturally sanctioned attention and social support through the adoption of the sick role.

Linda Amy Kimball and Shawna Craig's chapter discusses the stress Brunei Malay women from all socioeconomic groups experience due to overwork. Overwork is a result of the hard physical labor that comprises their daily routine, the demands of full-time parenting, and Islamic marital and religious obligations. That this stress is underreported in the literature is seen as a function of a Western bias towards culturally defined "woman's work." Stress-reduction mechanisms include reliance on traditional healers or *dukuns* for herbal remedies and massages, and the use of extended kin relations to provide socioemotional support.

For various reasons, the Vietnam conflict has had widespread consequences for the people who served in it. A common belief is that the military nurses who served in Vietnam now suffer from Post Trauma Stress Disorder (PTSD). Elaine Fox examines this stereotype in her chapter on Vietnam nurse veterans. She discusses the kinds of stresses experienced by a group of nurses while they were in Vietnam and their postconflict adjustment. This group of nurses belies the stereotype. While acknowledging that service duty in Vietnam was stressful, they emphasize the sense of competence, responsibility, and independence they acquired while there. Since then, this level of assertiveness and confidence is helping them make career choices and achieve personal satisfaction, though at times exacting a price in the difficulty of adapting to the civilian role.

The chapters in this section share a concern for women who experience stress caused by sex-role conflicts and socioeconomic change. These stressors affect their psychological and physical well-being. The means these women use to alleviate the stress vary in effectiveness. Some women redefine traditional social support networks, become assertive as a response to stress, or adopt the sick role in order to reduce it and gain attention from their peer group. They actively pursue and redefine the coping strategies available to them from within their cultures.

10

COMPADRAZGO AS A PROTECTIVE MECHANISM IN DEPRESSION

Anna Baziak Dugan

Indigent single mothers are at high risk for clinical depression in the contemporary United States. Dugan examines a group of poor, single, Mexican American mothers living in Detroit, who, despite the stress in their lives, do not appear to experience depression. Their effective antidepression strategy involves a redefinition and application of a traditional social support mechanism: *compadrazgo*. *Compadrazgo*, a traditional Latin American social institution of fictive kinship, provides either an adult male (*compadre*) or female (*comadre*) who may act as a surrogate parent figure for the woman's children, and an adult, nonsexual friend for the mother. Thus, the mother receives adult male and female social support for herself which does not violate the norms of proper behavior. The support may extend to her children or help her to parent. Redefining social networks is a strategy which effectively inhibits depression for an otherwise high-risk group of women.

Do elements of social systems act to support an individual's health? A good deal of observed data shows that well-being is closely linked with social reciprocity, and there is increasing interest in research to clarify these inferred health benefits.

Data on the Latin American kinship system, *compadrazgo*, are typical of such qualitative, observational data, but this social practice, to date, has not been studied from a quantified, correlational perspective. A social alliance with roots in feudal Europe, *compadrazgo* is presented in the literature as a reciprocal practice of considerable social and emotional benefit (Kemper 1982; Mintz and Wolf 1950; Thompson 1973). Embedded in Latino culture, *compadrazgo* is a fictive, or voluntarily created, kin tie that is neither biological nor legal. It may have a ritualistic aspect, with the bond formed by a religious ceremony such as the baptism of an infant or blessing a house, but ritual is not always involved. Whatever the initiating occasion, the im-

143

portant relationship established is that between the individuals and their supportive persons, called a *comadre* when a woman, or a *compadre* when a man. These are terms of deeply felt regard and respect, and are employed in same gender and cross-gender relationships, both of which are possible within the system of *compadrazgo*.

Knowledge about the impact of social alliances on illness can be substantially improved in terms of the juxtaposition of quantitative and qualitative data, so that the explanatory power of each is enhanced by the other. This study reports on qualitative and quantitative data collected to determine the impact *compadrazgo* has on depression. Women of Mexican heritage, raising children alone, were chosen for several reasons. Mexicans are reported to maintain strong kin and fictive-kin ties even under conditions of migration and assimilation. Women raising children alone in the United States are reported to be under considerable stress in such an undertaking, and stress is shown to be related to mental and physical disorders. Lastly, studies in the United States and elsewhere report the incidence of depression for women to be double that of men (Arce 1981; Keefe 1980; Rabkin and Struening 1976; Rothblum 1983). Thus this is a problem worthy of investigation from many perspectives.

The central question, then, is: Will those women of Mexican heritage who are raising children alone and who utilize *compadrazgo* have fewer symptoms of depression than those who do not have the social and emotional support of this reciprocal system? The relationship of social systems to health requires an appreciation of the particular place individuals occupy within their cultural spheres and the ties forged through exchange and reciprocity. While the interconnections and adjustments of groups within social organizations are used to explain how a society functions, network analysis calls attention to the power of personal relationships within formal social organizations (Boissevain and Mitchell 1973).

It is difficult to establish specific links between elements of social organization, social networks, well-being, and illness. Yet it could be of considerable practical benefit if such relationships are made clear. Alexander Leighton, known for his examination of the interaction of individuals and their social environment, asserts that

> the malfunctioning of social institutions and high prevalence rates of mental illness is one of the strongest associations that has so far been uncovered in psychiatric epidemiology . . . . With poverty areas . . . the most outstanding examples of where badly functioning social institutions and people with mental illnesses congregate together (1984:195).

Those with marginal status in society, such as ethnic minorities who are rejected by the dominant majority in their neighborhoods, those from broken homes, or those in isolated living circumstances, are found to have consistently higher rates of tuberculosis, schizophrenia, alcoholism, accidents, and suicide (Dugan 1984; Mishler and Scotch 1963).

Women are finding themselves in the vulnerable categories of being both poor and marginal, as increasingly they become heads-of-household and single parents. The number of women in this situation continues to increase. One-quarter of all family groups, over five and one-half million families, are poor and headed by a single parent (United States Department of Commerce 1985:46). Kosa and Zola (1975) call attention to the fact that families with a female head are three and one-half times as likely as families with a male head to fall into the category of poor. As noted earlier, the improverished for numerous reasons appear to be more susceptible to all types of illnesses than the more affluent.

MEXICAN WOMEN, *COMPADRAZGO*, AND DEPRESSION

This study was carried out in a *barrio* located in a Midwestern metropolis, Detroit. From a total urban population of 1,203,339, those identifying themselves as Latinos numbered 28,970 (United States Department of Commerce 1981:16). Latinos are one of the smaller minorities in this urban area. How many of the 28,970 cite their heritage as Mexican is unknown, but Mexicans are the predominant Latino group in the city as well as the state.

Those of Mexican heritage in this area trace their origins to the early 1900s, when large parts of the United States were being urbanized and increasing rapidly in size. The migration of Mexicans to mechanized farms in the Southwest and then on to agricultural and industrial opportunities in the Midwest and the Northeast, took place at that time (Alvarez 1973). The Detroit group had in the past an urban orientation; many were recruited first for the sugar beet industry, but upon their initial trip north gravitated to nonfarm jobs in Detroit (Baba and Abonyi 1979). Several generations are represented in the *barrio* near the city center. This area has long served as a transitional "zone of passage" for new arrivals from other countries and from the southern United States. In addition, Mexicans live in suburbs adjoining the metropolitan core and throughout the state, but no *barrios* are known to exist in outlying areas.

Methodology

Data were collected over a two-year period between 1980 and 1982. Participant observation, key informant interviews, life histories, and interview questionnaires were the means of gathering data. Fifty women of Mexican heritage, who were heads-of-household raising children alone, were located first by referrals of key community informants, a priest, a Mexican social worker, and then by "snowball technique," i.e., each person interviewed was asked if she knew of anyone like herself who might be approached for inclusion in the study.

Participant observation was conducted in a health clinic, a central park, restaurants, churches, community recreational and aid centers, doctors' offices, grocery stores, and pharmacies, all of which are located within and serve a predominately Latino neighborhood. In nearly every instance, interviews were conducted in the homes of respondents where the nuances of life style were observed. The investigator rented a room in a private home in the neighborhood, and this enhanced participant observation opportunities.

The questionnaire used four categories of variables, three independent and one dependent. The first independent variables included age, education, income, marital status, number of children living at home, and country of birth. Social support resources were also utilized, both personal ones—kin and friends, and professional ones—curandero, doctors, priests, or teachers. For each social support identified, it was noted how often such a person was used over a six-month period, as well as the gender and ethnic identity of the individual social supporter. The third set of independent variables was a family history of depressive symptoms.

The dependent variable, depression, was examined using the Beck Depression Inventory, a 21-item, self-report schedule designed specifically to measure depth of depression in an individual. It includes the major components of depression: a "central mood factor" which is associated with feelings of hopelessness, despair, and lowered self-esteem; a "self-accusatory factor" which encompasses guilt and worthlessness; a psychomotor factor which extends from agitation to general motor retardation; and a somatic component which includes a variety of bodily and sleep disturbances (Katz 1971). This depression inventory is based on extended trials with both depressed and normal populations, and has undergone rigorous tests for reliability and internal consistency (Beck and Beamesderfer 1974).

In addition to completing the questionnaire, narrative notes were made of stories and elucidations offered by the women when answering specific survey questions. This added appreciably to other qualitative data collected.

Findings

Quantitative data revealed that 10 percent of the women in this study fell into the serious range of depression. They are in the low range of expected depression for women in the general population whose prevalence rate is 11 percent to 24 percent (Boyd and Weissman 1981:1041).

Among all considered possible personal social supports, individuals of Mexican heritage are used most frequently (92 percent), and of these, female supports predominate over male supports by a 4:1 ratio. Non-Mexican social

TABLE 10.1 SUMMARY OF REGRESSION OF DEPRESSION ON
DEMOGRAPHIC, SOCIAL SUPPORT, AND
FAMILY HISTORY VARIABLES

Demographic = 13%	
Age (older/more depression)	10% p<.05*
Martial Status (never married/more depression	3% N.S.
Social Support Resources = 7%	
Personal (*compadre* support is 2% of this figure)	
(more supports/less depression)	6% p<.05*
Professional (more support/more depression)	1% N.S.
Family History = 4%	
Depressive symptoms (more family depression/more personal	
depression)	4% N.S.
TOTAL	24%

N = 50
*P<.05 significance level indicates that if there was no relationship, these results would be obtained less than one in 20 samples, suggesting that some kind of nonrandom relationship exists between two variables. In this case, the relationship is between depression and age and between depression and personal social support resources.

supports are much less frequent, comprising 23 percent of the available support.

Multiple regression analysis reveals the dependence of depression on the presence of the other variables. In the statistical analysis the variable found to explain the greatest connection with depression is identified first, then the variable that next accounts for some variance in depression, and so on. Old age is the strongest predictor of depression. Personal social supports account for the next largest amount of explained variance and of this, *comadre/compadre* support accounts for one-third (see Table 10.1). When regressed separately, neither achieves statistical significance; together they show a relationship to depression—i.e., more supports, less depression. The *comadre/compadre* support, thus, could be an important contributor to emotional stability.

RESULTS OF STUDY

As a group, the fifty women in this study reflect the total range of risks that are associated with higher depression rates for women within the general United States population. They are separated, divorced, or never married; single heads-of-household; all raising children, with one-half the group earning low income; and 12 percent of the group older than forty-six. Yet, these women of Mexican heritage fare well with respect to depression, a prevalent disorder of modern times. Qualitative data both support and illuminate these findings. Life histories, open-ended interviews, and participant observation data reveal an interesting mix of urban American and traditional Mexican traits in this group of women. Of the fifty women, forty-three were born in the United States, half of these in the Detroit area, and some were third-generation Americans. They have attended schools, movies, sports, and shopped in major retail centers of an urban metropolis. Despite this, Mexican and Anglo paths do not often cross, and few friendships are forged across ethnic lines. A type of closed society of Mexican only social contacts prevails. This exclusiveness could have been a type of backlash by these women of Mexican heritage in response to long-standing expectations of deviousness and hostility from Anglos. When asked about her use of the term *whites* in general conversation, one woman said:

> We're only white when someone wants to use us. Take the busing to schools here in Detroit—they counted us as white so that they could even out the schools with blacks. It was *our* neighborhoods that were destroyed while the white kids could stay in their own schools. I could give you a lot of other examples. But, in jobs, other good things, we don't get that designation. That's why we look at others as "white" and keep to our own Mexican identity. We're not wanted unless someone wants something from us.

Observations made clear that few non-Mexicans penetrate the *barrio* with the exception of "eat and run" activities at restaurants with reputations that have spread to other areas of the city.

The seven women who were born in Mexico varied little, if at all, from their United States-born counterparts. Dress, home, jobs, bilingualism are all similar. What is most interesting is the degree to which ethnic traits are retained in the group as a whole. All respondents speak Spanish in addition to English and so do their social contacts. They favor Mexican food, listen to Mexican music on the radio, and attend Mexican dances. They appear to identify strongly with Mexican traditions of gaiety, sensualism, and fatalism which is reinforced repeatedly in their *barrio* surroundings, recreation, and friendships. Gaiety is noted in Mexican music playing in the background during visits to homes, and also in the distinctly joyous selection of Spanish music at church services that have people clapping, stamping, and chanting in time with the music. Many of the women are quick to smile and laugh when telling about a holiday, party, or weekend dance they attended, invariably described as "Mexican" in music, food, and participants. Sensualism is perceived, in nearly every case, in a manner of dress that is both polished and form revealing—in long, shiny, usually curly hair, hoop earrings, attractively applied facial makeup, and a languid, though alert manner of conversing. There is a mixture of gaiety and liveliness in home decor with a profusion of color in spreads and rugs, velvets and brocades predominating, and artificial flowers tucked behind picture frames and other places, even in homes that are very poor.

Fatalism is noted in expressions about "God's will" and an acceptance of harsh experiences in their youth, or current "hard times" as a "way of life." The women in this study frequently cite the necessity to avoid shame by efforts of their own, at the same time they presumably protect themselves from shame and guilt by reference to an inexorable fate, powerful and unalterable. Such a fatalistic philosophy may serve as a protective strategy. For example, some women talk about the poor reflection on their families that resulted from their single-status motherhood. While they might justify the need they felt to end their marriage, they do not minimize the embarrassment or pain this action has caused their families. Nor is there any indication that they are veering from traditional Mexican values of inculcating respect, obedience, and family centeredness in raising their children. They display fatalistic dependence on God, and strong tendencies toward selfless nurturing. These women may have become "trapped" at an early age by pregnancy, but they are "redeemed" by how they cope with the responsibilities of motherhood.

It is within this context that gender distribution in personal supports can be considered. These are predominately female supports except in the case of older, depressed women, where greater use of both male supports as well as professional social support are found. It is considered unseemly for a woman without a spouse to be involved with men except under prescribed conditions. They can, for example, visit the homes where male and female kin reside, but return visits to their single-parent abodes are infrequent. On the other hand, public dances are acceptable for meeting and socializing with men, but these are not places that foster the kind of intimacy that can be considered as socially supportive in the sense intended by the interview questions.

There is, in addition, an overriding tendency to long for traditional roots. Frequent visits to Mexico, telephone calls to kin there, and attempts to resettle in Mexico following several generations removed from their forebears' land of origin attest to this. One woman, who holds a graduate professional degree, has a well-paying position, and chooses to remain in the *barrio*, expresses this kind of tension:

> Only a person who has traveled back and forth across the border in an attempt to find out where they really fit in would know how I feel about what it is like to be caught between two cultures—a hyphenated American. I wonder if we listen to, or sing, the National Anthem and feel a swelling of pride and patriotism rise within us, or if we do the same to the *Hymno Naciónal*? Is it possible to

feel the same way for both? I would say it's possible to feel the same about both countries, because I most certainly do. Yet, I don't really feel I "belong" to either.

The importance of *compadrazgo* within this overtly supportive milieu cannot be overemphasized. Eighty percent of the group has *comadres/compadres*. These are forged from early adulthood or when one decides to deepen and extend contact with someone and asks that person to act as honorary sponsor for some event. An individual may have a number of *comadres* and *compadres*. Sometimes these relationships emerge with no event initating the connection. "It just happened. We got closer and closer and now we tell each other everything, we help in every way we can. *Sure she's my comadre!*" With a single exception, references to these relationships bring glowingly expressed responses such as:

"It's like having a grandmother, aunt, sister, mother all wrapped up in one."
"This is something that is so deep it goes to the soul."
"It's hard to describe it because it's something deeply felt."
"Nothing can destroy it because it grows and goes deeper all the time."
"You might be close to your brother but not like this—with your brother you have fights or bad times, with your *compadre* it is only good—respect, honor, good things always."

In a number of instances, the geniality of such interactions was observed. In one case, where the women were having considerable difficulty arranging for basic subsistence, an afternoon was spent, nevertheless, around a kitchen table laughing uproariously over one amusing story after another. It seemed quite likely that this pleasant interlude, in a somewhat grim reality, was a frequent occurrence. The supportive ties of *comadres* and *compadres* alleviate the harrassments of daily urban living. For example, "My *comadre* never let me down. When I needed to get to work and I had no way, she came in her car every day for two weeks, back and forth, and took me to work." There is advice on where to get bargains in prized material goods. These are fenced items, T.V.s and stereos, for example, that have been stolen. As one woman said:

Probably [they were stolen], but we never know that, and how else could we afford these things; you know the best bargains in the big stores are advertised one day and you have to get there the next. Well, what are you supposed to do when they won't give you a charge card because your income isn't enough? Come up with the cash just like that? Don't make me laugh.

The capacity to engage in such close, caring, loving relationships may be an important legacy of the *compadrazgo* experience. In that sense, its influence is much more far reaching than what is measured when examining the strength of its practice as a variable separated from other social expressions. The system of *compadrazgo* may have a socializing effect that enables those brought up in it to extend themselves and know how to make friendships even when these are not formalized as fictive kin. There is one interesting account of this with a respondent counting as her *compadre* an older Italian man she met at a bus stop and with whom she now has frequent contact. There has been no symbolic, ritualistic ceremony through which the choice was made, but he is as surely her *compadre* as if there had been such a ceremony.

Field experience provides ample evidence of the extension of respect, regard, and helpful consideration even to those outside kin boundaries. In nearly all of them, formal or casual, considerable warmth and geniality are extended. In one instance a troubled, harassed mother of twelve, having finished the interview, sent her daughter and son out of their very poor flat to be sure the investigator would have no difficulty getting to her car. In homes headed by a woman alone with small children and at times supported entirely by public assistance, the atmosphere is one of considerable tension, in some cases bordering on despair. Broken kitchen chairs, spilled food, empty cans, discarded paper wrappings on the kitchen table, and a sink overflowing with dirty dishes are observed. In one case, a youngster was sleeping at midday in a curtained alcove off the main entryway to a basement apartment that seemed filled with children of all sizes. The children were neatly dressed in clothes of current youth fashion. The teenaged girl was prettily made up with facial color and a shiningly clean long hairdo. All this flourished amidst the cramped and dirty combination kitchen, dining, living room which was about ten feet square. A cockroach ran over the multipurpose table in the center of the room. A kerosene or oil heater was in use in a crowded corner and looked like a fire hazard. During the course of the interview, the children argued loudly, and the mother periodically screamed at them, all the while trying to respond attentively to the interview questions. While it could be argued that such considerate behavior toward a stranger is a reflection of cultural values distinct from *compadrazgo*, the impression is strong that there is a presumptive carry-over of fictive kin behaviors to other social interactions. There is, among Mexicans, a perceived respect and caring about another's well-being that emerges so often and in such different circumstances, the likelihood is strong that it is culturally embedded. It is not unusual, for example, to encounter warm, generous assistance from strangers who, noting a puzzled expression, explain and guide one towards what appeared to be a missing house number.

CONCLUSION

Women in this study experience considerable economic and interpersonal stresses, yet they cope with these well enough so that depression, the "common scourge" of women, does not emerge as a response. Both quantitative and qualitative data support *compadrazgo* as a significant addition to an array of potential social support resources.

It is important to learn how women of other ethnic and social groups fare who do not have *comadres* and *compadres* and have similar serious life stresses. This study presents one quantitative/qualitative test of the impact of *compadrazgo*, but continuing refinement, control, and comparison are obviously required. Settled Americans, as well as acculturating peoples worldwide, might benefit from learning about traditional social forms that have potential value for health, and thus move to retain or to seek fictive kin ties and other sources of support rather than to fully assimilate into Western social patterns. In the case of Americans, a model for non-kin-based social support already exists in the California subculture where there is widespread adoption of Eastern philosophy and lifestyle. What are lacking are measures of the influence on health when such lifestyles are adopted.

Equally important and related to *compadrazgo* is the development of tools to gauge the contribution to wellness of other aspects of traditional Mexican culture, such as retention of use of the Spanish language, identification with Mexican heritage, such as eating Mexican foods and relaxing in a unicultural Mexican ambience at parties. Measures that would tap an array of potentially protective behaviors, perhaps more readily visualized in closed ethnic groups such as in this study, would have great relevance for the study of other, less cohesive groups. Beyond this, one can investigate whether there are differences in health between those who choose to stay in ethnic enclaves and those who believe that they are trapped within them.

The issue of locus of control with respect to life events is a prime area for study. To what extent are events perceived to be influenced by one's self or by external forces? Depression that is not biologically grounded may well be stimulated by situations of shame and guilt. If efforts such as avoidance of shame, through fatalistic acquiescence to disturbing life events does, indeed, offer some protection in regard to depression, more should be learned about this. A recent trend has been away from studies of the psychology of behavior with respect to social imperatives, part of which is in the values domain. This declining interest is to be regretted. Anthropologists once consistently studied peoples' values and belief systems. This aspect of data collection should be restored and given methodological development.

NOTE

This study was supported by National Research Service Award (NRSA) #1 F31 NU05132-04, USPHS DHEW, Division of Nursing.

11
THE PRICE OF POWER: GENDER ROLES AND STRESS-INDUCED DEPRESSION IN ANDEAN ECUADOR

Ruthbeth D. Finerman

Nervios, a psychosomatic illness resembling depression, is a culture-based syndrome affecting women in an Ecuadorian village. Women exposed to rapid cultural change experience sex-role confusion and conflict. As a consequence, some of these women develop *nervios,* which results in their receiving attention and social support, and helps them to alleviate the stress created by the changes and responsibilities arising from the process of culture change.

Insights into role allocation often result from the study of breakdowns in role performance. Failures may occur when individuals are unable to meet personal or community expectations because of incompetence, or because requirements for role fulfillment change, or are excessive, or unreasonable (Parsons and Fox 1952).

A number of studies suggest that health and illness present one possible causal or consequential link to failure in role performance (e.g. Brenner 1981; Lebra 1972; Marsella et al. 1985; McKinlay 1981; Parsons 1951; Rubel, O'Nell, and Collado-Ardon 1984; Uzzel 1974). Illness can directly incapacitate individuals, hindering their role performance (Alexander 1982). In other instances, illness may be exploited as an excuse for inadequate execution of duties, or because of frustration or stress in attempting to satisfy role demands (Foster and Anderson 1978). Many of these studies indicate that illness is most frequently associated with role demands and stress among women (Brown, Bhrolchain, and Harris 1975; Edgerton 1985; Rubel 1964; Uzzell 1974). Health care would therefore provide a socially acceptable means of disrupting the self-perpetuating chain of illness and role failure.

My own research suggests that a strong correlation exists between role performance and health among adult Saraguro Indian women in Ecuador. Data that I collected in this population over a six-year period from 1978

153

through 1984 indicate that Saraguro women suffer from a high frequency of the stress-related disorder *nervios*, which causes symptoms paralleling those of depression. This disorder appears to function as a coping mechanism for stress, allowing opportunities for Saraguro women to attract sympathy and support for their attempts to accommodate changing family and community demands. The following text explores Saraguro sexual division of labor and gender roles, the etiology and treatment of *nervios* in the indigenous population, and the relationships between changing gender roles and the appearance of this stress-related depression disorder among adult Indian women. Recent changes in gender roles in activities such as production, domestic labor, and family health are identified as key factors influencing stress and illness in Saraguro.

SARAGURO CULTURE

Of the estimated fifteen to eighteen thousand Saraguro Indians of southern Ecuador, only five to eight thousand reside in the Andean county seat of Saraguro. Other Saraguros have migrated in the past century to cities and parishes scattered throughout highland and tropical forest territories in the southernmost province of Loja. The Indian population is thought to represent a racially assimilated group composed of natives indigenous to southern Ecuador, and transplanted individuals or *mitimaes*, relocated in the Saraguro area during Incan rule (Belote 1984). The majority of Saraguros are fully bilingual in Quichua and Spanish.

The town center of Saraguro supports nearly 2000 non-Indian residents, referred to locally as *blancos* (literally, "whites"). The majority of *blancos* work as artisans and merchants. Saraguro Indians live outside the town in rural districts or *barrios* where they labor as agriculturalists, cultivating maize, beans, squash, and potatoes. In the past century Saraguros have also adopted pastoralism, raising sheep and cattle for sale or trade primarily within the Indian population. Opportunities for Saraguro men and women to participate in education, politics, and religion, the distribution of property among men and women, and changes in the allocation of responsibilities in production and domestic activities provide insights into gender roles and expectations in the community.

Education

In the past two decades, Saraguros have increasingly encouraged both men and women to complete formal education. Economic opportunities have opened up in the community for Indian residents with advanced educational degrees. Indigenous nurse practitioners have worked in Indian *barrios* around Saraguro for the past two decades, and the first Saraguro Indian physician opened a practice in the community in 1984. A number of Saraguros teach in local Indian primary and secondary schools, and others have recently been hired by the Ecuadorian government as instructors in a Quichua language standardization and proficiency program. A few Saraguro men and women have also pursued university studies in Quito, seeking degrees in engineering and architecture.

Community expectations have risen for Saraguro men and women in response to new economic and educational opportunities. A number of young Indian mothers have been encouraged to return to school. Many Saraguro women now leave children under the care of mothers or in-laws while they attend evening courses to complete their secondary school degree. Nevertheless, a majority of Saraguro families resist the notion of Indian women pursuing nondomestic careers. Most favor traditional roles of marriage and childbearing, and many Indian parents oppose efforts to send daughters to schools in other cities. This ambivalence towards economic advancement presents conflicting role expectations for young Saraguro women seeking educational degrees and careers.

Politics

Saraguro men and women both take an active role in community development projects. Indian men belong to work cooperatives, or *mingas*, in each *barrio*, where they contribute to projects such as road construction, irrigation and drainage ditches, and construction of community meeting houses. Indian women attend weekly health and development meetings where they organize funding drives for projects such as construction of health clinics and water storage tanks, and installation of water and power lines. All men's and women's groups elect their own *barrio* presidents, who supervise meetings and projects. Indian men and women achieve prestige and status by participating in, and, especially, by heading political organizations.

As in many peasant societies, political and voluntary groups in Saraguro are highly fissionable, with membership, attendance, and cooperation fluctuating from year to year (Wolf 1966). Friction between members of community groups may generate public conflict, gossip, and negative social opinion. Consequently, participation in voluntary community groups poses a risk for male and female members, creating the potential to enhance or damage social status.

Religion

Saraguros describe themselves as devout Catholics. However, religion as practiced by Indians in the community can best be described as a syncretism of Catholic and pre-Conquest animistic beliefs. Most Indian residents attend Mass every Sunday, and many serve as major financial supporters of the

Catholic church. Saraguro men and women participate actively in the church, but the roles assigned to members differ by gender.

A select group of Saraguro men assist with communion, collection of donations, and other duties during Mass. Attendants recruited by priests are highly respected members of the Indian community, and participation in Mass enhances their status. Indian women do not assist in services, but many are enlisted to lead processions at the end of Mass. Saraguro women also volunteer to sweep out the building, and others prepare ornate floral displays for Sunday services.

Both men and women in Saraguro are eligible for membership in *fiesta cargo* systems, whereby individuals sponsor religious celebrations in the community (Belote and Belote 1977). The Spanish term *cargo* refers to a burdensome management position. *Cargo* offices are ranked hierarchically, with prestige levels organized by degree of financial responsibility for holiday events. Potential sponsors must satisfy selection criteria to enter *cargos*. Qualifications include possession of adequate capital to pay for feasts and a respected position in the church. Since access to *cargo* offices is restricted, membership enhances the status of male and female members (Vogt 1970).

Fiesta cargo duties in Saraguro differ for men and women. Males provide liquor and meat for celebrations and participate in ritual dance performances. Female *cargo* members are responsible for food preparation, and only the highest-ranked members of the women's *cargo* are eligible to participate in public dance performances.

Indian men commonly achieve greater status than women in the religious *cargo* system, since membership in men's *cargos* requires a greater monetary investment and because women perform a less visible role in *fiestas*. Still, religious service incurs substantial economic costs for both men and women, and it takes years for many Saraguro families to recover financially after supporting feasts. Consequently, pressures to sponsor religious activities are accompanied by fears of incurring long-term debts.

Property and Inheritance

Both men and women in Saraguro obtain property through family inheritance and economic transactions. However, the kinds of wealth men and women possess and the value of their holdings often vary. Some differences can be noted in male and female ownership of land, livestock, domesticated animals, and household goods.

Saraguro women and men both own land in diverse climatic zones throughout the county seat. Saraguro families practice a limited form of verticality (Brush 1977). Verticality increases diversification of property holdings and production as individuals exploit lands in the fertile valley basin for habitation and cultivation, and in the higher *paramo*, an area of high altitude scrub and grass, for grazing pasture. Many Indian women own more cultivated land in Saraguro than their husbands do. In the past century, however, Saraguro men have extended the practice of verticality by leaving homes and families in Saraguro to exploit territory in the Amazonian tropical forest where they have taken ownership of additional grazing and crop land. As a result, Saraguro women now own proportionately less land than their husbands and brothers do.

Saraguros also own a number of domesticated animals such as cattle, sheep, pigs, chickens, and guinea pigs. In addition, some families have acquired horses, and a few individuals raise rabbits. Saraguro women, as with women in many societies, remain near the house to attend to children and domestic activities (Brown 1970; Freidl 1975; Nag, White, and Peet 1978). Since most grazing lands are located in the Amazon or several miles away from their homes, Saraguro men commonly take charge of cattle- and sheep-herding duties. The sexual division of labor in pastoralism thus leaves males in charge of marketing and exchange of sheep and cattle. As a result, men tend to acquire more livestock than do their wives. Women frequently engage in the sale of swine, chickens, and guinea pigs, but these animals have little value compared to larger domesticated animals.

Saraguro girls inherit other valued goods through their mothers. Indian women in the community continue to wear traditional dress, including hand-spun and woven skirts and shawls, large silver earrings, and shawl pins. The jewelry is passed on from mother to daughter as family heirlooms, and the silver antiques have become very valuable. While Saraguro men also wear traditional dress, few inherit any expensive heirlooms. Women thus possess more valuable personal goods than men. Unlike cattle, however, jewelry cannot be used as stored wealth for sale or exchange. Mothers are expected to hold jewelry in trust for their daughters. Women who sell family silver are severely castigated by relatives and friends.

Saraguro men and women differ, then, in the types and value of property they own. Both own land, but most avoid selling it, preferring to hold lands in trust for children. Men and women can both obtain cash by selling animals, but men tend to own a larger number of valuable animals such as cattle and horses, giving them more stored wealth. Saraguro women do own some cattle, and they express constant anxiety about losing herds to theft or disease. Women also own valuable jewelry, but they are not free to sell or exchange heirlooms. Many women also fear the theft of family jewelry, an increasingly common occurrence, which would leave little to pass on to daughters. Consequently, many Saraguro women are preoccupied by thoughts of misfortune and poverty.

Labor and Production

The sexual division of labor for economic and subsistence production is relatively flexible in Saraguro (Finerman 1985). Indian men and women participate together in most agricultural duties, although some of the more strenuous cultivation tasks, such as plowing, are usually performed by men. As noted earlier, males assume greater responsibility for cattle herding since women must remain near home. Still, Saraguro women take charge of all agricultural and pastoral duties when spouses and other male relatives are not available to assist them. In the last century, Saraguro men have left the community to seek work in other cities or in the tropical forest. As discussed above, migration of males has also risen dramatically in the past thirty years as Saraguro men have become increasingly involved in land development and cattle-herding programs in the Amazon. These men have been forced to leave wives in charge of homes, families, agricultural production, and livestock.

Indian men and women also engage in a number of economic ventures. Saraguro men and a few women sell or trade cattle and sheep with their neighbors or in the town market. In one *barrio*, Indian men have formed a weaving cooperative, selling ponchos and other items to neighbors, town residents, and the occasional tourist. Saraguro women are less organized, but many have become successful parttime merchants. Some women set up small stores in their homes while others sell chickens, guinea pigs, eggs, and dairy products to town residents, and wool, bead necklaces, and small weavings to Indian neighbors and tourists. Other women periodically accept wages for completing small tasks such as spinning wool or sewing garments for neighbors. In this way both males and females participate in economic production.

Increased responsibility for subsistence and economic production has created new pressures for Saraguro women. Since their husbands are working elsewhere and are no longer available to assist in cultivation and herding, many women have recently been forced to abandon some production activities. Others have had to depend more heavily on the cooperation of children and available family members. In many homes, daughters have been left to supervise domestic and childcare duties while their mothers attend to cultivation tasks. In other instances, sons have been assigned greater responsibility for herding to leave their mothers free to pursue other economic activities. Thus, while new economic opportunities have opened for Saraguros, changing gender roles and increasing responsibilities have created new burdens and stress for women.

DOMESTIC ACTIVITIES AND THE HEALING ROLE

Saraguro gender roles are more strictly delineated within the domestic sphere. Men's household activities are limited to collecting and splitting firewood and weaving fabric. Indian women are expected to manage all childcare and household duties and manufacture family clothing. Children learn appropriate gender roles for both production and domestic work by assisting parents. Sons help their fathers with cultivation and herding tasks, while daughters remain at home to assist their mothers with domestic activities.

Saraguro mothers also accept responsibility for family health as part of the domestic childcare role (Finerman 1983). The Indian women have extensive knowledge of the cultivation of herbs and preparation of herbal remedies, and they provide preventive care and treatment for a broad range of family health complaints (Finerman 1983, 1985). My research indicates that, despite availability of numerous traditional and modern biomedical health services, Saraguro mothers are the primary source of family care. Data suggest that during the period surveyed, Saraguro mothers were found to have treated nearly 86 percent of 2460 illness episodes which were surveyed in 140 families over a one-year period between 1980 and 1981. Moreover, Indian mothers acted as the first consultant for nearly 75 percent of all complaints reported during this period (Finerman 1985). Follow-up studies undertaken during the summers of 1982 and 1984 indicate that Indian mothers remain the primary healers for family members, and they continue to pass on curing information to daughters as part of their instruction in domestic activities.

In Saraguro, control over family health accords social status. Responsibility for therapeutic decisions and the outcome of care gives Indian mothers power within the domestic sphere, and successful healers attract credit and prestige within the community. Saraguro women express public approval for proper childcare by complimenting each other on the healthy appearance of family members, and female friends and neighbors often consult mothers with healthy children for curing advice (Finerman 1985).

While the healer role confers status for successful treatment, responsibility for family health can be a burden for women with sick children. Saraguro mothers consider themselves liable for illness as well as health, and women with chronically sick children often become targets of gossip and ridicule within the Indian community. Consequently, Saraguro women demonstrate a preoccupation with family health. Indian mothers exhibit extreme anxiety during periods of family illness. They also invest substantial time, money, and effort in health-related activities, discussing new remedies with female friends and relatives, and purchasing and preparing herbs or medications for preventive and therapeutic care (Finerman 1983, 1985).

Changing gender roles and new demands placed upon Saraguros create stress for many indigenous women. Stressors may, in turn, generate health problems for those unable to fulfill family and community expectations. Data indicate that Saraguro women suffer from disorders associated with stress and role performance.

NERVIOS AS STRESS-RELATED DEPRESSION

Nervios, or "nerves," has been identified in a number of studies as a psychosocial disorder associated with a range of symptoms expressing emotional distress (Barlett and Low 1980; Davis 1985; Guarnaccia 1985; Low 1985; Nichter 1981; Van Schaik 1985). The disorder has been identified in such culturally diverse populations as India (Nichter 1981), Newfoundland (Davis 1983), Eastern Kentucky (Ludwig and Forrester 1981), and among Greek residents in Montreal (Dunk 1985). It has been particularly well documented in Latin America among communities in Costa Rica (Low 1981), the Peruvian Andes (Stevenson 1977), the Ecuadorian Andes (Butler 1982), Guatemala (Low 1985), and mainland Puerto Ricans (Garrison 1977; Guarnaccia 1985; Harwood 1981).

Nervios represents a common health complaint in Saraguro, having one of the highest incidence rates in the indigenous community. Symptoms of the disorder appear to be consistent with those for depression. Data indicate that the onset of *nervios* is correlated with stress and changing or unrealistic role demands.

As noted earlier, a one-year survey of family illness in Saraguro households was undertaken with 140 Indian mothers in the community between 1980 and 1981 (Finerman 1985). Health complaints and therapeutic care were documented. During this period, participants reported that family members suffered from 2460 episodes of illness. Of these 2460 health complaints, 154 cases involved *nervios*, and the disorder was the sixth most frequently reported health complaint in the survey. While children were the most common victims of a majority of recorded ailments, nearly all victims of *nervios* were female heads of household (survey participants, or the mothers of survey participants). Survey data indicate, furthermore, that *nervios* was the third most common health complaint for adult Indian women in the study.

I collected detailed information on *nervios* in a 1984 follow-up study in Saraguro (Finerman 1985). An open-ended questionnaire on the disorder was administered to thirty-one Indian mothers. Participants were asked to describe the etiology, symptoms, course, and treatment of *nervios*, and personal histories of encounters with the condition were recorded.

All participants in the 1984 study stated that they had suffered from *nervios* at some point in their lives. In fact, I was unable to locate a single adult Indian woman who had never claimed to suffer from the condition. Most Saraguros questioned about *nervios* described the disorder as gender-linked. A majority of participants in the 1984 study (twenty-seven out of thirty-one volunteers, or 87 percent), identified women as the most frequent victims of *nervios*. However, four individuals stated that men and women of all ages can suffer from the disorder. All participants stated that humans are the only victims of *nervios*, although animals are said to suffer from other culture-specific disorders.

The tendency for Saraguros to describe *nervios* as a women's disorder may be explained, in part, by differences in gender role expectations in the display of emotion. Saraguro males indicate that they value stoicism and discourage public expressions of pain and sorrow. Nevertheless, Indian men appear to use alcohol as an outlet for depression and repressed emotions. In recent years, alcohol abuse by adult Indian males has become a major health concern in the community.

Participants were asked to describe the general etiology of *nervios*. All thirty-one informants reported that the main cause of the disorder is *sufrimiento* or "suffering." However, fourteen (45 percent) of the women stated that *rabia* (anger) and *susto* (extreme or magical fright) can also precipitate or aggravate the condition. In addition, two women reported that physical illness and deaths in the family can generate the disorder, and one informant suggested that gossip, theft, or financial hardship may provoke an episode of *nervios*.

Six Indian informants indicated that *nervios* has a biolgical or organic etiology as well as an emotional one. This concept is consistent with the perspective in many societies that illness is the result of physiological rather than psychological dysfunction, indicating absence of body mind dualism in the perception of disease causation (Foster 1953; Helman 1984; Katon and Kleinman 1981; Kleinman 1980). Somatization is common in Saraguro, where social and emotional problems are converted into physical manifestations of distress. Saraguro informants who cited organic causes for *nervios* attributed the condition to dislocation of an organ refered to as *nervios* or *pulsario* (roughly translated as "pulsation"). Women suggested that the organ moves up and down inside the body of troubled individuals, making them tense, nauseous, and weak.

Participants in the 1984 study were questioned about the onset and course of *nervios*, but less consistency was noted between informants on this topic. Approximately 74 percent of the women (23 of 31 participants) indicated that *nervios* has a slow or gradual onset. However, 22.6 percent (7 of 31 informants) stated that the condition begins rapidly, and one woman suggested that the speed of onset varies. When questioned further, all participants stated that the speed of onset can vary by the cause of the disorder and by the victim's ability to tolerate suffering. Chronic or long-term problems progressively induce the condition, while sudden tragedy or fright precipitates a rapid onset. Informants suggested that, since most cases occur when victims gradually succumb to prolonged suffering, onset is usually slow.

Individuals participating in the 1984 study were more divided about the speed of recovery from *nervios*. More than half of the participants (16 of 31 women) indicated that victims recover slowly from the disorder. Over one-third of the women (12 of the 31 participants) stated that recovery can be rapid, while only a few informants (3 of the 31 participants) suggested that recovery speed varies. More extensive questioning about the course of *nervios* resolved some of the disparity in perspectives on speed of recovery. All participants indicated that the course of *nervios* is accelerated by conflict resolution and proper treatment. They suggested that effective treatment and settlement of problems leads to rapid recovery, while inadequate care and failure to resolve disputes or misfortune prolongs illness. Since many conflicts cannot be quickly or fully rectified, recovery from *nervios* is usually slow and incomplete.

Symptoms associated with *nervios* were also recorded in the 1984 questionnaire. Participants were asked to detail general physical and emotional sensations associated with the condition. Individuals reported that victims of the disorder may suffer from the following symptoms (since informants listed multiple features of *nervios*, the total number of symptoms recorded exceeds 31):

NERVIOS SYMPTOMS:	NUMBER OF RESPONSES:		*NERVIOS* SYMPTOMS:	NUMBER OF RESPONSES:	
sad/depressed	31	(100%)	preoccupied	16	(51.6%)
no appetite	31	(100%)	feverish	14	(45%)
unable to sleep	30	(96.8%)	feelings of guilt	13	(42%)
unable to work	29	(93.5%)	sweating	10	(32.2%)
fatigue, tire easily	29	(93.5%)	hot (humoral imbalance)	7	(22.5%)
headaches	28	(90.3%)	heart pains	6	(19.3%)
confused/can't concentrate	27	(87%)	cold (humoral imbalance	5	(16%)
lack interest	26	(83.8%)	act "crazy"	5	(16%)
tremble/agitated/nervous	25	(80.6%)	dizziness	5	(16%)
menstrual cycle			blurred vision	4	(13%)
irregularity	23	(74%)	weakness	3	(9.6%)
cry continually	22	(70.9%)	skin blisters	3	(9.6%)
nightmares	21	(67.7%)	nausea	2	(6.4%)
body aches	20	(64.5%)	bloody nose	1	(3.2%)
irritable	19	(61.2%)	dark circles under eyes	1	(3.2%)
stomach aches	18	(58%)	blood is "eaten" (lost)	1	(3.2%)

In addition to the above symptoms, eighteen women (58 percent) reported that *nervios* can be fatal in some instances, particularly if a woman suffering from the condition is also pregnant.

Symptoms reported in the 1984 questionnaire closely parallel those currently associated with depressive disorders (American Psychiatric Association 1980; Kleinman and Good 1985) and reflect some of the characteristics of the culture-specific depression syndrome *susto* as described in *mestizo* (Indian-Spanish) populations throughout Latin America (Rubel, O'Nell and Collado-Ardon 1984). However, it is important to note that Saraguros view *susto* as a disorder quite distinct from *nervios*. Saraguros describe *susto*, or magical fright sickness, as a childhood ailment which causes physical pain and diarrhea. Twenty cases of *susto* were recorded in the 1980–1981 family health survey, and children were the reported victims in nineteen of these episodes. Symptoms of magical fright are distinct from those listed above for *nervios*, although, as mentioned in the discussion on etiology, *susto* can aggravate or precipate some cases of *nervios*.

Saraguro women were questioned in both the 1980–1981 and 1984 studies about therapeutic care for *nervios*. In the 1980–1981 family health survey, Indian mothers indicated that they themselves were the preferred source of care for all forms of illness in the family. The mothers reported in the 1980–1981 survey that they had treated nearly 86 percent of their own health problems and those suffered by spouses and children (Finerman 1985). This pattern of therapeutic resort remained consistent in the case of *nervios*, where self-treatment was employed for 131 of the 154 *nervios* cases reported during the one-year survey (eleven episodes did not receive treatment). Mothers noted in the survey that they had also consulted neighbors (in fifty-nine cases) and pharmacists (in eighty-two cases) to obtain additional ingredients for home remedies in *nervios* treatment. A few Saraguro mothers sought additional consultations with one or more health specialists for cases of *nervios*, but specialized care was rare in comparison with self-treatment. Only twenty-three of the 154 *nervios* episodes were presented to physicians, and Indian nurse practitioners were consulted for only fifteen of the episodes. Another eight cases were treated by herbalists; a midwife and a *curandero*, or traditional healer, were each consulted for one *nervios* case in the 1980–1981 survey.[1] All thirty-one Indian women participating in the 1984 survey supported the notion that home or self-treatment was the preferred method of care for *nervios*. Five of the participants indicated that they had consulted physicians for the treatment of the condition, but all five stated that doctors had been unable to relieve their symptoms. Saraguro women employ a number of techniques in treating *nervios*. A number of Indian residents purchase pills, liquids, and other pharmaceuticals to treat the conditions. However, the most common form of care involves use of *remedios casseros*, or home-made herbal remedies. Indian women prepare and administer plant remedies in the form of teas, decoctions, plasters, baths, and flotations. Numerous plants may be employed in treatment (see Appendix). One informant suggested, however, that the best therapy for *nervios* is distraction. As she stated:

> How can you cure *nervios* if you sit at home and think about how much sadness you have? When you have the *nervios* all you want is to sit on your bed and stare at the walls or into your heart and think of how unhappy you are, how many problems you have, and cry and cry. But this is foolish. I know a woman who does this—just sits and cries—but it is crazy. You must get up and leave the house; the house is where *nervios* begins. You must get up and go out; go to a fiesta and dance and eat and forget your problems.

DEPRESSION AND GENDER ROLES IN SARAGURO

Nervios and depression appear to be associated with changing gender roles in Saraguro. Links between role fulfillment and depression in Saraguro are revealed in *nervios* case histories. Participants in the 1984 study were asked to recall events which precipitated the disorder, as well as details of onset, symptoms, treatment, and recovery. Representative examples of *nervios* case histories (identified with pseudonyms) follow.

Case 1

Carmen, a 20-year-old woman, became ill during her first pregnancy. She lacked the strength to walk, work, or eat. As her illness continued, she began to fear that her first child would be sick or stillborn. Carmen blamed her child for her sickness and believed that the child had purposely made her ill. She grew anxious, suffered from nightmares, and was eventually unable to sleep for more than a few hours a night. She went to the doctor for a check-up and some pills, but did not feel better. Finally, she prepared an herbal remedy and recovered, but she remains apprehensive about future pregnancies, and views her child as a burden.

Case 2

Maria, a 35-year-old mother, has suffered from a chronic case of *nervios* since one of her three children died from measles. Maria sat in her son's room for a week after the boy died, crying and praying for her own death. For the first month after her son's death, Maria was unable to eat, sleep, or work regularly; her hands trembled, she sweated constantly, felt weak, and suffered blinding headaches. Maria stated that she nearly went crazy after the death because she had failed to protect the boy, and had not given him adequate care. She relieves symptoms of her condition by taking home remedies, but symptoms recur, especially during periods of family sickness and misfortune.

Case 3

Luz, a 38-year-old mother of eight, suffered her first case of *nervios* when she was a child. When Luz was eight years old her father drowned in a lake. After the death, Luz cried for days, refused to eat, became weak, had nightmares and debilitating headaches. After her father died, Luz's mother had to take charge of work, and Luz was left to raise her brothers and sisters. She continues to take herbal remedies, which control the symptoms of *nervios*. Still, Luz said that since her father died she has felt alone in the world, and she suffers recurrent episodes of *nervios* when her husband drinks or argues with her, and when family members are ill.

Case 4

Rosa, a 42-year-old mother of five, suffers from *nervios* caused by her children's sickness. She indicated that her children are often sick because they ignore her warnings to dress warmly and eat properly, and they play with other children who are ill. Rosa stated that she feels responsible for her children's sickness, and worries about gossip for being an inadequate mother with a chronically sick family. During these periods she gets headaches, feels weak, and cannot eat or sleep. She takes herbal remedies which relieve the symptoms of her disorder, but because her children continue to fall ill, the condition recurs.

Case 5

Angelina is a 65-year-old woman with three living children. After her marriage at age 16, her husband left for the tropical forest to find work. Angelina was orphaned and had no living relatives, so she took sole charge of her home and children. After her husband returned, she began to argue with him over his drinking. Angelina has suffered periodically from *nervios* for the past fifty years because of loneliness and the "bad comportment" of her husband. During these periods she has head, body, and stomach aches, cannot eat, sleep, or work, and cries constantly. She said that after years of suffering she has also lost her vision. She takes home remedies and pills which help to relieve symptoms, but stated "there is no cure for a bad life."

Case 6

Juana, a 28-year-old mother of two, has an eight-year-old daughter who has suffered from *nervios* all her life. Juana said an herbalist told her that the child has had the condition since she was in the womb. Juana explained that when she was nearly six months pregnant with her daughter she was bitten by a dog, and then she fainted and fell into a river. Juana suggested that her extreme fright gave the fetus *nervios*, and that the girl has suffered since that time. Juana said her daughter cries constantly, has persistent colic, stomach aches, and nightmares. Juana stated that there are good herbal remedies for *nervios*, but thus far she has been unable to cure the girl.

These examples suggest a link between role expectations and depression in Saraguro. Informants attribute *nervios* to excessive demands for maintaining family health and marital harmony and supervising domestic and economic production.

In the first four cases, women cited health-related factors which placed excessive demands upon them and precipitated episodes of *nervios*. In the first case, *nervios* was associated with personal illness during pregnancy and was aggravated by the victim's anxiety over the health of her fetus and by feelings of resentment toward her child. The second and third cases were generated by grief and, in the second case, guilt over the death of a family member. These chronic cases recur during periods of family illness, discord, or misfortune. The fourth case of *nervios* was attributed to the high incidence of health problems in the victim's family. Despite indications that the woman blamed her family for bringing sickness upon themselves, she continued to assume personal liability for their illness. The fifth case of *nervios* concerned inability to maintain marital harmony and meet domestic and economic responsibilities. The victim in this instance succumbed to depression caused by marital discord and and by the burden of assuming sole charge of home, family, and production duties. The sixth case, involving both a mother and her daughter, was caused by *susto*. As with the first four examples, this case is also associated with role demands to maintain family health. The daughter's condition was attributed to prenatal exposure to magical fright, while the mother's condition was aggravated by her daughter's persistent illness.

Case histories of all women participating in the 1984 *nervios* study suggest that inability to meet excessive role expectations may be associated with stress and depression disorders among adult Saraguro women. Specific events which had led to personal or family experiences with *nervios* were evaluated for all participants. A total of forty-one *nervios* cases were recorded among the thirty-one participants. The most frequent cause of *nervios* reported in interviews was family illness, which accounted for twenty-five episodes (61 percent) of the disorder. Husbands' drinking, abusing, or arguing with their wives was the second most frequent source of *nervios*, precipitating eleven cases of the condition (26 percent). Other causes of the disorder were less common. Four of the forty-one episodes (9 percent) were attributed to magical fright, but three of these cases involved the children of informants. Only one adult Indian woman in the 1984 study reported that she had suffered from *nervios* as a result of *susto*. Finally, two cases (4 percent) were reportedly induced by theft.

These data suggest that Saraguro women face pressure to fulfill role expectations with respect to family health, marital and domestic relations, and economic production. It may be expected, then, that recent changes in the allocation of traditional gender role responsibilities and excessive new demands on indigenous women to compensate for male migration outside the community have intensified role pressures and elevated incidence rates of stress-related disorders among adult Indian women. Interviews with Saraguro women tend to support this perspective. These women indicate that mothers face new pressures and demands. They also suggest that, while individuals have always suffered from *nervios*, recent years have seen more women suffering from the condition more frequently.

CONCLUSION

Saraguro women currently face an accelerated rate of change, requiring rapid accommodation to continually shifting gender role demands. New economic opportunities have forced Indian men and women to redefine traditional roles in education, politics, religion, production, and family care.

As Indian women assume responsibility for domestic and nondomestic production duties, they encounter stress in their efforts to fulfill excessive and unstable gender role expectations. This stress, in turn, appears to have contributed to the elevated incidence of depression disorders among adult Indian women.

It would be a mistake, however, to interpret increased *nervios* rates as evidence that Saraguro women have failed in their efforts to adapt to change. Quite the contrary, my data indicate that *nervios* represents an adaptive device which aids Indian women in the transition from traditional to contemporary gender roles.

Nervios appears to provide an effective means for the expression of a "language of distress" (Low 1985:187). Carr and Vitalliano define distress as "a complex of biobehavioral responses to antecedent stressors (perceived as well as real) mediated by vulnerability to stress . . . and psychological and social resources (coping strategies, social supports)" (1985:246). (see also Helman 1984; Kleinman and Kleinman 1985; Lewis 1981.) A number of studies suggest that depressive disorders act as culturally sanctioned coping mechanisms for distress (see Bandura 1977; Carr and Vitalliano 1985; Good and Kleinman 1985; Suarez, Crowe, and Adams 1978). As Schieffelin indicates,

> [A] person is likely to become depressed when placed in a situation in which his or her social moves are repeatedly frustrated and in which unhappiness and mental suffering are grounds for legitimately obtaining sympathy and support by entering the illness role. The rewards of entering this role in this situation are such that the individual develops a kind of "learned helplessness" in which motivational passivity and depression become a kind of self-perpetuating coping strategy (1985:116).

Since virtually all Saraguro Indian women suffer from *nervios* at some point in their lives, the disorder provides a nonstigmatizing means of articulating feelings of distress, frustration, and low self-esteem, and allowing opportunities to garner the sympathy of relatives and community members during periods of rapid change and stress. Saraguro women may actually exploit their newly elevated position of social responsibility, demonstrating the indispensible quality of their contribution to the family once they become temporarily incapacitated by an illness which is thought to be caused by "suffering."

The nonstigmatizing nature of *nervios* is further reflected in the fact that Saraguros view the condition as a sign of emotional sensitivity, a trait which, though disparaged in Saraguro males, is culturally valued in Indian women. Studies indicate that a number of cultures encourage diverse expressions of depression as an index of character strength or religious salvation (cf. Good, Good, and Moradi 1985; Kleinman and Good 1985). For Saraguro women, periodic susceptibility to transient episodes of *nervios* provides public affirmation of emotional depth, while women unacquainted with the condition may be viewed as callous and detached.

While chronic dependency on the sick role may damage individual status (Alexander 1982), short-term episodes of *nervios* entitle Saraguro women to the attention of family members, exempt them from failure in role performance, and provide temporary relief from responsibilities and time to adjust to gender role alterations (Foster and Anderson 1978). It is expected that, denied the opportunity to express frustration with new responsibilities, Saraguro women would become less capable of adapting to change within the community.

APPENDIX: Medicinal Plants and Ingredients Employed by Saraguros for the Treatment of *Nervios*.

Plants are listed alphabetically by their Spanish or Quichua name along with the number of times each ingredient was reportedly used to treat *nervios*. English and scientific names are included for those plants which could be identified.

PLANT	NUMBER OF TIMES REPORTED:
aleli (*Mathiola annua*)	14
alfalfa [alfalfa] (*Medicago sativa*)	1
ataco/sangurache [amaranth] (*Amaranthus caudatus*)	4
begonia [begonia] (*Begonia sp.*)	80
berro [watercress] (*Cardamine nasturtioides*)	5
boraja [borage] (*Borago officinalis*)	16
canela [cinnamon] (*Nectandra connamomoides*)	1
cerro grande	1
clavel [carnation] (*Dianthus sp.*)	7
cola de caballo [horsetail] (*Equisetum arvense L.*)	2
culantrillo [maidenhair] (*Adiantum aethiopicum*)	2
escancel (*Aerva sanguinolenta*)	21
flor de espiritu (*Epidendrum sp.*)	5
hierbabuena [peppermint] (*Mentha pipertita*)	1
limon [lemon] (*Citrus limonum*)	8
linaza [linseed] (*Linum usitatissimum*)	3
llanten [plantago] (*Plantago major*)	5
malva (*Malva sp.*)	53
manzanilla [chamomile] (*Matricaria chamomila*)	21
monte de perro	1
mora [blackberry] (*Rubus fructicosus*)	2
mortino [nightshade] (*Solanum nigrum*)	8

PLANT	NUMBER OF TIMES REPORTED:
ortiga [nettle] (*Urtiga urens*)	1
pacunga (*Piperomia peltigera*)	1
pelo de choclo [corn silk] (*Zea mays*)	6
pena [fuschia] (*Fuschia sp.*)	57
pimpinela [pimpernel] (*Poterium sanguisorba*)	41
poleo/tipo (*Bistropogon mollis*)	2
retama [Spanish broom] (*Spartium junceum*)	2
romero [rosemary] (*Rosmarinus officinalis*)	1
rosa [rose] (*Rosa sp.*)	6
sauco (*Cestrum sp.*)	5
segroron	1
shullo (*Oenothera sp.*)	4
tamarindo [tamarind] (*Tamarindus indica*)	1
tigresillo, sauce [willow] (*Salix sp.*)	10
toronche	12
toronjil [lemon balm] (*Melissa officinalis*)	99
valeriana (*Valeriana sp.*)	8
violeta [violet] (*Violeta sp.*)	5

OTHER INGREDIENTS

assorted pills	72
bottled herbal preparations	65

NOTES

Research funding was provided, in part, by the UCLA Committee for Health Services Research and the UCLA Department of Anthropology. The assistance of the Museo de Antropologia of the Banco Central del Ecuador and the Instituto Naciónal de Patrimonio Cultural is gatefully acknowledged. I greatly appreciate the assistance of Allen Johnson, Ph.D., Douglass Price-Williams, Ph.D., Carole Browner, Ph.D., and Ross Sackett, M.A., all of UCLA, and Tom Collins, Ph.D., and Charles McNutt, Ph.D. of Memphis State University, who read drafts of this manuscript or shared many thoughts with me about my research. Nevertheless, opinions expressed in this chapter are my own, and I assume responsibility for all errors and omissions. Additional thanks are extended to Miss Toreda Earls of Memphis State University, who typed early drafts of this chapter. As always, deepest gratitude is owed to the people of Saraguro, without whose generous support this research would not have been possible.

1. Several illness expisodes were treated by more than one practitioner, so that consultation totals exceed 154.

12
WOMEN AND STRESS IN BRUNEI

Linda Amy Kimball and Shawna Craig

Brunei Malay women portray stereotypically overworked and under appreciated females. Overwork is a function of the hard physical labor involved in daily life, including parenting responsibilities as well as strict Islamic marital and religious obligations. The degree to which overwork as a source of stress has been ignored in the anthropological literature is related to biases about "women's work." Women of all socioeconomic groups among the Brunei are negatively affected by overwork and have various mechanisms to cope with this stress. Coping mechanisms include the use of traditional healers or *dukuns* for herbal remedies and massages and social support from extended female kin.

Brunei is a small country situated on the northwest coast of the island of Borneo in Southeast Asia. Malays represent one of a number of cultures living in Brunei, including Europeans, Chinese, Kadayans, and Dusun. Brunei Malay culture is distinct from the other cultures of the Malay Peninsula (West Malaysia). Yet Brunei Malay women, like women everywhere, experience stress in their lives, and use various means to cope with it.

Very little of the extensive literature on Island Southeast Asia deals directly with the stresses women face. One exception is Laderman (1982, 1983), who provides a detailed discussion of stresses faced by women in Trengganu, West Malaysia. Others (R. I. Firth 1966; R. M. Firth 1966; Fraser 1966; Geddes 1957; Hudson 1972; Sutlive 1978; Williams 1965) describe women's work and roles in Malay or non-Malay cultures in Borneo and West Malaysia, but do not discuss stress as being a part of women's life. Danaraj (1980) and Skeat (1967) discuss mysticism, traditional medical practices, poisons, and amulets as found among the Malays of the Malay Peninsula, but do not discuss their relationship to stress.

A dual bias in much of the literature on Southeast Asia conceals the

170

stresses women face. The first bias is that women, and women's activities, are often taken for granted

> or discounted as "women's work" and hence underreported or not mentioned. . . . Anthropologists in writing about human culture have followed our own culture's ideological bias in treating women as relatively invisible and describing what are largely the activities and interests of men (Rosaldo and Lamphere 1974:2).

The second bias is more subtle. Most authors from an urban, Western background are unaware of the enormous drudgery of life for both men and women in much of the world. That drudgery implies very real stress. The basics of obtaining food, shelter, and clothing require immense physical labor and exact a physical toll from both men and women. The stress placed on women, however, has further dimensions. "Work is defined as activity that is related to the production of goods and services" (Madeira and Singer 1975:490). The domestic tasks associated with women's work are not seen as being contributions to economic development, nor are they valued as "work." Women's tasks are highly diverse, yet share a core of common features. These center about the household and its management, including the production and rearing of children, and cooking (Bourguignon 1980). Men's work in the public domain is culturally valued and materially rewarded, while women's work in the domestic domain is culturally undervalued and symbolically rewarded. This dichotomy appears in those cultures where there is a sexual asymmetry associated with a definite division of labor and roles based on gender (cf. Rosaldo and Lamphere 1974). Such is the case in Brunei.

The women described here live in a rural village in the Tembourong District of Brunei. The data reported here were gathered by participant observation and interviews conducted during fieldwork in 1969–1971, and more recently in 1983. As part of this research, I was apprenticed to a *dukun* (traditional healer), and observed her rituals and ministrations. I lived with and was adopted into a family of good common ancestry background where I observed and participated in daily family life, focusing on child enculturation. The people in this study were rice farmers until recently, but vary in wealth from rather poor to economically comfortable. They are all of good commoner ancestry; they are not of the royal or noble classes.

This chapter focuses on the stresses that rural women must cope with throughout their lives. Urban women, and women of royal or noble blood, face different sets of stresses than those encountered by rural Brunei Malay women.

Younger women, especially those in the city who hold jobs in addition to being wives and mothers, have the fulltime demands of work as well as the demands of household and family. They have to purchase everything they need, not having the fishing and gathering resources of the rural village available to them. On the other hand, they do not have heavy farm chores to do, and thus are spared some of the physical stress placed on rural women.

Very high-status and royal women face many stresses, which include dealing with intense rivalries and jealousies, establishing and maintaining status, ensuring personal safety and security, and observing intricate court etiquette, dress, and behavior. Their very high social rank means that, unlike lower-status women, they have almost no one to turn to to help relieve stress due to cultural values, which will be discussed later.

It is impossible to address the issue of stress among all these different groups of women in a brief chapter. Thus, my focus will be on rural Brunei Malay women of common ancestry. One thing all Brunei Malay women share in common is that modernization has brought new sets of stressors. Increasing emphasis on materialism has led to the desire to accumulate goods, and a breakdown of traditional sharing. Some people prefer a new car or piece of furniture to helping their elders or other family members. The family network is one of the important ways in which women cope with stress in Brunei. Widespread education is another force of modernization which creates stress. Although schooling is free, uniforms and supplies must be bought. More importantly, children are no longer available to help with domestic chores, and thus another link in the family network is lost to Brunei Malay women.

Before discussing the particular causes of stress among Brunei Malay women and the ways they cope with it, however, it is necessary to consider the meaning of stress itself, and its relationship to their culture.

STRESS AND BRUNEI MALAY WOMEN

The Brunei Malay language has no word which corresponds to the English word stress. Consequently, in studying stress among Brunei Malay women we are applying a non-Brunei concept to the study of one aspect of their life. Also, the fact that no word in Brunei Malay corresponds to the English word stress means that women do not cope with a unified entity, but rather with various manifestations of what in English has a specific definition. The closest the Brunei Malay language comes to this term is the concept of *susah-payah*, "hard and difficult," or "difficult and troubled."

Stress has been defined in many ways. In his classic study, Seyle (1976:1) provides two definitions of the word: "the rate of wear and tear on the body" and "the nonspecific response of the body to any demand."

However, the more traditional common meanings of the word are better suited to the study of stress among Brunei Malay women. The Oxford English Dictionary defines stress as (1) "the overpowering pressure of some adverse force or influence," (2) "a condition of things compelling or characterized by strained effort," and (3) "strain upon a bodily organ or a mental power."

The verb "to stress" is defined as, "to subject (a material thing, a bodily organ, a mental faculty) to stress or strain; to overwork, fatigue" (1961:1110–11).

Examined from the perspective of the common definitions above, several types of stress can be seen to affect Brunei Malay women. First and foremost is overwork. Other sources of stress include family difficulties, illnesses, accidents, and societal and religious pressures. Women use various strategies to cope with each of these stressors. To understand how they do this, it is necessary to consider the cultural background of the Brunei Malays.

Cultural Demands

Brunei Malays traditionally lived primarily in Brunei-town (now Bandar Seri Begawan), engaging in trading, fine craftsmanship, and fishing. They traded with the Kadayans (Moslem rice farmers), and they feared the headhunting Muruts of the hinterlands. However, a smallpox and cholera epidemic in the early 1900s seriously reduced the Murut population. This, combined with the advent of European rubber tapping, led to dramatic subsistence changes for the Brunei Malays. Some Brunei Malays moved upstream into the Tembourong district, formerly the land of the Muruts, and became rice farmers, traders, and rubber tappers.

All Brunei Malays are Moslems. Islamic life is a total way of life which regulates a woman's being on all levels, from personal habits and family relationships to community and national life (Tweddell and Kimball 1985). The expected cultural role for a Brunei Malay women is that of wife and mother. Important cultural values include being a good member of society, not showing anger, and having polite manners and refined speech. Brunei Malays would agree with the statement that:

> [S]ocial man's supreme achievement [is] a stable culture with a tradition that has persisted relatively unchanged for generations. It is by tradition and culture that a man weaves his separate activities into the whole cloth of a great cultural canon—the living fabric of civilization (Henry and Stephens 1977:234).

A rural Brunei Malay woman must meet all cultural expectations and perform her role well or face *malu* ("shame"). If a woman does not dress her children properly, keep the house clean in a prescribed manner, or keep her husband from straying, she will be ashamed and have *malu*. Therefore, no matter how *susah-payah*, "hard or difficult," her life may be, the woman must maintain the status quo or face ridicule, gossip, and possible abuse from her husband.

In the years since World War I, change has slowly altered traditional female values and behaviors. Women can enter the male public domain, such as on shopping trips to the city accompanied by children or other females. Girls can now go to school, and can even be in the same class as boys. The older women say that females used to be meek, quiet, retiring, and not forward (Kimball 1980:47). This follows the Koranic precept that women be modest and circumspect.

Yet much remains basically the same as it was in the past. The woman's domain is the domestic sphere of life with an occasional foray into the fields to work with her husband. The expected cultural role is still that of an obedient wife and dutiful mother. At age five or six, girls are expected to care for their younger siblings. After age seven, girls are expected to do their share of the household chores and are scolded if they do not. A girl in her teens may be taken out of school in order to help her mother at home.

The duties, responsibilities, and obligations of a Brunei Malay woman are ordained from birth. No matter how "hard" life becomes, a woman must persevere and perform her cultural role. However, a woman has access to three main stress-reducing, coping mechanisms: female networks, the *dukun*, and the strength of her own faith in Allah. An examination of the need for these coping mechanisms in dealing with stress follows.

Work Demands

One word summarizes the life of a rural Brunei Malay woman—work. The work is endless, often boring, and often physically demanding. Women's tasks include cleaning, bearing and raising children, and preparing, cooking, and storing food. They must also plant and harvest food, care for animals, and gather fruit and eggs. Brunei women collect firewood and water, sew clothes, weave baskets and mats, and tap rubber if needed. They must care for children and elderly kin alike. Various communal rituals such as births, weddings, and funerals require additional work.

Underlying the stress of overwork is the stress of never receiving a reward for one's efforts. After tirelessly working from dawn to dusk, there is always something left undone. The Brunei Malay woman is subject to frequent interruptions. These interruptions produce stress because the woman may then be unable to perform all the necessary tasks of the day, and thus feel *malu*, shame, at not doing all her appointed duties.

Little wonder, then, that overwork and attendant exhaustion are prime stress factors for women. A woman can do little to cope with the stress of overwork, for the work must be done. Work not done today will be added to tomorrow's tasks. A woman may fall ill, but she still performs her chores unless she is too ill to rise from her bed. Everyone from time to time experiences *malas*, or lassitude. This is an utter physical disinclination to work. Cumulative exhaustion ages women rapidly.

Economic concerns tie in with both work and family problems. Women are the family treasurers; it is the Brunei Malay woman who holds the purse strings and manages the family finances. Money is considered "hot," and it is therefore bad if the man holds the money. If the man controls it, the family will be poor or lack adequate sustenance. The men acknowledge that women perform the managerial and advisory functions of handling the purse strings very well (Strange 1981). Yet this financial control brings with it the resultant responsibilities and stress of managing the family money.

Women take three basic approaches to economic problems. First, they try whatever practical means are available to solve them. Women often work to make small crafts that earn money or that can be bartered for goods and services. Second, they may simply fall into despair. Third, they may accept the attitude of *alhamdullilah*, "as Allah wills." If the family has adequate sustenance, their basic health and vigor level will be reasonable. But if the family has too little to eat, as is common, lack of energy becomes a factor.

Religious Obligations

The religion of Islam imposes its own stressors. Women, like men, are required to pray five times daily, though the demands of childcare often make it impossible to say all the prayers, or to fast during the month of Ramadan. Ramadan, the ninth month of the Muslim lunar calendar, is the fasting month. Women must continue their daily duties while fasting and must perform additional chores including preparing a special meal, *sahur*, and serve it nightly at 2 A.M.

A menstruating woman is forbidden to fast or pray. Making up the fast later is a stressor. Pregnant or lactating women are not supposed to fast, though many do because they say it is too hard to make up the missed fast. It is not unknown for women to welcome menstruation because they are then freed from one duty.

Older Brunei Malay women say that Islam used to be lighter on women, because "Allah made them that way." "He understands," meaning that if women missed praying or fasting because of familial duties or pollution taboos, it would be acceptable. But such is not the strict orthodox interpretation of Islam espoused today. A man and a woman sometimes face the choice of observing religious duties or providing food for the family to survive. This creates a conflict with no resolution, adding another source of stress for women.

Marriage Demands

The primary role of a Brunei Malay woman is that of wife. Women usually marry between the ages of fifteen and twenty. After marriage, a woman is under her husband's care and command, both by Brunei Malay cultural expectations and by Islamic law. Once she is married, the ideal behavior for a woman is that she seek her husband's permission before going anywhere, even to visit her mother. She needs her husband's permission to undertake any major activity outside the home (Kimball 1980; Strange 1981). Mutual respect between husband and wife are emphasized, but as the Brunei Malay point out (according to the Koran), men are in charge of women. However, men also have to financially support women (Strange 1981:23). This is the ideal behavior, however, and most women go about their own business. This ideal behavior is most carefully observed by new brides. Women who have been married several years acquire some freedom, yet still remain beholden to their husbands.

Family matters and problems often are a source of stress. In Brunei Malay society most women are, or have been, married. This means that relationships with the husband form a major part of life. Traditional marriages were arranged by the parents of the couple, though theoretically the couple had rights of refusal.

> Women—mothers, grandmothers, and matchmakers—are pivotal to the mate selection process when it is carried out in the traditional manner. And it is the women's network that possess [sic] information within and between the villages about who is seeking a wife or husband for a child (Strange 1981:104).

Today marriages are often semiarranged, and schooling has introduced some Western expectations into the marriage relationship. For example, some couples meet in high school and make a match based on romantic love. Traditionally, romantic love was not a part of the marriage relationship, and "happiness" in marriage was not expected. It was enough to fulfill one's role and be a good spouse.

Women say that it is important to be sexually pleasing to their husbands. This is a stress factor in many marriages, for if the woman is not sexually pleasing, then the man may have affairs or take on a second wife. This would bring shame to the woman.

Brunei Malay women say that their husbands do not beat them the way some non-Malay husbands beat their wives. One of the things a bride is taught, as part of her premarital preparation, is how to make poisons that will sicken or kill. (Poisons are used elsewhere in the Malay world. [See Gimlette 1981.]) Husbands know that their wives can poison them if they are violent.

Divorce does occur among the Brunei Malays, but it is comparatively rare, and is not an expected part of the marriage pattern. Brunei Malay women explain that the high *berian*, "bride price," discourages divorce. If the man divorces the woman for any reason except adultery on her part, he forfeits the *berian*. Therefore, men rarely seek divorce.

For various reasons, some women never marry. Either their fiancé died or their parents were too choosy about mates; in a few cases the women were terrified of the idea of sex, and their parents did not force them to marry. These older women live as maiden aunts with one of their relatives. They care for the children and are valuable in relieving the mother of work. Their position, however, always remains somewhat anomalous. In one sense, they have never been adult, that is, they have never married and had children. This sometimes causes a sense of strain, as does their somewhat tenuous position in the household. Some of them become skilled in needle-work or other crafts and some take refuge in religious devotions as a way to relieve the stress.

Demands of Child Rearing

The Koran, the sacred text of Islam, states that a woman's most important duty is to bear children to her husband. As soon as a Brunei Malay woman has married, older women begin to look for signs of pregnancy. Couples want children, as having children is the full mark of adulthood. A couple who remain childless after several years of marriage usually adopt a child. A widow who is still in her childbearing years is expected to remarry.

Children are Allah's gift to the couple and the couple's *harta*, "wealth." Women warn their childless daughters that men do not like barren women. Fertility can also be a stressor. The Moslem belief is that one should accept all the children that Allah chooses to bestow on you, but privately women say, "Enough is enough." Some women reportedly take herbal medicines to prevent pregnancy.

Children are hard work. Women spend the greater part of their lives raising children. The Brunei Malay concept of *kapunan* is a stressor. *Kapunan* means "very vulnerable to becoming sick or injured." *Kapunan* usually occurs because a desire, especially for food or beverage, was not fulfilled; if children do not receive the attention they want they become *kapunan*. Thus, a crying child or infant is immediately tended to (Kimball 1979). Not only does *kapunan* apply to crying, but to all the child's needs. If a child wants something, he must have it or be subject to possible illness. Four or five young children place interminable strain upon the mother, who must tend to them in addition to doing all her other chores.

A bright youthful bride tends to look worn and no longer young after six or seven childbirths, even though she is in her twenties (Kimball 1980). Women say that in the old days having children was a happy thing, the children were company, and soon learned to help out with the neverending chores. Today, however, because of school, children cannot help with the work and are more of a financial burden than a help. This adds to the stress.

Weddings

Weddings are the largest, most elaborate ceremonies in the Brunei Malay life cycle. Women begin preparations a year or more ahead of time. They must do extra work to save money for purchases, make as many things as they possibly can, and prepare ahead for the feast. This means planting an extra large rice crop, with all the attendant work, and selecting a water buffalo, cow, or steer to fatten for a meal a year hence, among many other preparations.

The woman instructs her daughter in housewifely arts and skills if she has not yet learned them, and gives the daughter special instruction on "how to be a wife." The kin group of all relatives linked to the parents of the bride must be visited to invite them to the wedding and to enlist their cooperation for it. There are many tasks to be done which include sewing the nuptial curtains, slaughtering and cooking the steer, and feeding the thousand or more wedding guests.

Death

A death in the family imposes other stresses on the woman. In addition to the sadness of the loss, there is the need to arrange for the memorial feasts to be held on the day of the death and burial, and on the third, seventh, and fortieth days after death. The fortieth day memorial feast is the final one and the largest. By then the affairs of the dead person should have been settled, the inheritance distributed. Relatives come from far and wide to attend the fortieth day feast. Many people may have to be fed—a small feast involves thirty people, a large one more than one hundred. It may also well be the woman who, several months later, purchases the gravestone and arranges for its emplacement.

Gossip

Social relationships and gossip may create stress. Gossip has a regulatory function. During female gatherings over tea, at wedding ceremonies, and at many ceremonies and rituals, women hear one another's opinion of each other. Late adolescent girls are usually present, and from the tenor of the conversation absorb the cultural values gossip reflects (Kimball 1980).

Some women gossip maliciously about others. In the world of the Brunei Malay, where public opinion is of great importance, gossip can create stress. The specific ways of coping with malicious gossip will be discussed later.

Illness

Children's health is an overriding concern. Traditionally infant diarrhea killed many infants in their first year; epidemic diseases such as malaria and smallpox killed others. Today Western maternity and child health services have cut the mortality rate drastically (Kimball 1979). Caring for a sick or injured child or family member may involve days and nights of constant care, while also performing as well as possible all the other demands of daily life. A sick child means an exhausted and sleepless mother, who in her turn may become sick.

A more insidious stress for women is malaise. This may result from several factors, including menstruation, hepatitis, or a recurring parasite, which may cause lassitude. The woman will try to get a little rest to relieve this stress, but often this is not possible. The stress may result in chores being done later, and an impatient attitude toward the family, especially toward the children. The basic attitude toward lassitude and pain is to put up with it—"What can you do?" A fair amount of hurts, pains, and feeling unwell are considered part of normal life. They occur frequently, and thus form a fairly consistent low-level source of stress, for which acceptance and forbearance are the only remedies.

Coping Mechanisms

There are three primary stress coping mechanisms available to a Brunei Malay woman. First, she may call on her female social network for help. Second, she may consult a traditional healer, female or male, for advice and massage. Finally, she may simply accept the stress, based on the religious belief that "Allah wills it so."

The female social network is made up of affinal and consanguineal kin, and friends. Women give and take emotional support, time, efforts, and food from each other (Strange 1981). Older women are instrumental in this network. As a woman ages, her life changes; she may now have long periods of free time. With the newfound freedom their age gives them, older women may spend much time visiting other women, or they may find work, such as that of masseuse. Their massages give physical relief from stress, while their advice based on the experiences of long life provide psychological help to younger women under stress.

By virtue of their age, old women are permitted to say things that would be improper for a younger woman to say. They may even "tell off" someone who is a malicious gossip or troublemaker. The presence of old women at weddings provides a respectable chaperone and a link with the past. They reinforce the fact that marriage joins together two kinship groups and continues the river of social and cultural life from the past to the present and future. Old women are the traditional ritual experts, who provide suggestions and guidance on the proper procedures. At weddings, these women discuss kinship connections and events of the past, thus providing an ongoing family link. This is important because for a Brunei Malay, to be cut off from the family and from tradition is extremely stressful.

When younger women talk to the older ones, they realize that, however great their troubles, others have survived equal, if not greater difficulties. By their "strength" in having lived so long, having weathered the storms of life, older women provide comfort and hope for the future. Older women sometimes provide relief for harassed mothers by taking care of children and performing other tasks. Thus, old women play a significant role in relieving stress. The younger female relatives, especially daughters, will take over the baby-tending chores. Other women may share tea with her and let her know that she is not alone in her overworked situation. The comradeship of her kin and friends helps to alleviate the boredom and the work load. There is the added benefit of enhancing the woman's self-worth as a female by identifying and communicating with other women.

Women try to control their men by being the perfect wife; however, some men stray. When this happens, the woman may try to talk things over in the family as a means of bringing social pressure to bear against the second marriage or the affair. But more likely she will consult a *dukun*, a traditional healer. The *dukun* will suggest various remedies, including special amulets and potions. The *dukun*'s advice also includes such practical suggestions as "fix more of his favorite treats," and "wear some fragrant oil at night to entice him."

To alleviate the stress resulting from overwork, boredom, and frustration, women call for help from their female networking system, and receive massages or counsel from the *dukun*. Female *dukun* massage women, male *dukun* provide counsel, medicines, and amulets. An older masseuse, who is always a woman, may provide massage and advice.

The resources available in the face of malicious gossip are the hope of enlisting public opinion, or consultation with a *dukun*. The *dukun* may give advice, but primarily provides empathic listening. Sometimes the *dukun* counters the gossip or counsels the woman to ignore such behavior. Withdrawing into oneself is not a culturally accepted response.

When a woman encounters economic difficulties, a main coping device, again, is consultation with the *dukun*. The *dukun* will make amulets which are believed to help the economic situation, perhaps by helping the fish catch to increase, the garden to produce more, or the market trade to be more profitable.

When a child or any other family member is sick or injured, home remedies are tried first, unless it is recognized immediately that the situation is serious. In the case of serious illness or injury the woman turns to the *dukun* or Western medicine, if it is available. The Brunei government provides free health care for all citizens, but in many villages there is little or no transportation to the district hospital, and the mobile clinic comes only once every six weeks or so.

While the women have recourse to the *dukun* or to the female network, the cultural constraint of shame means that most women have only themselves to rely on. Thus, faith in Allah sustains many believers. In the end, the woman has to find her strength in herself and in Allah. Among the Brunei Malay women, prayer relieves stress. The familiarity of chanting, the comfort of one's God, and the faith that prayer works are coping factors. Religious ritual allows the woman to feel that she is doing all she can, and that whatever then happens must be accepted as the will of Allah, somehow "right" in a way beyond human comprehension.

In addition to the three primary stress-coping mechanisms discussed above, a few others exist. "The major physical method of dealing with stress is exercise. Other forms of exercise in addition to physical activity are laughing, crying, shouting, screaming, singing, whistling, and massage" (Morse and Furst 1982:394). Brunei Malay women use these outlets at various times. Since larger cultural values of shame limit real intimacy or sharing, a woman needs to "let off steam" through outbursts of frantic physical activity such as sudden housecleaning binges or by crying and shouting.

Singing releases inner tension (Morse and Furst 1982:402). A mother who is up at night with a sick child sings both to comfort the child and to relieve her own anxiety; thus singing to the child serves as an emotional catharsis.

CONCLUSIONS

Two biases exist in the literature on stress for Island Southeast Asia. The first is the fact that "women's work" is not seen as work, and hence is underreported or not mentioned at all. The second bias is the Western authors' failure to comprehend the drudgery of women's lives.

It is likely that both of these biases are common in the literature for other areas of the world as well. It is to be hoped that the reader, having become familiar with the types of stress that face women in Brunei and the ways they cope with them, will be able to perceive the existence of stress in other cultures, even where it is not reported or is only hinted at, and will come to understand how women in other cultures successfully cope with it.

Women's work can be drudgery. The sheer physical onslaught of the long hours and physical difficulty of their tasks age many women rapidly. For example, the energy expended in climbing house and dock stairs in the course of daily chores for one year is equivalent to scaling Mount Everest.

However, women who perform these tasks do not perceive them as menial, nor do they regard themselves as mere beasts of burden. Gratification arises from the ethical value of work related to women's roles and cultural expectations, a sense of competence and pride in the ability to fulfill the role of wife and mother, and the symbolic value associated with raising children and having a happy family.

Rural Brunei Malay women cope daily with physical, psychological, and social stress. The most obvious physical stressor is that of unrelenting tedious overwork. Morse and Furst (1982:33), in discussing the stress of American women's occupations state that "the housewife/mother typically has the task of raising the children, balancing the budget, keeping the house clean, feeding and clothing the family, catering to the husband's associates, being a lovable wife, and trying to stay slim and beautiful." As discussed, the Brunei Malay women's physical tasks are more arduous and tedious. Rural village Brunei Malay society also places high cultural expectations upon the women.

The stress-coping mechanisms for physical stress involve using the resources of the female networking system, consulting a *dukun*, or accepting stress based on religious belief in Allah's will. However, women often hesitate to consult their female network or to consult with a *dukun* because of the concept of *malu*, "shame." A woman does not want others to know that she is unable to handle the demands of her role as wife and mother. Having friends and being a part of a female network can be psychologically rewarding and act to reduce stress. Most Brunei Malay women, however, confide their *susah-payah*, "troubles and difficulty," and their intimate thoughts to only one or two very close friends, usually their mother, adult daughter, sister, or cousin.

Consultation with the *dukun* for overwork occurs only if the woman is unable to cope with the cultural expectations regarding work. The *dukun* offers psychological support and physical relief through massage, medicine, amulets, and counsel. Massage relieves primary muscular contractions, induces relaxation, and allows the woman to be the recipient of special attention. Counsel provides psychological comfort and sound advice, medicine gives physiological relief, and amulets are believed to provide protection against harm or to help bring about a desired event such as increasing a husband's fondness.

While many stresses confront a Brunei Malay woman during the course of her life, she does not remain passive. She accepts and copes with her difficult world as best she can by resorting to the *dukun*, her female networking system, and her faith in herself and Allah.

NOTE

We wish to thank Carson Lee Riley for her assistance.

13
WOMEN IN VIETNAM: THE WAR WITHOUT AND THE WAR WITHIN

Elaine Fox

A tour of armed forces duty in Vietnam has generally been viewed as stressful, with the effects of the stress carrying over to civilian life. In this article, Fox examines the sources of stress female nurses experienced while they were in Vietnam and their postconflict adaptation. She challenges the stereotype that all these nurses suffer from Post Trauma Stress Disorder (PTSD), and claims that most of them have adjusted well. Many of the nurses interpret the Vietnam-induced stress positively. It is perceived as having provided them with a sense of competence, responsibility, and independence as professionals and individuals.

Since 1970 there has been a plethora of research related to the Vietnam War. Within academic circles much of this work has concentrated on identifying adjustment problems associated with returned veterans (Bourne 1970; Egendorf 1981; Figley 1978, 1980; Horowitz and Soloman 1975; Lifton 1973; Wilson 1978). Despite this rather intensive output of Vietnam-related material, with few exceptions, little published work as yet has focused specifically on female Vietnam veterans.

It is estimated that some six thousand military nurses served in Vietnam, as well as an unknown number of civilian females (Christie 1982; Schnaier 1982; Vietnam Veterans of America 1981). The majority of females in Vietnam appear to have functioned in some medical capacity, although a few served in administrative support positions. The military kept no records of gender participation, so despite significant female participation, little is known of the female experience in Vietnam.

While popular literature has periodically addressed female participation in Vietnam, women's magazines and newspaper articles have generally concentrated on female adjustment to Post Traumatic Stress Disorder or PTSD (Early 1982; Podesta 1982; Tutelian 1981; Van Devanter 1983). Three studies of female Vietnam veterans recently have been completed (Jacobs 1983; Paul and O'Neill 1983; Schnaier 1982). All samples used were primarily comprised of female military nurse veterans, and the inquiries focused on identifying signs, symptoms, incidents or treatment strategies for women PTSD sufferers. These studies attempted to identify major areas of stress experienced by female Vietnam veterans during their tour of duty in Vietnam.

The three studies agree that females in Vietnam, along with male cohorts, appeared to experience stress due to their presence in the dangerous environment of a war zone. Female nurses, in addition, experienced anxiety related to specific nursing/medical functions. Both Schnaier (1982) and Paul and O'Neill (1983) indicate that the latter problem was most often associated with two major areas: inadequate medical supplies, and the number, youth, and severity of those injured. Paul also found that additional stress was associated with sexual harrassment. Fifty-one percent of that sample listed exposure to sexual harrassment as being problematic. These studies also suggest that a certain amount of cynicism towards the government may well be a legacy of Vietnam for female veterans.

While the concurrence of findings on major areas of stress for women in Vietnam strengthens the reliability of these results, some limitations are present. First, many of the women who participated in these studies were still closely affiliated with the military, either as voluntary members in veterans' organizations or as patients undergoing psychiatric treatment for PTSD. This prevented a more complete understanding of the cause of stress for typical women nurses in Vietnam. Second, the authors explored only the relationship between stress and the female gender role. This current study attempts a broader account of the Vietnam experience for women nurses, and analyzes stress as a product of multiple role maladaptation.

THEORETICAL CONSIDERATIONS

Thornton and Nardi (1975) point out that traditional role theory views role acquisition as synonymous with the acquisition of a new position. Implied in this perspective is the notion that when individuals assume new positions in a social system, the participants immediately conform to expectations associated with the new positions (Linton 1936; Sherif 1936). More recent works incorporate the notion that role acquisition is a developmental process and includes a psychological element (Becker et al. 1961; Goffman 1961; Olesen and Whittaker 1968). This approach has been demonstrated in studies which focus on socialization into a new professional role, particularly those in the medical field (Becker et al. 1961; Davis 1972; Freidson 1970; Levine 1975; Mechanic 1978).

Role acquisition for nurses also has encompassed socialization into the female gender role. Nurses generally are expected to be caring, compassionate, nurturing, and are taught to be subservient, especially to physicians, who have traditionally been male, older, more educated, and of a higher socioeconomic status (SES). The tendency of nurses to comply with authority figures has been noted by several researchers (Bates 1970; Rank and Jacobson 1977; Stein 1967). Mauskch (1972) points out that such a perception creates a woman who serves sacrificially, who supports and protects a dominant male, and who identifies her success as a nurse with her successes as a woman. Mauskch further suggests that the objectives of a majority of nursing students are to be needed and to engage in personal helping relationships.

In one sense, the study of stress factors for female Vietnam veteran nurses is an exploration of the role of women in a war zone, as well as a study of an occupational category. Vietnam represented a special situation for these nurses, since, unlike males, these women should not have been prepared for the "masculine endeavor" of war. This does not deny the dangers and stress of war for men. However, while women most certainly shared the similarities of a dangerous environment with their male cohorts, women also faced situations which were unique to both the roles of female and nurse. Additionally, these women were military officers and, as such, were expected to perform competently in that arena.

Socialization into the gender role of female is a lifelong process. Nursing, as an occupational choice, in many ways reinforces femininity. For young Vietnam nurses the role of military officer was a relatively new one; they spent only a few months as an officer prior to arriving in the war zone.

Thornton and Nardi (1975) suggest that role acquisition can be thought of as a multicomponent process prior to full adaptation. Social adjustment and psychological adjustment are two of the important components which culminate in a personal stage of acquisition. While social adjustment, the adequate performance of role expectations, can be fairly easily met by a competent performer, psychological adjustment, the achievement of congruity between individual psychological needs and the role, is more difficult to master. From their perspective, the personal stage of role acquisition is crucial, for it is here that one is able to fit together individuality with the role. Thornton and Nardi caution that:

> The individual cannot be ignored, for his personality, past experiences, unique abilities and skills and culturally defined values and beliefs affect how he enacts his role. It is not enough to view individuals as simply carrying out formal and informal expectations. Incongruence of self and role often result in perfunctory role enactment and in problems of social and psychological adjustment (1975:881).

Stress experienced by women nurses in Vietnam may be viewed as a by-product of an inability to adequately achieve congruency of self and role.

Additionally, any theoretical consideration of the role of women nurses in Vietnam should take into account the complementary or contradictory nature of multiple role requirements. Role conflict often results in stress. Women nurses were expected to successfully fulfill requirements of three roles simultaneously, that of woman, nurse, and military officer.

METHODOLOGY

The limitations of previous studies' sample size reflect the difficulty of securing women veterans as respondents. The approach used in this study to generate a sample of female nurse veterans was novel. Utilizing a physician's scrapbook list of all personnel assigned to a particular evacuation hospital in Vietnam during 1968–1970, the names and addresses of all fifty-six female nurses who served there during this time were obtained. Letters explaining the nature of the research and asking for participation in the study were sent to these women. Although responses were often delayed because of dated addresses, thirty-one nurses were eventually contacted.

An open-ended, in-depth questionnaire was devised. In addition to collecting the usual demographic variables, respondents were asked to write narrative replies to a series of questions designed to elicit some generic understanding of their perceptions of the Vietnam experience. The questionnaire was comprehensive in nature. However, the data to be discussed at this time center around the major topic area of stress and role adaptation associated with serving in Vietnam. At the completion of the study, an analysis of the self-reported data was undertaken, and commonalities of response were identified.

Completed survey questionnaires were obtained from twenty-six of the original group. Clearly the sample employed for this study is not random, so generalizations are limited. However, from the data gathered one can gain a general understanding of the Vietnam environment for women serving in one evacuation hospital.

By combining age and military status, respondents can be categorized into two groups. The first grouping of nine respondents consists of older career military women, whose average age was forty-one, and who had at least ten years of active military duty prior to serving in Vietnam. The second group of respondents was younger (the average age was twenty-two), and generally they graduated from nursing school no more than six months prior to serving in Vietnam. Eight respondents noted that they had joined the military as a way to obtain funding for nursing school. The rest indicated they had joined the military in order to gain nursing experience, had a "desire to help," and felt "patriotic."

Ten of the respondents still practice nursing. Five are retired from nursing, and five identified themselves as housewives. The rest are currently employed in a variety of occupations, having discontinued nursing shortly after fulfilling their military obligations. Of these six employed in other occupations, five noted that their Vietnam experience directly affected their decisions to leave nursing. This issue will be addressed at a later point.

FINDINGS

The most typical areas of stress for women in Vietnam have been identified previously. Data from respondents in this study, to a large extent, validated previous research findings. However, interesting differences were noted in the present group. In previous studies, inadequate medical supplies were found to be a major cause of stress for Vietnam nurses. That finding was not as significant for this sample; inadequate medical supplies were deemed to be an area of concern, but only within parameters of the medical environment. It was not reported as an overall concern related to the female experience in Vietnam. Only when asked specifically about stress associated with medical work did personnel and supply shortages emerge as a primary area of stress.

All but two of the respondents indicated that their Vietnam experience was stressful, and most cited multiple areas of stress. Analysis of the narrative responses yielded twelve primary categories of stress as outlined in the following list; the right-hand column indicates the number of respondents citing each.

1. Physical Environment (heat, humidity, rain, etc.)	4
2. Physical Fatigue	5
3. Youth of Casualties	5
4. Fear for Personal Safety	5
5. Mass Numbers of Dead Casualties	8
6. Physical Separation from Family	5
7. Suffering of Civilians (poverty, injuries)	5
8. Social Environment of the Compound (no privacy, typical military restrictions)	8
9. Severity of Injuries of Wounded (amputations, head wounds, quality-of-life issues)	9
10. Vietnamese Casualties (injured noncombatants)	2
11. Emotional Isolation from Peers	5
12. Political or Ideational Confusion (anxiety, anger, or cynicism regarding justification of war)	11

Philosophical Confusion

As noted previously, most of the respondents mentioned several areas of stress. The pattern of responses fell loosely into two major groupings: those females who said that being separated from their families was stressful also indicated that living on a military compound was problematic. They tended to include social isolation from peers as a primary area of stress. Observation of the youth, their numbers, and the severity of casualties were generally cited together as a second stressor. Respondents, noting these reasons as major stress areas, were also likely to indicate that they experienced some political or philosophical confusion. The quotes below demonstrate this association.

The waste of human life in its prime—with no justification.

Death, not being able to help and not knowing why.

Dealing with dead and dying GI's for a questionable and uncertain cause.

Sensory overload and a feeling of helplessness. The insanity of war—the endless "whys."

Anger when U. S. papers denied the invasion of Cambodia, when we had numerous casualties, resulted in personal disillusionment with the government.

The stress of Vietnam? The pain and suffering of our patients. The deprivation of the Vietnam people.

The loss of youth in all of us.

One might ask why philosophical confusion over the incidence of casualties and the death rate should arise. Surely these women must have supported or at least considered the moral implications of the Vietnam War effort prior to entering active military duty. Interestingly, only thirteen of the respondents indicated that they had personal doubts regarding the political or moral justification of the war prior to serving in Vietnam. Of these, eleven made clear that despite reservations about the morality of the war, they felt patriotic allegiance to their country and saw a situation in which they could "serve" without engaging in an act of war. With the exception of two career military nurses who considered a Vietnam tour as "just another duty assignment," the rest of the respondents stated that they had seen Vietnam as an opportunity for "helping wounded soldiers" and considered themselves apolitical. In essence, these women went to Vietnam to engage in a "helping role," and only after exposure to war conditions were they forced to confront the effects of war from a philosophical/political standpoint. One respondent described her disillusionment with the war in this way:

I went to Vietnam because I thought as a nurse I could help. I didn't see myself as supporting the war because I was there. I wasn't fighting. If the U.S. was in Vietnam, then Americans needed medical care and I could give that. I didn't come to realize until later that I shouldn't have been in Vietnam because we [United States] shouldn't have been in Vietnam. The first night, I helped put a young G.I. in a body bag and I wondered how anybody could explain his death to his mother in a way that made any sense to her. I knew no one could make it make sense to me either. I remember thinking that night about a slogan that was popular then, "What if somebody gave a war and nobody came?" For the first time I really understood what that meant.

Others indicated that the stress they experienced from the large numbers of dead casualties was associated with philosophical confusion.

Being alive while in the middle of death constantly created problems for me. The constant "why." Why was this occurring?

Why couldn't we help them? Why couldn't we prevent so much death, and the not knowing why there was so much death.

Being so intimately involved with death on a day-to-day basis was disturbing for the respondents, but without an accompanying justification for continual exposure to death, stress became very high. Having been trained as nurses, these women expected to deal with death during the course of their nursing careers. However, the frequency of casualties and the severity of injuries combined with a weakening ideological allegiance to the government's war effort proved emotionally disabling for many of them. Indeed, most (twenty-three) of these respondents at a later point in the questionnaire reported a residual cynicism towards the American political system for creating a situation which was responsible for massive numbers of dead.

The category "severity of casualties" was also associated with ideational confusion and was directly concerned with nursing philosophy. Those who noted "severity of casualties" as a primary stress area tended to be concerned with whether medical technology may have functioned in a beneficial manner.

It got so I couldn't stand the maimed bodies.

The severe injuries . . . . What did we do saving them to live with what was left over.

I know we were there to save lives—and we did save lives, but I wonder if we saved people.

The stress was watching young men suffering . . . seeing some of the very severely injured we "saved."

Paul and O'Neill (1983) found that most women went to war as humanitarians, yet were denied this role due to the circumstances of war. "Quality of life" issues forced these women into situations leading them to question their humanitarian endeavors. This seems to be an issue which remains unresolved for those women in the present study who cited this category as a primary area of stress in Vietnam. Only one of the respondents also indicated that closure on this philosophical concern had subsequently been achieved:

> The nursing experience in Vietnam aged me over twenty years. I now feel I can meet any obstacle in nursing and survive. It identified my belief about what is life and at what point nurses leave resuscitation to God.

Thorton and Nardi (1975) note that some roles, such as the soldier's, are more institutionally rooted and defined than others, and should therefore provide for easier role acquisition. The career nurse officers who regarded Vietnam as "just another tour of duty" and denied experiencing any political/ philosophical confusion, may well have given priority to the soldier's role, one which does not call for ideological questioning. Hewitt (1976) suggests that conceptions of self are linked to ideal conceptions of what the person ought to be, and that many definitions of the ideal self are linked to group membership, which is dependent on a "we-they" contrast between groups. For the majority of the respondents, Vietnamese casualties as well as injured Americans were seen as wounded patients, a situation which called out the "helper role" of the nurse, rather than the political allegiance of the soldier. In essence, for most of the nurses, the ability to simply "do their duty" as defined by the military officer role was achieved and represents adequate social adjustment to expectations. However, most additionally found themselves unable to "do their duty without questioning," a failure in part in terms of psychological and personal role acquisition to the military role. Precedence was given to the nurse role and these respondents found themselves in situations of role conflict.

Additionally, quality of life issues appear to have contributed to role stress. Conflict due to the discrepancies involved in performing as a humanitarian in a situation which brought forth doubts as to the value, worth, or humanitarian result of such action prevented these women from achieving congruency of self and role. Philosophical confusion again expresses an incomplete personal and psychological stage of role acquisition.

Coping Strategies

Both Schnaier (1982) and Paul and O'Neill (1983) report that the stress of the war generated emotions which tended to be overwhelming for their respondents at times. Schnaier suggests this created a motivation to negate emotion and explains, "Unlike men who had traditionally been taught a certain stoicism, women are more often taught to express these emotions, yet during the war, the women were forced to negate these emotions in order to attend to the higher tasks at hand" (1982:7). Having given priority to acting as a nurse-soldier, despite ambivalence associated with this behavior, women in Vietnam were additionally forced to deny aspects of their traditional gender role. How then did nurses in Vietnam handle the stress? When asked to reflect on strategies used to deal with the stress generated by Vietnam, eleven of the respondents noted that they attempted to minimize stress levels by spending time with friends, although much of the time spent with friends involved "partying." Five of the respondents also indicated that while "partying" they consumed more alcohol than they used to prior to Vietnam. One respondent explained the tendency to party in this manner: "It was so damn bad dealing with so many young men dying. I realized that they wanted to live but didn't, so I needed to live a little more for them."

Three nurses indicated that they sought out close friends to discuss feelings but, given the stress everyone experienced, it was difficult to use this as an adequate coping mechanism. Eight respondents indicated their major coping strategy was to continually emphasize to themselves the short-term nature of the assignment to Vietnam. As one respondent noted, "When things got rough and I felt like I couldn't take it anymore, I kept telling myself over and over that I could put up with anything for a year. Whenever things got bad, I would count the days left until I got to go home."

Clearly, these respondents also gave indications of having negated the emotions generated by the stress of war. Denied the more traditional emotional outlets of their gender by the need to give priority to the nurse-soldier role, stress management mechanisms assumed a masculine flavor, as in partying and drinking, or stoicism. Vietnam nurses were again caught in a tangle of role conflict.

Van Devanter (1983) shares Paul and O'Neill's (1983) and Schnaier's (1982) conclusions that postwar adjustment problems for women veterans may well be associated with the inability to have managed stress effectively. Understandably, these women were placed in situations which could conceivably strain the coping powers of persons not enmeshed in the role conflicts or maladaptation these nurses endured.

Given the ongoing stress women were forced to confront on a daily basis, one is drawn to ask how successful these various coping mechanisms were. Earlier studies have suggested that as many as 30 percent of returned veterans experienced postwar adjustment problems (Borus 1973; Christie 1982; Figley 1978). In the present sample, twelve of the respondents evaluated their post-Vietnam adjustment to the stress of Vietnam as "good" to "successful." Seven additional respondents acknowledged their adjustment as fairly satisfactory with some residue. One respondent described her residue this way: "I think I handled my stress fairly well. Sometimes, when I think about Vietnam I get sad." Four of the respondents indicated that they continue to suffer from some form of emotional/psychological maladjustment due to war-induced stress. The remaining respondents simply noted in their narrative accounts that they "survived."

AREAS OF NURSING STRESS

Paul and O'Neill (1983), Schnaier (1982), and Jacobs (1983) all reported tremendous stress associated with nursing care or tasks in Vietnam. In their studies, stress was commonly associated with the following areas:

1. Acute shortages of medical supplies
2. Inadequate staffing of medical personnel
3. Working under conditions of severe mental or physical fatigue
4. Being subjected to mass casualties
5. Youth and severity of casualties

As mentioned earlier, the present sample of respondents viewed the last two stress areas more holistically, and these concerns were listed under general areas of stress rather than being specifically identified as occupational concerns. When the present sample was asked to describe stress areas or concerns regarding nursing tasks while in Vietnam, the following categories emerged as most prominent:

1. Supply, equipment, and personnel shortages   18
2. Primitive working conditions (e.g., too little rest, long hours,
   inadequate climate control)   8
3. Inexperienced medical personnel   8
4. Morale (i.e., demoralized by other nursing problems to the extent
   it affected work)   5

Obviously, in validation of previous research, problems associated with too little equipment, supplies, and trained personnel emerged as primary stress areas. However, seven respondents indicated that they experienced no problems associated with completion of nursing responsibilities. This appears to contradict the reactions of other nurses. However, this is not necessarily the case. While the majority of respondents did indicate difficulty in carrying out nursing care tasks, all but three of the respondents also included in their narrative accounts some statement regarding the quality of care patients received, in spite of problems such as lack of adequate equipment. It may well be that those respondents who did not indicate any problems associated with administering nursing care in Vietnam either perceived none, or given the eventual outcome of good nursing care, chose not to indicate problems encountered in the successful completion of duties.

This may also be the case in the category "Inexperienced medical personnel." Each of the eight respondents who indicated that giving good nursing care while working with inexperienced medical personnel was extremely stressful for them, was quick to point out also that neither they nor new staff remained inexperienced very long. Twenty-two of the respondents, regardless of their citing of "inexperienced medical personnel" as a stress area, remarked on various training mechanisms employed for adjusting to inexperience. Most cited the intensive, one to-one teaching programs which provided the basis for most of the on-the-job training in Vietnam as a primary strategy for overcoming inexperience:

> We had the only neurosurgeon in I Corps. He would be in surgery for hours at a time. We had to be good nurses. He trained us, he taught us, and then he trusted us. We weren't his handmaidens; we were his right hand.

> In Vietnam there wasn't time for a slow in-service orientation to the place. You learned quick by watching and helping. The first mass casualties and you got overwhelmed. Some nurse who had been there a bit longer would begin saying, "Do this, do that!" and you did exactly what you were told. After the patients were taken care of you asked why this way, why that way. Any nurse with a bit more experience was willing to share some of that knowledge with you, and before long, you were the one with the experience passing it along to another brand new nurse.

In some ways, it appears that adjusting to the stress associated with providing adequate nursing care in Vietnam, while difficult, was manageable. Nurses were able to cope by relying on mechanisms which were appropriate for their gender and occupation. Much of the work of nursing, regardless of work environment, necessarily requires a hands-on approach and one-on-one training. Women have also traditionally turned to each other for knowledge in day-to day living skills outside the work environment. Nurses in Vietnam may have found the work role difficult and stressful, but in this area role expertise as both nurses and women helped them to accommodate stress.

Nursing in Vietnam was unlike nursing situations typically found in the United States. From the accounts given by the respondents, nurses found themselves in medical situations which taxed their educational preparation as well as strengthened their clinical experience. Many, while still maintaining that such stress areas as inadequate supplies were burdensome at the time, now view aspects of the Vietnam experience positively. With few exceptions, the nurses described Vietnam as an unparalleled opportunity for developing superior nursing skills.

> When a new graduate tells me she can't do a task because she does not have the equipment, I generally laugh. I know better. I can remember filling canteens

and water jugs with sand to use as traction. I guess everyone in this hospital thinks I am a skinflint. I am always on everyone to conserve and not be wasteful. Vietnam taught me that. Because I am this way and preplan, I have what I need when I need it. I found myself doing things in Vietnam I always believed only doctors could or should do. But when all the docs were tied up in triage or OR, then no one was left to do it but me. I didn't know I could perform in all the ways I was forced to—to accept all that responsibility, but when push came to shove, I could and I did.

The words most often used by the respondents to describe their nursing experience in Vietnam were creativity, flexibility, improvisation, and management skills.

This perceived increase in nursing skills also appears to be a double-edged sword. Most of the nurses in this sample noted that the nature of the work in Vietnam compelled them to assume a work style which was basically more independent and autonomous than they were accustomed to or had been trained as professional nurses to expect. For some, this assumption of sharpened clinical skills resulted in atypical relationships with medical doctors in Vietnam, often a colleague relationship rather than the more traditional, subservient, nurse role. Of course, after Vietnam, some of these nurses encountered problems with their new roles. The autonomy and independence which were the legacies of socialization into wartime nursing care were viewed in civilian institutions as "outspokenness" and "being difficult." Six of the respondents who remained in nursing after Vietnam commented on the difficulty they experienced attempting to portray the more traditional role expected of nurses. They stated that they still find themselves more likely to challenge the routine nature of physicians' orders. Being forced, in post-Vietnam nursing, to accept orders from interns or "antiquated" physicians is an untenable position; thus these nurses are often in conflict with the medical power structure. Four of the respondents indicated that decisions to leave nursing altogether after Vietnam included some component of rejection of the passive role expected of them as nurses back in the United States. As one respondent, now a practicing attorney, explained: "I experienced disillusionment with nursing. I left because I wanted to exercise more independence within my career."

Stein (1967) described the traditional interaction between nurse and physicians in his classic "Doctor-Nurse Game" paper. He points out that nurses are to be bold, show initiative, and make recommendations to the doctor in a manner which is passive and totally supportive of the physician. He predicts that nurses who don't play the game very well suffer severe consequences. Overall, this sample of Vietnam nurses, after returning from Vietnam, did not play the game very well. Socialization into the role of Vietnam nurse, while effective during the war, created maladaptation upon returning home.

Sexual Harassment

The Paul and O'Neill (1983) and Schnaier (1982) studies reported relatively high incidences of sexual harassment of women nurses in Vietnam. This study does not validate those findings. Again, this difference may well be a product of an alternative manner of addressing the question. In the earlier studies, respondents were asked to choose from a list of sexual harassment behaviors they had been subjected to while in Vietnam. In the present study, a list was not provided. Instead, respondents were asked to describe in narrative form their response to being female in a predominantly male environment.

Nine of the respondents simply noted that this had not been an area of concern and did not address the issue further. The remainder of the respondents did remark that this had been problematic for them in some ways. Eleven stated that they were uncomfortable with the special attention they received from males, and three commented that being female in a predominantly male environment created the potential for vulnerability to sexual liaisons. However, four of the respondents also noted that this situation provided them with an environment in which they gained more confidence in themselves as women. Only three respondents reported specific episodes of sexual harassment.

In analyzing the narrative data, one is left with a sense that the respondents more or less expected such difficulty under battlefield circumstances and, with few exceptions, it was not an overwhelmingly troublesome area when compared to other concerns. Interpretational as well as methodological differences may account for the conflicting findings reported on sexual harrassment. Areas of stress associated with the Vietnam experience most often involve aspects of role conflict or role maladaptation for women veterans. Undesired sexual overtures by men, while unpleasant, do not fall outside the experience of most women. Socialization into the feminine sex role should have provided these women with some typical coping mechanisms to use and does not represent role conflict, but rather an intensification of the role expectations women hold.

CONCLUSION

With some interesting differences, this study validates previous research. Definitive statements of theory or generalization appear a bit premature given the current state of social science knowledge about women Vietnam veterans. However, some suggestive interpretations of the current data are indicated.

This chapter has explored the experiences of women nurses in Vietnam and attempted to link stress associated with that experience with role maladaptation or role conflict. As discussed earlier, role acquisition can be

considered a developmental process which incorporates a psychological element with a functional behavioral component for complete role congruency.
This notion suggests that one may assume the behavioral tasks of a new
role and complete these tasks successfully, while not yet having the ability
to successfully fit together the individual with the role. For women in Vietnam, adjustment to the roles of nurse, military officer, and woman was a
strain. These nurses were adequate role performers in a functional sense—
they "got the job done"—yet apparently were not able to create congruency
with the self role. Getting the job done while struggling with the conflicting
nature of divergent roles produced high levels of stress for these women.

Paul and O'Neill's (1983) assertion that females went to war as humanitarians, but were denied that role due to the circumstances of war,
appears most relevant. The present study, as well as previous work, suggests
that being denied the opportunity to act out the humanitarian role may well
prove to be a focal point for the study of female veterans. The political/
philosophical confusion expressed by participants in this study indicates
some further questioning of the humanitarian role. Polner (1971) and Defazio
(1975) both make reference to the moral doubt associated with serving in
a war regardless of its ideological justification. It may be that females are
subject to this type of moral doubt even while serving in noncombatant roles.
As Lifton points out, "Albert Camus urges that men be neither victims nor
executioners. In Vietnam we have made our young men into both"
(1973:495). With regard to the issues of "quality of life" for those who were
severely wounded as well as implicit positions of support of war by non-
combatants, it may well be that Lifton's charge holds true for women veterans
as well.

"Quality of life" issues joined with high levels of political/philosophical
confusion reflect an area of stress produced by role conflicts. As military
officers, these women should never have responded to the etiology of casualties; rather, they should have simply viewed their care of wounded
patients as a duty to be completed. As nurses they had been taught not to
make moral judgments on the etiology of disease, but rather had been
socialized simply to enact the helper role. As women, the nuturing, compassionate nature of their gender role perhaps allowed them to become
emotionally involved in a situation which continually produced such casualties, and may possibly have been the generating force behind the philosophical confusion expressed by so many of the respondents. Combining
this with the demand to fulfill the "helper role" as nurse, questions the
validity of "helping" certain kinds of severely injured patients, and produces
maladaptation to the psychological component of the military officer role.

Vietnam service results in increased nursing skills and a sense of competency and is seen as a positive reflection of Vietnam. However, for some
women, the increased skill levels created difficulty in adjusting to the demands of routine nursing care after Vietnam. Borus has suggested that for

many veterans, adjustment after returning home was difficult because skills employed while in Vietnam "had little immediate relevance or status" (1973:503). He, of course, was referring to learned military skills utilized by military men serving in Vietnam. The basic platform of his argument, however, holds true for the medical skills achieved by nurses. Women in Vietnam learned superior role performance as nurses only to discover upon returning home that this achievement carried with it costs.

In this particular case, a strong psychological commitment as well as social adjustment to the role of competent nurse proved dysfunctional for some of the respondents. Criticism for adhering to this role upon their return to the United States produced sufficient levels of stress to motivate some nurses to totally reject nursing as an occupation.

The major areas of stress associated with Vietnam for the present sample of women veterans can be attributed to role conflict or inadequate role socialization. Vietnam nurses learned to cope quickly and well to role performance expectations with regard to carrying out nursing tasks and duties. Personal and psychological adjustment to the role of military officer was incomplete; commitment to the "helping role" as nurse was paramount. Stress was also associated with denial of traditional gender-role coping mechanisms. Negating emotions during Vietnam still impacts on some of these women today. In essence, the job of the military nurse in Vietnam was multidimensional, encompassing various degrees of competency in fulfilling the often conflicting roles of woman, nurse, and soldier.

This chapter attempts to create a greater understanding of the social situation of women nurses who served in Vietnam. As an exploratory study, the data are too tenuous to form connecting hypotheses between role adaptation and PTSD (Post Trauma Stress Disorder). However, the stress produced by the Vietnam experience for these respondents does suggest that the contradictory nature of divergent roles may operate at times to prevent total role adjustment. The Vietnam experience for these women was undoubtedly stressful for most, and perhaps still remains personally destructive for a few.

SUMMARY

While anthropological and nonanthropological interest in women's lives has increased since 1970, until recently, most of the literature in women's health has been focused on either gynecologic or psychiatric issues. Overall, women's health has not been considered from a multidimensional approach. This volume is an attempt to broaden the scope and depth of research into women's health. The book examines a variety of contemporary health care concerns which affect both Western and non-Western women. The papers integrate theoretical concepts related to health with practical health care issues women face. When possible, resolution of health care problems or alternatives to dealing with specific issues are discussed. As such, this volume on women's health is distinct from the more strictly theoretical works in medical anthropology, and from many of the available self-help books.

A positive focus is found in this volume. While serious health care situations exist, women are discussed relative to how they confront and resolve their problems. The problems are related to situations of stress, issues which are a function of the life cycle, and culture change. Regardless of the specific situation, women are active, decision-making participants who utilize resources within their social, symbolic, and economic systems in order to achieve and maintain health. Within their given social systems, these behaviors are defined as rational, goal oriented, and decisive. Specifically, in situations of change or stress which affect health, women redefine appropriate sex-role behavior and social institutions, as well as expand their economic and personal boundaries. Their strategies are similar, despite a diversity of issues which confront them.

Examples of women who meet their health care needs and who use similar strategies to do so can be found in each section of the book. Newfoundland fishing women and Maya Mexican women adopt modern means of birth control and obstetric practices within their traditional concepts of appropriate and supportive behavior relative to these issues. In culture change situations, Turkish migrant women and wives of British coal miners redefine acceptable female roles in order to meet their needs and deal with the stress inherent in culture change. Mexican-American single mothers living in Detroit and Brunei Malay women both rely heavily on female-based networks to reduce stress and provide sociopsychological support. Women redefine behavior, use supportive female relations, and incorporate change and new technology into familiar contexts to address their health care problems.

Emphasizing the positive means which women use to manage their health neither negates nor mitigates the problems which global economic, political, and social chnages have on societies or women as members of

198

these larger groups. Consistently, culture change of any sort is disturbing to groups and individuals. A continuous, common dimension of this disturbance is stress. Ideally, in situations of culture change, modernization and Western medicine would be syncretized with traditional health practices so that the strengths of both systems are retained and the weaknesses in each minimized. In reality, as shown in the chapters by Faust, Davis, Van Esterik, and Miller and Kearney, this is not the case. Misapplication and misunderstanding of Western medical techniques, as well as inadequate training in them, health care provider insensitivity and ethnocentrism, and loss of traditional, familiar social support systems result in serious miscommunication and consequent health problems. Western health care planners and providers also need to be sensitive to the uniqueness of each cultural situation. Because cultures may share a similar value such as female modesty does not mean that they act on that shared value in comparable ways. This is exemplified by the different reactions to and use of male physicians by Turkish and Maya women. Health care providers need to be aware of the problems they may inadvertently create by trying to "help" people in traditional societies (Romanucci-Ross, Moerman, and Tancredi 1983; Angeloni 1986).

Culture change does not occur evenly, nor does it present the same options for everyone, as is shown in the chapters by Szurek, Marmor, and Fox. While stressful, moving into middle-class British society doesn't incur the same kinds of costs for coal-mining women as assimilating into urban Berlin society does for Turkish women. Turkish women who assimilate must renounce a valued cultural identity and to a large extent leave behind their native culture. In the Fox chapter, assertive nursing which is adaptive to a combat situation does not transfer positively to a peace-time hospital social structure that is based on subordinate-superordinate nurse-doctor roles. This conflict resulted in some nurses changing careers. In any culture change situation, costs in terms of stress and questions of personal identity exist as traditional roles and values are questioned, transformed, or eliminated.

The chapters in this volume reflect a range of personal costs, coping mechanisms, and adaptive strategies. As expected in a volume of this nature, some articles reflect more of a traditionalist perspective (e.g., Miller and Kearney), while others show a more Western bias (e.g., Szurek, Faust). This range of perspectives is commonly found in anthropology and is due to a variety of factors. Some of these include the researchers' professional training and field experiences, the degrees of cultural relativism they achieve in any given situation, and the degree of cultural differences between the group studied and the anthropologists' own culture. All the chapters address health dilemmas late twentieth-century women face, and offer coping strategies that will be functional in each specific situation.

While this book addresses some of the current issues in women's health which include gynecologic and affective concerns as well as those more directly related to situations of culture change and stress, there are other women's health care issues which require further research and resolution. Examples include premenstrual syndrome (PMS), work-related health problems, and drug abuse. While research is ongoing in each of these areas, the importance of these topics as possible culture-bound phenomena needs to be examined. Expanding on these examples, suggested areas for future research include the extent to which PMS is universal as a biochemical response or a culture-specific reflection of our attitudes toward menstruation, discomfort, nutrition, and lifestyle.

As women worldwide increasingly work outside the home, the health concerns unique to their work environments as well as those engendered by dual role requirements (working and taking care of home and children) need to be addressed. The effects of drug use on women's health is another area of investigation. This includes not only prescription drugs, but the use of recreational and over-the-counter drugs available to women everywhere. These latter concerns range from alcoholism to use of birth control devices to medications used to relieve indigenous ailments.

A holistic approach, which examines the physical, cultural, and psychological aspects of health care issues is needed. As part of the holistic approach, culture-specific methods of resolution which complement individual societal belief systems and socioeconomic structures are required. The universality or frequency of a health problem does not belie the unique situation in which it is found. As Klee, Davis, Faust, and others show, perceptions of the issue by the participants are critical to its resolution, acceptance of relevant new ideas, and positive adjustment to change. The chapters in this volume reaffirm the importance and need for this perspective.

Finally, a consideration of women's active role in culture change is important in formulating theoretical concepts of health as well as treatment plans. New coping mechanisms may incorporate familiar insitutions which are defined in an innovative way as in the case of Dugan's presentation of *compadrazgo*. Traditional role boundaries are stretched to accommodate personal growth and well-being as discussed by Szurek. Women in this volume are active, involved participants who seek to meet their health needs within culturally defined contexts, but who also reinterpret and redefine these contexts as necessary.

CONTRIBUTORS

Elyse Ann Barnett received her Ph.D. in anthropology from Stanford University, having spent fifteen months studying women's health at midlife in various communities throughout Peru. Dr. Barnett is currently a health educator at Foothill College in California and is actively involved in teaching and research in the field of women's health.

Shawna Craig holds a M.A. in anthropology from the University of Texas at Austin and has done fieldwork with the *Fidencista* movement in Mexico. She is co-author of *Anthropological World: An Introduction to Cultural Anthropology*. Currently, she is working with computers at the University of Texas, Austin.

Dona Lee Davis received her Ph.D. from the University of North Carolina at Chapel Hill in 1980. She is currently an associate professor of anthropology at the University of South Dakota in Vermillion. Her areas of research and publication include maritime anthropology, human sexuality, women's studies, and aging. She has written a book on menopause, *Blood and Nerves: An Ethnographic Focus on Menopause*, and has recently finished editing (with Jane Nadel) a volume entitled *Women in Fishing Economies*.

Anna Baziak Dugan, Ph.D., is a professor at the Oakland University School of Nursing (Rochester, MI). She is also a professional nurse, having received a M.S. in psychiatric mental health nursing from Yale University. She was formerly nursing director at the Yale Psychiatric Institute and nursing consultant with the Alaska Division of Mental Health, dealing with problems of dysfunctional families among Alaskan Natives living in remote areas of the state. Her major area of interest is the study of cross-cultural behavioral motivators related to health enhancement.

Betty B. Faust is a Ph.D. candidate in anthropology at Syracuse University and holds M.A. degrees in Spanish language and literature, anthropology, and public administration. She has taught both at the State University of New York at Potsdam, and at Mater Dei College (Ogdensburg, NY). She received a fellowship from Syracuse University for 1985–1986 to do fieldwork for her Ph.D. dissertation on native interpretations of the effects of modernization on family life in a Campeche-Maya village.

Ruthbeth D. Finerman received a Ph.D. in anthropology from U.C.L.A. and is an assistant professor of anthropology at Memphis State University.

201

For the past ten years she has been conducting research on women's roles in health and reproduction, indigenous curing systems, and therapeutic decision-making strategies among Amazonian and Andean populations in Ecuador.

Elaine Fox completed her graduate work at Oklahoma State University. In addition to holding a doctorate in sociology, she has been a registered nurse for over fifteen years. She is the author of one book and a number of articles focusing primarily on aspects of medical sociology and the sociology of the family. She is an associate professor at the University of Central Arkansas, where she teaches courses in medical sociology, the family, and death and dying.

The late **Robert N. Kearney** was a professor of political science, Maxwell School, Syracuse University. He wrote extensively on politics and society in Sri Lanka, including *Communalism and Language in the Politics of Ceylon* (Dune University Press, 1967), *Trade Unions and Politics in Ceylon* (University of California Press, 1971), *The Politics of Ceylon (Sri Lanka)* (Cornell University Press, 1973), and *Social Change and Internal Migration in Sri Lanka*, coauthored with Barbara D. Miller (Westview Press, forthcoming). His most recent research interests centered on suicide and rapid social change and the social and political bases of democracy in Sri Lanka.

Linda Amy Kimball holds a Ph.D. in cultural anthropology from Ohio State University and is an associate professor of anthropology at Western Washington University. She was a Fulbright exchange lecturer in Malaysia from 1972–74. Her fieldwork among the Brunei Malays was conducted between 1969 and 1971, and in 1983. She has authored articles and books about the Brunei Malays.

Linnea Klee, a Ph.D. in medical anthropology, has worked as a cultural and medical anthropologist for eleven years on projects examining a variety of issues, principally in applied anthropology. Her current research interests include examination of the medical and mental health problems of children in foster care, the effects of layoffs and unemployment on families of industrial workers, and women's health with regard to childbirth and gynecological surgery decision making. Her dissertation research investigated health beliefs and practices in nineteenth century San Francisco, with emphasis on popular professional interpretations of infectious disease prior to understanding of bacteriology. Presently, she is the program development coordinator at the Center for the Vulnerable Child, located at Children's Hospital Medical Center, Oakland, California.

Judith A. Marmor received her B.A. from Pomona College and her

M.A. from the University of Connecticut, where she is a doctoral candidate. She has done field research with Turkish migrants in Germany. Her research interests include migrants' health, women's health, and the Near East.

Barbara D. Miller, an anthropologist, is an associate researcher in demography, Graduate Group in Demography, at the University of California, Berkley. She has done research on children's health and women's status in India, sociocultural aspects of local public finance in Bangladesh, and low-income households in Jamaica. Her publications include *The Endangered Sex* (Cornell University Press, 1981) and *Social Change and Internal Migration in Sri Lanka*, coauthored with Robert Kearney (Westview Press, forthcoming).

Dana Raphael, a Ph.D. in anthropology and director of the Human Lactation Center, is a noted researcher in lactation studies. She has written the now-classic book, *The Tender Gift: Breastfeeding*, as well as many popular and scholarly articles on the subject. She is the editor of *Being Female: Reproductive Power and Change* and is currently writing a book on new approaches to mothering.

Jane Szurek received her Ph.D. from Brown University. Her dissertation, "I'll Have a Collier for My Sweetheart: Work and Gender in a British Coal-Mining Town," was completed in 1985. While at Brown she also conducted research on childbirth rituals and practices in Latin America. Currently she is teaching anthropology at the Rhode Island School of Design and Rhode Island College. For the summer of 1986, she was part of the N.E.H. seminar on China at Columbia University, where she has done research on health and change in work roles for women in Chinese society.

Penny Van Esterik received her Ph.D. from the University of Illinois and is an associate professor of anthropology at York University, Toronto, Canada. Her principal areas of interest include nutritional anthropology, particularly infant feeding, Southeast Asia, cognitive and symbolic theory, and advocacy anthropology. In addition to past fieldwork on Thai symbolism, religion, and cultural history, she has recently worked with an interdisciplinary team studying the determinants of infant feeding in several developing countries.

Patricia Whelehan received her Ph.D. from the State University of New York, Albany and is a certified sex therapist with the American Association of Sex Educators, Counselors, and Therapists. An associate professor of anthropology at the Potsdam College of the State University of New York, she is an adjunct with the college's counseling center and does research on various aspects of sexuality in the United States.

REFERENCES

Abbott Laboratories. 1978. "The Volume of Human Milk Produced by Malnourished Mothers." (Xerox copy)

Alderdice, K., et al. 1973. Attitudes Toward Family Planning in Newfoundland. In: *The Family Planning Association of Newfoundland and Labrador Report*, 31–35. St. John's Provincial Family Planning and Sex Education Conference. St. John's, Newfoundland.

Alexander, L. 1982. Illness maintenance and the American sick role. In: *Clinically Applied Anthropology*, ed. N. Chrisman and T. Maretzki. Boston: D. Reidel.

Allen, H. L. 1983. Fathers in the delivery rooms—survey results of anaesthesia departments. *Anesthesiology*. 59:152.

Alvarez, R. 1973. The psycho-historical and socioeconomic development of the Chicano Community in the United States. *Social Science Quarterly*. 53:920–42.

American Psychiatric Association. 1980. *Diagnostic and Statistical Manual of Mental Disorders*. 3d ed. Washington, D.C.: American Psychiatric Association.

Angeloni, E., ed. 1986. *Annual Editions-Anthropology 86/87*. Unit 7:206–42. Guilford, CT: Dushkin.

Antunes, C., et al. 1979. Endometrial cancer and estrogen use. *New England Journal of Medicine*. 300:9–13.

Arce, C. H. 1981. "A Reconsideration of Chicano Culture and Identity." In: Americans, Indians, Blacks, Chicanos, and Puerto Ricans. *Daedalus*. 110:177–91.

Archer, J., and B. Lloyd. 1985. *Sex and Gender*. New York: Cambridge University Press.

Arms, S. 1975. *Immaculate Deception*. Boston: Bantam Books.

Atchley, R. C. 1971. Retirement and leisure participation: Continuity or crisis? *The Gerontologist*. 1:13–17.

Baba, L. M., and M. H. Abonyi. 1979. Mexicans of Detroit. In: *Peopling of Michigan Series Ethnic Studies*. Wayne State University, Center for Urban Studies, Detroit.

Bagana, E., et al. 1982. *Treff-und Informationsort für Frauen aus der Türkei (TIO)*. Berlin: Berlin Verlag.

Bancroft, J. 1976. Research on Menopause. In: *Research on Menopause*. Geneva: World Health Organization.

Bandura, A. 1977. *Social Learning Theory*. Englewood Cliffs, NJ: Prentice-Hall.

Barbach, L. 1976. *For Yourself: The Fulfillment of Female Sexuality*. Garden City, NY: Anchor Books.

Barker-Benfield, G. J. 1975. *The Horrors of the Half-Known Life*. New York: Harper and Row.

Barlett, P., and S. Low. 1980. *Nervios* in Rural Costa Rica. *Medical Anthropology*. 4:523–59.

Barnett, E. 1986. The importance of role satisfaction in a Peruvian town. Ph.D. diss., Stanford University, Palo Alto, CA.

Baron, E. L. 1977. Hysterectomy: The relationship between occupational role and emotional, behavioral, and attitudinal outcomes. Ph.D. diss., Northwestern University, Chicago, IL.

Bart, P. 1969. Why women's status changes in middle age. *Sociological Symposium*. 3:1–18.

Bart, P. B. 1977. Biological Determinism and Sexism: Is It All in the Ovaries? In: *Biology as a Social Weapon*, 69–83. [The Ann Arbor Science for the People Editorial Collective.] Minneapolis: Burgess.

Bates, B. 1970. Doctor and nurse: changing roles and relations. *New England Journal of Medicine*. 283:129–34.

Beck, A. T., and A. B. Beamesderfer. 1974. Assessment of Depression: The Depression inventory. In: *Psychological Measurements in Psychopharmacology. (Modern Problems of Pharmacopsychiatry.)* vol. 7, 151–69. P. Pichot and R. Olivier-Martin, eds. Paris: S. Karger.

Becker, H., et al. 1961. *Boys In White*. Chicago: University of Chicago Press.

Belote, J. 1984. Changing adaptive strategies among the Saraguros of southern Ecuador. Ph.D. diss., University of Illinois, Champaign-Urbana.

Belote, J., and L. Belote. 1977. El sistema de cargos de fiestas en Saraguro. In: *Temas sobre la continuidad y adaptacion cultural Ecuatoriana*. ed. N. Whitten, Jr. Quito, Ecuador: University Católica.

Benedek, T. 1950. Climacterium: A developmental phase. *Psychoanalytic Quarterly*. 19(1):1–27.

Benton, D. 1975. The role of the infant food industry in promoting desirable policies and practices in feeding of infants and children. *Protein Advisory Group Bulletin*. 5(1):20–24.

Blaxter, M. 1983. The causes of disease: women talking. *Social Science and Medicine*. 17(2):59–69.

Blumhagen, D. W. 1980. Hyper-tension: a folk illness with a medical name. *Culture, Medicine, and Psychiatry*. 4:197–227.

Bohannan, (Bowen) L. 1964. *Return to Laughter*. New York: Harper and Row.

Boissevain, J., and J. C. Mitchell, eds. 1973. *Network Analysis: Studies in Human Interaction*. The Hague: Mouton.

Bolande, R. P. 1969. Ritualistic surgery-circumcision and tonsillectomy. *New England Journal of Medicine*. 280(1):591–96.

Bombardier, C. A., et al. 1977. Socioeconomic factors affecting the utilization of surgical operations. *New England Journal of Medicine*. 297(13):699–705.

Borus, J. 1973. Reentry: adjustment issues facing the Vietnam returnee. *Archives of General Psychiatry*. 28:501–6.

Boston Women's Health Book Collective. 1973, 1976, 1984. *Our Bodies, Ourselves*. New York: Simon and Schuster.

Bourguignon, E., ed. 1980. *A World of Women: Anthropological Studies of Women in the Societies of the World*. New York: J. F. Bergin.

Bourne, P. G. 1970. *Men, Stress, and Vietnam*. Boston: Little, Brown.

Boyd, J. H., and M. M. Weissman. 1981. Epidemiology of affective disorders. *Archives of General Psychiatry*. 38:1039–46.

Brack, D. C. 1978. Why women breast-feed: The influence of cultural values and perinatal care on choice of infant feeding methods and success at breast-feeding. Ph.D. diss., City University of New York.

Bradley, R.A. 1965. *Husband-Coached Childbirth*. New York: Harper and Row.

Brenner, M. H. 1981. Importance of the Economy to the Nation's Health. In: *The Relevance of Social Science for Medicine*. ed. L. Eisenberg and A. Kleinman. Boston: D. Reidel.

Broeg, W., et al. 1980. Befragung deutscher und ausländischer Haushalte zur Ausländerintegration in Berlin. Senatskanzlei-Planungsleitstelle. Ausländerintegration No. 3, Berlin.

Brown, G., M. Bhrolchain, and T. Harris. 1975. Social class and psychiatric disturbance among women in an urban population. *Sociology*. 9:225–54.

Brown, J. 1970. A note on the division of labor by sex. *American Anthropologist*. 72:1073–78.

Brown, J., and V. Kerns, eds. 1985. *In Her Prime: A New View of Middle-Aged Women*. So. Hadley, MA: Bergin & Garvey. (Intro. by J. Brown.)

Brush, S. 1977. *Mountain, Field, and Family: The Economy and Human Ecology of an Andean Valley*. Philadelphia, PA: University of Pennsylvania Press.

Bryant, C. A. 1984. Implication of Support Networks on Breastfeeding Practices: Implications for Program Development. In: *Helping Mothers to Breastfeed. Program Strategies for Minority Communities*. 162–75. ed. J. D. Gussler and C. A. Bryant. HAP Health Action Papers No. 1.

Bunker, J. P. 1976. Elective hysterectomy: pro and con. *New England Journal of Medicine*. 295(5):264–68.

Bunker, J. P., K. McPherson, and P. L. Henneman. 1977. Elective Hysterectomy. In: *Costs, Risks, and Benefits of Surgery*, 262–76. ed. J. P. Bunker, P. B. Barnes, and F. Mosteller. New York: Oxford University Press.

Burmeister, I., et al. 1981. Gesundheit und Lebensverhältnisse türkischer Frauen: eine empirische Untersuchung in Berlin. Grant Proposal. Fachhochschule für Socialarbeit und Socialpädagogik, Berlin.

Burmeister, I., et al. 1984. *Regionalanalyse von Totgeburtlichkeit und Säuglingssterblichkeit in Berlin (West) 1970–1980*. Stuttgart: Verlag W. Kohlhammer.

Butler, B. 1982. Anger Sickness: Social Stress and Native Diagnosis among Ecuadorian Indians. In: *Women, Health, and Development*. ed. M. Aguwa. [Women in International Development.] Ann Arbor: University of Michigan Press.

Cain, E., et al. 1983. Psychosocial reactions to the diagnosis of gynecologic cancer. *American Journal of Obstetrics and Gynecology*. 62(5): 635–41.

Carr, J., and P. Vitalliano. 1985. The Theoretical Implications of Converging Research on Depression and the Culture-bound Syndromes. In: *Culture and Depression: Studies in the Anthropology and Cross Cultural Psychiatry of Affect and Disorder.* ed. A. Kleinman, and B. Good. Berkeley: University of California Press.

Center for Disease Control. 1980. *Surgical Sterilization Surveillance: Hysterectomy in Women Aged 15–44, 1970–1975.* Atlanta: USDHHS Public Health Service, Family Planning Evaluation Division.

Christie, J. 1982. Women in Vietnam. Presentation to National Association of Concerned Veterans' Convention. New Haven, CT, June.

Cobb, S. 1976. Social support as a moderator of life stress. *Psychosomatic Medicine.* 38(5):300–14.

Cole, J. P. 1977. Breastfeeding in the Boston suburbs in relation to personal-social factors. *Clinical Pediatrics.* 16:352–56.

Cole, P., and J. Berlin. 1977. Elective hysterectomy. *American Journal of Obstetrics and Gynecology.* 29(2):117–23.

Corea, G. 1977. *The Hidden Malpractice.* New York: Jove.

Cosper, B., S. S. Fuller, and G. J. Robinson. 1980. Characteristics of Post Hospital Recovery Following Hysterectomy. In: *The Menstrual Cycle.* Vol. 1, 328–36. ed. A. J. Dan, E. A. Graham, and C. P. Beecher. New York: Springer.

Cox, D. 1972. Problems related to marketing and promotion practices of foods for infants and young children—Industry's view. Paper presented at PAG/UN Conference of Pediatricians and the Food Industry on Problems of Infant Food Marketing and Promotion, 16–17 June, Paris.

Cox, D. 1980. A perspective on infant formula in developing countries. Paper presented at the MIT-Harvard International Nutrition Planning Seminar, 12 May, Cambridge, MA.

Cronenwett, L. R., and L. L. Newmark. 1974. Father's responses to childbirth. *Nursing Research.* 23:210–17.

Dale, L. 1984. Women's health project: An evaluation. Prepared for the Atlantic Office of the Health Promotion Directorate. (Manuscript on file). The Newfoundland Collection. Queen Elizabeth Library, Memorial University. St. John's, New Foundland.

Dan, A. J., E. A. Graham, and C. P. Beecher, eds. 1980. *The Menstrual Cycle.* Vol. 1. New York: Springer.

Danaraj, A. G. S. [1964] 1980. *Mysticism in Malaya.* Reprint. Singapore: Asia Publishing.

Datan, N. 1971. Women's attitudes toward the climacteric in five Israeli subcultures. Ph.D. diss., University of Chicago, Chicago.

Davies, M. E. 1983. A consumer's guide to hysterectomy. *Medical Self-Care.* 21(Summer):32–37.

Davis, D. L. 1979. Social Structure, Sex Roles, and Female Voluntary Associations in a Newfoundland Fishing Village. Paper presented at the annual meeting of the Canadian Ethnology Society, Banff, Alberta.

Davis, D. L. 1980. Women's Experience of Menopause in a Newfoundland Fishing Village. Ph.D. diss., University of North Carolina, Chapel Hill.

Davis, D. L. 1983a. Blood and Nerves: An Ethnographic Focus on Menopause.

St. John's Memorial University of Newfoundland, Institute of Social and Economic Research.

Davis, D. L. 1983b. The family and social change in a Newfoundland outport. *Culture*. 3(1):19–32.

Davis, D. L. 1983c. Woman the worrier: confronting archetypes of stress. *Women's Studies*. 10(2):135–46.

Davis, D. L. 1984. Medical misinformation: communication difficulties between Newfoundland women and their physicians. *Social Science and Medicine*. 18(3):273–78.

Davis, D. L. 1985a. Belligerent legends: bickering and feuding among outport octogenarians. *Aging and Society*. 5(4):431–48.

Davis, D. L. 1985b. Newfoundland Nervosity: Victorian Legacy or Thoroughly Modern Folkway? Paper presented at the 85th annual meeting of the American Anthropological Association, Washington, D.C.

Davis, D. L. 1986a. Changing Self-Image: Studying Menopausal Women in a Newfoundland Fishing Village. In: *Sex and Gender-Role Boundaries in Cross Cultural Encounter*. 240–62. ed. T. Whitehead and M. Conaway. Urbana: University of Illinois Press.

Davis, D. L. 1986b. The meaning of menopause in a Newfoundland fishing village. *Culture, Medicine, and Psychiatry*. 10(1):73–94.

Davis, F. 1972. *Illness, Interaction, and the Self*. California: Wadsworth.

Defazio, V. 1975. The Vietnam era veteran: Psychological Problems. *Journal of Contemporary Psychotherapy*. 7(1):9–15.

de la Fuente, J. 1967. Ethnic Relationships. In: *Handbook of Middle American Indians: Social Anthropology*. vol. 6, 432–48. ed. R. Wauchope. Austin, TX: University of Texas Press.

Delaney, J. M., J. Lupton, and E. Toth. 1976. *The Curse: A Cultural History of Menstruation*. New York: New American Library.

Dennerstein, L., and G. D. Burrows. 1978. A review of studies of the psychological symptoms found at menopause. *Maturitas*. 1:55–64.

Dennerstein, L., C. Wood, and G. Burrows. 1982. *Hysterectomy*. Melbourne: Oxford University Press.

Department of Census and Statistics, Sri Lanka. (1971–1985) *Statistical Abstract of Sri Lanka*. Annual. Colombo: Department of Government Printing.

Department of Census and Statistics, Sri Lanka. 1974. *The Population of Sri Lanka*. Colombo: Department of Census and Statistics.

Department of Census and Statistics, Sri Lanka. 1981. *Census of Population and Housing, Sri Lanka, 1981*. Preliminary Release No. 1. Colombo: Department of Census and Statistics.

Department of Census and Statistics, Sri Lanka. 1982. *Census of Population and Housing, Sri Lanka, 1981: Population Tables Based on a Ten Percent Sample*. Preliminary Release No. 2. Colombo: Department of Census and Statistics.

Department of Census and Statistics, Sri Lanka. 1983. *Census of Population and Housing, Sri Lanka, 1981: The Economically Active Population. Tables Based on a Ten Percent Sample*. Preliminary Release No. 4. Colombo: Department of Census and Statistics.

Deppe, H. 1973. Arbeitsunfälle bei "Gastarbeitern." In: *Industriearbeit und Medizin*. 101–11. ed. H. Deppe. Frankfurt, Germany: Athenaeum.

Der Senator für Inneres. 1982. Yabancilar icin Oturma Hukuku. Berlin.

Der Senator für Gesundheit, Soziales und Familie. 1982. Miteinander Leben: Ausländerpolitik in Berlin. Berlin.

D'Esopo, D. A. 1962. Hysterectomy when the uterus is grossly normal. *American Journal of Obstetrics and Gynecology*. 83(1):113–22.

Deutsch, H. 1945. Motherhood. In: *Psychology of Women*. 456–85. ed. H. Deutsch. New York: Grune and Stratton.

Deykin, E. Y., et al. 1966. The empty nest: psychosocial aspects of conflict between depressed women and their grown children. *American Journal of Psychiatry*. 122:1422–26.

Dicker, R. C., et al. 1982. Complications of abdominal and vaginal hysterectomy among women of reproductive age in the United States. *American Journal of Obstetrics and Gynecology*. 144(7):841–48.

Dissanayake, S. A. W., and P. de Silva. 1983. Sri Lanka. In: *Suicide in Asia and the Near East*. 168–209. ed. L. A. Headley. Berkeley: University of California Press.

Dixon, R. B. 1971. Explaining cross-cultural variations in age at marriage and proportions never marrying. *Population Studies*. 25(2):215–34.

Dixon, R. B. 1978. *Rural Women at Work: Strategies for Development in South Asia*. Baltimore: The Johns Hopkins University Press.

Douglas, M. 1966. *Purity and Danger: An Analysis of Concepts of Pollution and Taboo*. London: Routledge and Kegan Paul.

Dow, J. 1986. Universal aspects of symbolic healing: a theoretical synthesis. *American Anthropologist*. 88(1):56–57.

Drellich, M. G., and I. Bieber. 1958. The psychologic importance of the uterus and its functions. *The Journal of Nervous and Mental Disease*. 126(4):322–36.

Dublin, L. I. 1963. *Suicide: A Sociological and Statistical Study*. New York: Ronald Press.

Dugan, A. B. 1984. *Compadrazgo*: A Caring Phenomenon Among Urban Latinos and Its Relationship to Health. In: *Care: The Essence of Nursing and Health*. 183–94. ed. M. M. Leininger. Thorofare, NJ: Slack.

Dunbar, R. I. M. 1983. Structure of gelada baboon reproductive units. Part 2: Social relationships between reproductive females. *Animal Behavior*. 31:556–64.

Dunk, P. 1985. Greek Women and Broken Nerves in Montreal. Paper presented at the 85th annual meeting of the American Anthropological Association, Washington, D.C.

Durkheim, E. 1966. *Suicide: A Study in Sociology*. New York: Free Press.

Dyck, F. J., et al. 1977. Effect of surveillance on the number of hysterectomies in the province of Saskatchewan. *New England Journal of Medicine*. 296(23):1326–28.

Early, P. 1982. Nurses haunted by memories of service in Vietnam. *American Nurse*. 14 (14 February):8.

Easterday, C. L., D. A. Grimes, and J. A. Riggs. 1983. Hysterectomy in the United States. *American Journal of Obstetrics and Gynecology.* 62(2):203–12.

Edgerton, R. 1985. *Rules, Exceptions, and Social Order.* Berkeley: University of California Press.

Egendorf, A., et al. 1981. *Legacies of Vietnam: Comparative Adjustment of Veterans and Their Peers.* Washington, D.C.: U.S. Government Printing Office.

Eisenberg, L. 1977. Disease and illness. *Culture, Medicine, and Psychiatry.* 1:9–23.

Elmendorf, M. 1976. *Nine Mayan Women: A Village Faces Change.* New York: Schenkman.

Eloff, F. 1973. Ecology and Behavior of the Kalahari Lion. In: *The World Cats* vol. 1, 90–126. ed. R. L. Eaton. Winston, OR: World Wildlife Safari.

Ennis, F., and D. Sherrard. 1984. Women's Resource Kit. A Final Product of the Women's Health Education Project in Newfoundland and Labrador. St. John's, Newfoundland: Jesperson's Printing Ltd.

Erikson, E. 1969. *Childhood and Society.* New York: Norton.

Ernst, S., ed. 1975. *Father Participation Guide.* Milwaukee, WI: International Childbirth Education Association.

Errera, D. W., ed. 1973. Prophylactic hysterectomy: pros and cons. *Hospital Topics.* 51(11):42–43.

Evans-Pritchard, E. E. 1937. *Witchcraft, Oracles, and Magic among the Azande of the Anglo-Egyptian Sudan.* Oxford: Clarendon Press.

Fabrega, H., Jr. 1974. *Disease and Social Behavior: An Interdisciplinary Perspective.* Cambridge, MA: MIT Press.

Farriss, N.M. 1984. *Maya Society Under Colonial Rule: The Collective Enterprise of Survival.* Princeton, NJ: Princeton University Press.

Fernando, D.F.S. 1975. Changing nuptiality patterns in Sri Lanka. *Population Studies.* 29(2):179–90.

Figley, C. R. 1978. *Stress Disorders Among Vietnam Veterans: Theory, Research, and Treatment Implications.* New York: Brunner-Mazel.

Figley, C. R. 1980. *Strangers at Home: Vietnam Veterans since the War.* New York: Praeger.

Finerman, R. 1983. Experience and expectation: conflict and change in traditional family health care among the Quichua of Saraguro. *Social Science and Medicine.* 17:1291–98.

Finerman, R. 1985. Health Care Decisions in an Andean Indian Community: Getting the Best of Both Worlds. Ph.D. diss., University of California, Los Angeles.

Firth, R. I. 1966. *Housekeeping Among Malay Peasants.* 2d ed. London: London School of Economics Monographs in Social Anthropology, No. 2.

Firth, R. M. 1966. *Malay Fishermen: Their Peasant Economy.* New York: Norton.

Flint, M. 1975. The menopause: reward or punishment? *Psychosomatics.* 16:161–63.

Fodor, J. G., E. Abbott, and I. Rusted. 1973. An epidemiologic study of hypertension in Newfoundland. *Canadian Medical Association Journal*. 108:1365–68.

Foster, G. 1953. Relationships between Spanish and Spanish-American folk medicine. *Journal of American Folklore*. 66:201–17.

Foster, G. 1965. Peasant society and the image of limited good. *American Anthropologist*. 76(2):293–315.

Foster, G., and B. Anderson. 1978. *Medical Anthropology*. New York: Wiley.

Franger, G. 1984. Schwangerschaft und Geburt-Wie erleben Türkinnen sie in der Heimat und Hier. *ISS Informations-Dienst zu der Ausländer Arbeit*. 4:29–32.

Fraser, T. M., Jr. 1966. *Fishermen of South Thailand: The Malay Villages*. New York: Holt.

Freedman, A., H. Kaplan, and B. Sadock. 1976. *Modern Synopsis of Comprehensive Textbook of Psychiatry II*. Baltimore, MD: The Williams and Wilkins Company.

Freidl, E. 1975. *Women and Men: An Anthropologist's View*. New York: Holt.

Freidl, J. 1982. Explanatory models of black lung: understanding the health related behavior of Appalachian coal miners. *Culture, Medicine, and Psychiatry*. 6:3–10.

Freidson, E. 1970. *Profession of Medicine*. New York: Harper and Row.

Fuller, N., and B. Jordan. 1981. Maya women and the end of the birthing period: Postpartum massage-and-binding in Yucatan, Mexico. *Medical Anthropology*. 5(1)(Winter):35–51.

Furst, P. 1976. *Hallucinogens and Culture*. San Francisco: Chandler and Sharp.

Garrison, V. 1977. "The Puerto Rican Syndrome" in Psychiatry and Espiritismo. In: *Case Studies in Spirit Possession*. ed. V. Crapanzano and V. Garrison. New York: Wiley.

Gath, D. 1980. Psychiatric Aspects of Hysterectomy. In: *The Social Consequences of Psychiatric Illness*. 33–45. ed. L. N. Robins, P. J. Clayton, and J. K. Wing. New York: Brunner/Mazel.

Geddes, W. R. 1957. *Nine Dayak Nights*. London: Oxford University Press.

Geertz, C. 1973. *The Interpretation of Culture*. New York: Basic Books.

Geertz, C. 1983. *Local Knowledge: Further Essays in Interpretive Anthropology*. New York: Basic Books.

Gerson, L., and J. Fodor. 1978. Family aggregation of high blood-pressure groups in two Newfoundland communities. *Canadian Journal of Public Health*. 66:294–98.

Gimlette, J. D. [1923] 1981. *Malay Poisons and Charm Cures*. Reprint. Kuala Lumpur: Oxford University Press.

Gluckman, M. 1964. *Custom and Conflict in Africa*. New York: Barnes and Noble.

Gluckman, M. 1965. *The Ideas in Barotse Jurisprudence*. New Haven: Yale University Press.

Gmelch, G. 1978. Baseball Magic. *Human Nature*. 1(8):32 33.

Goffman, E. 1961. *The Presentation of Self in Everyday Life*. New York: Doubleday.

Good, B. 1977. The heart of what's the matter: the semantics of illness in Iran. *Culture, Medicine, and Psychiatry*. 1:25–58.

Good, B., and M. J. Good. 1981. The Meaning of Symptoms: A Cultural Hermeneutic Model for Clinical Practice. In: *The Relevance of Social Science for Medicine*. ed. L. Eisenberg and A. Kleinman. Hingham, MA: Kluwer Academic Publishers.

Good, B., M. J. Good, and R. Moradi. 1985. The Interpretation of Iranian Depressive Illness and Dysphoric Affect. In: *Culture and Depression*. ed. A. Kleinman and B. Good. Englewood Cliffs, NJ: Prentice Hall.

Good, B., and A. Kleinman. 1985. Epilogue: culture and depression. In: *Culture and Depression*. ed. A. Kleinman and B. Good. Englewood Cliffs, NJ: Prentice Hall.

Goodman, M. 1980. Toward a biology of menopause. *Signs*. 5(4):739–53.

Gossen, G. 1986. From Ethnography of Tzotzil Communication to Historical and Political Action. Paper presented at the 85th Annual Meeting of the American Anthropological Association, Philadelphia. 3 December.

Greiner, T., P. Van Esterik, and M. Latham. 1981. The insufficient milk syndrome: an alternative explanation. *Medical Anthropology*. 5(2):233–48.

Grossman, M., and P.B. Bart. 1979. Taking the Men out of Menopause. In: *Women Look at Biology Looking at Women*. 163–84. ed. R. Hubbard, M. S. Henifin, and B. Fried. Cambridge MA: Schenkman.

Grottian, G. 1984. Einige Aspekte zu Gesundheit und Lebensverhältnissen türkischer Frauen in Berlin. In: *Krankheit in der Fremde*. ed. A. Geiger and F. Hamburger. Berlin: Express Edition.

Guarnaccia, P. 1985. *Ataques de Nervios*: An Idiom of Distress in the Latino Community. Paper presented at the 85th annual meeting of the American Anthropological Association. Washington, D.C.

Gussler, J., and L. Briesemeister. 1980. The insufficient milk syndrome: a biocultural explanation. *Medical Anthropology*. 4(2):3–24.

Gutman, R. 1963. Population Mobility in the American Middle Class. In: *The Urban Condition*. ed. L. J. Duhl. New York: Basic Books.

Hahn, R. A., and A. Kleinman. 1983. Biomedical practice and anthropological theory: frameworks and directions. *Annual Reviews in Anthropology*. 12:305–33.

Hamilton, S., B. Popkin, and D. Spicer. 1984. *Women and Nutrition in Third World Countries*. New York: Praeger.

Harris, M. 1983. *Cultural Anthropology*. New York: Harper and Row.

Harwood, A. 1981. *Ethnicity and Medical Care*. Cambridge, MA: Harvard University Press.

Hatcher, R. A., et al. 1976 continuous. *Contraceptive Technology*. New York: Irvington Publ.

Headley, L.A., ed. 1983. *Suicide in Asia and the Near East*. Berkeley: University of California Press.

Heckmann, F. 1978. Socio-Structural Analysis of Immigrant Worker Minorities: The Case of West Germany. Paper delivered at the 9th World Congress of Sociology, Uppsala, Sweden.

Helman, C. G. 1978. "Feed a cold, starve a fever"—folk models of infection in an English suburban community, and their relation to medical treatment. *Culture, Medicine, and Psychiatry*. 2(2):107–37.

Helman, C. G. 1984. *Culture, Health, and Illness*. Littleton, MA: PSG Publishing.

Henneborn, W. J., and R. Cogan. 1975. The effect of husband participation on reported pain and probability of medication during labor and birth. *Journal of Psychosomatic Research*. 19:215–22.

Henry, J. P., and P. M. Stephens. 1977. *Stress, Health, and the Social Environment: A Sociobiologic Approach to Medicine*. New York: Springer-Verlag.

Hewitt, J. 1976. *Self and Society: A Symbolic Interactionist Social Psychology*. Boston: Allyn and Bacon.

Hite, S. 1976. *The Hite Report on Female Sexuality*. New York: Macmillan.

Hoffman, L. 1978. Erkrankungen bei Ausländer in der BRD. *Medizinische Klinik*. 73:571–78.

Hommel, F. 1971. Twelve Years Experience in Psychoprophylactic Preparation for Childbirth. In: *Psychosomatic Medicine in Obstetrics and Gynecology*. ed. N. Morris. London: Basel, Karger.

Honigman, J. J. 1959. *The World of Man*. New York: Harper and Row.

Hopper, K. 1979. Of language and the sorcerer's appendix: a critical appraisal of Horacio Fabrega's *Disease and Social Behavior*. *Medical Anthropology Newsletter*. 10(3):9–14.

Horowitz, M. J., and G. F. Soloman. 1975. Prediction of delayed stress responses in Vietnam veterans. *Journal of Social Issues*. 31(4):67–80.

Horton, R. 1967. *African Traditional Thought and Western Science*, 50–187. Bobbs-Merrill Reprint Series in Black Studies. Indianapolis, IN: Bobbs-Merrill.

Hudson, A. B. 1972. *Padju Epat: the Ma'anyan of Indonesian Borneo*. New York: Holt.

Huff, B.B., ed. 1976. *Physician's Desk Reference*. Oradell, NJ: Medical Economics Co.

Hull, D. 1979. Migration, adaptation and illness: a review. *Social Science and Medicine*. 8:421.

Hull, V. 1981. The effects of hormonal contraceptives on lactation. *Studies in Family Planning*. 12(4):134–55.

Hunter, D. E., and P. Whitten. 1976. *Encyclopedia of Anthropology*, 93–94. New York: Harper and Row.

Imanishi, K. 1957. Social behavior in Japanese monkeys, *Macaca fuscata*. *Psychologia*. 1:47–54.

Itani, J. 1954. Japanese monkeys. In: *Takasakijama 'Nihon-dobutsuki'*. vol. 2. ed. K. Imanishi. Tokyo: Kobunsha. (In Japanese)

Jackson, M. N., et al. 1978. Elective hysterectomy: a cost-benefit analysis. *Inquiry*. 15(3):275–80.

Jacobs, M. 1983. Culture and Illness: An Analysis of Post-Traumatic Stress Disorder Among Women Veterans of Vietnam. Master's thesis, Washington State University. Pullman, WA.

Jacobson, S., and G. L. Klerman. 1966. Depressed patients' home visits. *Journal of Marriage and the Family*. 26(February): 94–101.

Jay, P. 1963. Mother-Infant Relations in Langurs. In: *Maternal Behavior in Mammals*. ed. H. L. Rheingold. New York: Wiley.

Jelliffe, D., and E. Jelliffe. 1978. *Human Milk in the Modern World*. Oxford: Oxford University Press.

Jessop, C. 1983. Women's curse: a general internist's approach to common menstrual problems. *Western Journal of Medicine*. 138:76–82.

Kaltreider, N. B., A. Wallace, and M. J. Horowitz. 1979. A field study of the stress response syndrome: young women after hysterectomy. *Journal of the American Medical Association*. 242(14):1499–1503.

Karmel, M. 1965. *Thank You, Dr. Lamaze*. New York: Doubleday.

Kasper, A. S. 1985. Hysterectomy as social process. *Women and Health*. 10(1):109–27.

Kasrawi, R., N. Labib, and H. Hathout. 1984. The premath of hysterectomy. *Journal of Psychosomatic Obstetrics and Gynecology*. 3:233–36.

Kato, H., M. Hirayama, and N. Kobayashi, eds. 1983. *Breast-feeding*. Tokyo: Medi-Science.

Katon, W., and A. Kleinman. 1981. Doctor-patient Negotiation and Other Social Science Strategies in Patient Care. In: *The Relevance of Social Science for Medicine*. ed. L. Eisenberg and A. Kleinman. Boston: D. Reidel.

Katz, M. M. 1971. The Classification of Depression: Normal, Clinical, and Ethnocultural Variations. In: *Depression in the 1970s: Modern Theory and Research*, 31–41. ed. R. R. Fieve. The Hague: Excerpta Medica.

Kearney, R. N. 1975. Educational expansion and political volatility in Sri Lanka: the 1971 insurrection. *Asian Survey*. 15:727–44.

Kearney, R. N., and B. D. Miller. 1985. The spiral of suicide and social change in Sri Lanka. *Journal of Asian Studies*. 45(1):81–101.

Keefe, S. E. 1980. Acculturation and the Extended Family Among Urban Mexican Americans. In: *Acculturation: Theory, Models, and Some New Findings*. AAAS Selected Symposium 39. Boulder, CO: Westview Press.

Kemper, R. V. 1982. The *compadrazgo* in urban Mexico. *Anthropological Quarterly*. 55:17–30.

Kessler, E. S. 1976. *Women: An Anthropological View*. New York: Holt.

Keyser, H. H. 1984. *Women Under the Knife: A Gynecologist's Report on Hazardous Medicine*. Philadelphia: George F. Stickley.

Kimball, L. A. 1979. *Borneo Medicine: The Healing Art of Traditional Malay Medicine*. Ann Arbor, MI: University Microfilms.

Kimball, L. A. 1980. Women of Brunei. In: *A World of Women: Anthropological Studies of Women in the Societies of the World*, 43–57. ed. E. Bourguignon. New York: J. F. Bergin.

Kleinman, A. 1980. *Patients and Healers in the Context of Culture*. Berkeley: University of California Press.

Kleinman, A. 1981. On illness meanings and clinical interpretation. *Culture, Medicine, and Psychiatry.* 5:373–77.

Kleinman, A., L. Eisenberg, and B. Good. 1978. Culture, illness, and care: clinical lessons from anthropologic and cross-cultural research. *Annals of Internal Medicine.* 88:251–58.

Kleinman, A., and B. Good. 1985. Introduction. In: *Culture and Depression.* ed. A. Kleinman and B. Good. Englewood Cliffs, NJ: Prentice-Hall.

Kleinman, A., and J. Kleinman. 1985. Somatization: The Interconnections in Chinese Society Among Culture, Depressive Experiences, and the Meanings of Pain. In: *Culture and Depression.* ed. A. Kleinman and B. Good. Englewood Cliffs, NJ: Prentice-Hall.

Kluckhohn, C. 1962. *Navaho Witchcraft.* Boston: Beacon Press.

Koepsell, T. D., et al. 1980. Prevalence of prior hysterectomy in the Seattle-Tacoma area. *American Journal of Public Health.* 70(1):40–47.

Kosa, J., and I. K. Zola, eds. 1975. [1969]. *Poverty and Health: A Sociological Analysis.* Revised. Cambridge, MA: A Commonwealth Fund Book, Harvard University Press.

Krystal, S., and D. A. Chiriboga. 1979. The empty nest process in mid-life men and women. *Maturitas.* 1:215–22.

Kupperman, H. S., et al. 1953. Comparative clinical evaluation of estrogenic preparation by the menopausal and amenorrheal invoices. *New England Journal of Medicine.* 15:688–703.

Laderman, C. 1982. Putting Malay Women in their Place. In: *Women of Southeast Asia.* ed. P. Van Esterik. Dekalb, IL: Northern Illinois University Center for Southeast Asian Studies. Occasional Papers No. 9.

Laderman, C. 1983. *Wives and Midwives: Childbirth and Nutrition in Rural Malaysia.* Berkeley: University of California Press.

Landis, J., and L. Stoetzer. 1966. An exploratory study of middle-class migrant families. *Journal of Marriage and the Family.* 28(1):51.

Langford, C. M. 1984. Sex differentials in mortality in Sri Lanka: changes since the 1920's. *Journal of Biosocial Science.* 16(3):399–410.

Latham, M. C., et al. In press. Infant feeding in urban Kenya: a pattern of early triple nipple feeding. *Journal of Tropical Pediatrics.*

Lawick-Goodall, J. van. 1967. Mother-Offspring Relationships in Free-ranging Chimpanzees. In: *Primate Ethology,* 287–346. ed. D. Morris. Chicago: Aldine.

Lebra, T. S. 1972. Religious Conversion and Elimination of the Sick Role: A Japanese Sect in Hawaii. Reprinted in revised form In: *Culture, Disease, and Healing.* ed. D. Landy. New York: Macmillan.

Leighton, A. H. 1984. Then and now: some notes on the interaction of person and social environment. *Human Organization.* 43:189–97.

Lettvin, M. 1980. *Maggie's Woman's Book.* Boston: Houghton Mifflin.

Levine, J., et al. 1976. *Physicians Desk Reference.* Oradell, NJ: Medical Economics.

Levine, S.V. 1975. Forging a feminine identity: women in four professional schools. *The American Journal of Psychoanalysis.* 35:63–67.

Lewis, G. 1981. Cultural Influences on Illness Behavior: A Medical Anthropological Approach. In: *The Relevance of Social Science for Medicine*. ed. L. Eisenberg and A. Kleinman. Boston: D. Reidel.

Lifton, R. J. 1973. *Home From the War*. New York: Simon and Schuster.

Like, R., and J. Ellison. 1981. Sleeping blood, tremor, and paralysis: a transcultural approach to an unusual conversion reaction. *Culture, Medicine, and Psychiatry*. 5:49–63.

Lilly, J. C. 1963. Distress call of the bottlenose dolphin: stimuli and evoked behavioral responses. *Science*. 139:116.

Linton, R. 1936. *The Study of Man*. New York: Appleton- Century.

Linton, R. 1973. Status and Role. In: *High Points in Anthropology*. 187–200. ed. P. Bohannan and M. Glazer. New York: Knopf.

Lock, M. 1982. Models and practice in medicine: menopause as syndrome or life transition? *Culture, Medicine, and Psychiatry*. 6:261–80.

Lorenz, K. 1959. The Role of Aggression in Group Formation. In: *Group Processes*. ed. B. Schaffner. New York: The Josiah Macy, Jr. Foundation.

Low, S. 1981. Meaning of *nervios*: a sociocultural analysis of symptom presentation in San Jose, Costa Rica. *Culture, Medicine, and Psychiatry* 5:350–57.

Low, S. 1985. Culturally interpreted symptoms or culture bound syndromes: a cross-cultural review of nerves. *Social Science and Medicine*. 21:187–96.

Lowenthal, M. F., et al. 1975. *Four Stages of Life*. San Francisco: Jossey-Bass.

Ludwig, A., and R. Forrester. 1981. The condition of "nerves." *The Journal of the Kentucky Medical Association*. 79:333–36.

Lyon, J. L., and J. W. Gardner. 1977. The rising frequency of hysterectomy: its effect on uterine cancer rates. *American Journal of Epidemiology*. 105(5):439–43.

Madeira, F. R., and P. Singer. 1975. Structure of female employment and work in Brazil. *Journal of Interamerican Studies and World Affairs*. 17:490–96.

Mair, L. 1969. *Witchcraft*. New York: McGraw-Hill.

Maoz, B., et al. 1978. The effect of outside work on the menopausal woman. *Maturitas*. 1:43–53.

Marieskind, H. 1975. The women's health movement. *International Journal of Health Services*. 5(2):217–23.

Marsella, A., et al. 1985. Cross-cultural Studies of Depressive Disorders: An Overview. In: *Culture and Depression*. ed. A. Kleinman and B. Good. Berkeley: University of California Press.

Martin, E. 1984. Pregnancy, labor and body image in the United States. *Social Science and Medicine*. 19(11):1201–06.

Martin, R. L., et al. 1977. Psychiatric illness and non-cancer hysterectomy. *Diseases of the Nervous System*. 38(12): 974–80.

Martinez, C., and A. Chavez. 1971. Nutrition and development in infants of poor rural areas. *Nutrition Report International*. 4(3):139–49.

Masters, W., V. Johnson, and R. Kolodny. 1982. *Human Sexuality*. Boston: Little, Brown.

Mauskch, H. 1972. Nursing: Churning for Change. In: *Handbook of Medical Sociology*. 2nd ed. ed. H.E. Freeman. NJ: Prentice-Hall.

McCarthy, E. G., and G. W. Widmer. 1974. Effects of screening by consultants on recommended elective surgical procedures. *New England Journal of Medicine*. 291(25):1331–35.

McClain, C. S. 1981. Women's choice of home or hospital birth. *The Journal of Family Practice*. 12(6):1033–38.

McClain, C. S. 1983. Perceived risk and choice of childbirth service. *Social Science and Medicine*. 17(23):1857–65.

McClain, C. S. 1985. Why women choose trial of labor or repeat cesarean section. *The Journal of Family Practice*. 21(3):210–16.

McKinlay, J. 1981. Social Network Influences on Morbid Episodes and the Career of Help Seeking. In: *The Relevance of Social Science for Medicine*. ed. L. Eisenberg and A. Kleinman. Boston: D. Reidel.

McKinlay, J. B. 1975. Who is really ignorant—physician or patient? *Journal of Health and Social Behavior*. 16(1):3–11.

Mead, M. 1978. On the Viability of Villages. In: *Village Viability in Contemporary Society*. ed. P. Copeland and B. Lenkerd. Boulder, CO: Westview Press.

Mead, M., and N. R. Newton. 1967. Cultural Patterning of Perinatal Behavior. In: *Childbearing—Its Social and Psychological Aspects*. ed. S. A. Richardson and A. Guttmacher. Baltimore: Williams and Wilkins Co.

Mechanic, D. 1978. *Medical Sociology*. New York: Toll Free Press.

Medical Anthropology. 1981. vol. 5.

Medical Anthropology Quarterly: International Journal for the Cultural and Social Analysis of Health. 1986 continuous. (Formerly *Medical Anthropology*).

Mehrländer, U., et al. 1981. Situation der ausländischen Arbeitsnehmer und ihrer Angehörigen in der Bundesrepublik Deutschland—Repräsentativuntersuchung 1980. Bonn.

Miller, A. B. 1981. *The Canadian Experience of Cervical Cancer: Incidence Trends and a Planned Natural History of Investigation*. Proceedings of the symposium on Trends in Cancer, Oslo, 1980. New York: Hemisphere.

Mintz, S. W., and E. R. Wolf. 1950. An analysis of ritual co-parenthood (*compadrazgo*). *Southwestern Journal of Anthropology*. 6:341–68.

Mishler, E. G., and N. A. Scotch. 1963. Sociocultural factors in the epidemiology of schizophrenia: a review. *Psychiatry*. 26:315–51.

Morgan, S. 1982. *Coping With a Hysterectomy*. New York: Dial.

Morse, D. R., and M. L. Furst. 1982. *Women under Stress*. New York: Van Nostrand Reinhold.

Nadarajah, T. 1983. The transition from higher female to higher male mortality in Sri Lanka. *Population and Development Review*. 9(2):317–25.

Nader, L., and H. F. Todd, Jr., eds. 1978. *The Disputing Process in Ten Societies*. New York: Columbia University Press.

Nag, M., B. White, and R. Peet. 1978. An anthropological approach to the study of the economic value of children in Java and Nepal. *Current Anthropology*. 19:293–306.

Nash, M. 1967. Witchcraft as a Social Process in a Tzeltal Community. In: *Magic, Witchcraft and Curing*. 127–33. ed. J. Middleton. Garden City, NY: The Natural History Press.

Neifert, M. 1985. "Every woman can breast-feed": doctrine or myth. *Breast-feeding Abstracts*. 5(1):1–2.

Neugarten, B. L., and F. J. Kraines. 1964. "Menopausal symptoms" in women of various ages. *Psychosomatic Medicine*. 27(3):266–73.

Neukirchen, M., and W. Haase. 1978. Beobachtungen über die Häufigkeit von Magenstörungen bei ausländischen Arbeitsnehmer. *Krankenhausarzt*. 51:922–29.

Newton, N., and E. Baron. 1976. Reactions to hysterectomy: fact or fiction? *Primary Care*. 3(4):781–801.

Newton, N., and M. Newton. 1950. Relation of the let-down reflex to the ability to breast-feed. *Pediatrics*. 5:726–33.

Nichter, M. 1981. Idioms of distress: alternatives in the expression of psychosocial distress: a case study from South India. *Culture, Medicine, and Psychiatry*. 5:379–408.

Olesen, V., and E. Whittaker. 1968. *The Silent Dialogue: A Study on the Social Psychology of Professional Socialization*. San Francisco: Jossey-Bass.

Ortner, S., and H. Whitehead, eds. 1981. *Sexual Meanings: The Cultural Construction of Gender and Meanings*. Cambridge, England: Cambridge University Press.

Oswalt, W. H. 1986. *Life Cycles and Lifeways: An Introduction to Cultural Anthropology*. Palo Alto, CA: Mayfield.

Parsons, T. 1951. *The Social System*. New York: Free Press.

Parsons, T., and R. Fox. 1952. Illness, therapy and the modern urban American family. *Journal of Social Issues*. 8:31–44.

Paul, E., and J. O'Neill. 1983. The Psychological Milieu of Nursing in Vietnam and Its Effects on Vietnam Nurse Veterans. (Xerox copy).

Paulshock, B. Z. 1976. What every woman should know about hysterectomy. *Today's Health*. 54(2):23–26.

Paz, O. 1961. *The Labyrinth of Solitude: Life and Thought in Mexico*. New York: Grove.

Peters, M. 1986. *Unquiet Soul: A Biography of Charlotte Bronte*. New York: Atheneum.

Pillsbury, B. L. K. 1982. Policy and evaluation perspectives on traditional health practitioners in national health care systems. *Social Science and Medicine*. 16:1825–34.

Podesta, J. S. 1982. The other Vietnam vets. *MS*. 10(June):23.

Polner, M. 1971. *No Victory Parades: The Return of the Vietnam Veteran*. New York: Holt.

Poloma, M. M., and N. T. Garland. 1971. Job or Career? The Case of the Professionally Employed Married Woman. In: *Family Issues of Employed Women*. ed. A. Michael. Leiden, Netherlands: Brill.

Polunin, I. 1977. The Body's Signs of Health and Disease. In: *The Anthropology of the Body*. ed. J. Blacking. New York: Academic Press.

Prados, M. 1967. Emotional factors in the climacterium of women. *Psychotherapy Psychosomomatic Medicine*. 15:231–44.

Presser, H. B., and L. L. Bumpass. 1972. Demographic and Social Aspects of Contraceptive Sterilization in the United States. In: *Demographic and Social Aspects of Population Growth*, 505–68. ed. C. F. Westoff and R. Parke. Washington, D.C.: Government Printing Office.

Prior, R. 1968. *The Roe Deer of Cranborne Chase: An Ecological Survey*. Oxford: Oxford University Press.

Prognos AG and Freie Planungsgruppe Berlin GmbH. 1980. Wohnraumversorgung von Ausländer und Entballung überbelasteter Gebiete durch städtebäuliche Massnahmen. Der regierende Bürgermeister von Berlin Senatskanzlei/Planungstelle. Berlin.

Quaquish, I., H. U. Burchardt, and K. L. Heilmann. 1979. Magenerkrankungen bei ausländischen Arbeitsnehmer in der Bundesrepublik Deutschland. *München Medizinische Wochenschrift*. 121:1563–65.

Rabkin, J. G., and E. L. Struening. 1976. Life events, stress, and illness. *Science*. 194:1013–20.

Rank, S., and C. Jacobson. 1977. Hospital nurses compliance with medication overdose orders: a failure to replicate. *Journal of Health and Social Behavior*. 18:188–93.

Raphael, D. 1966. The Lactation-Suckling Process within a Matrix of Supportive Behavior. Ph.D. diss., Columbia University, New York.

Raphael, D. 1969. Uncle Rhesus, Auntie Pachyderm, and Mom: all sorts and kinds of mothering. *Perspectives in Biology and Medicine*. 12(Winter):2.

Raphael, D. 1976. *The Tender Gift: Breastfeeding*. New York: Schocken Books.

Raphael, D. 1983. New Breastfeeding Patterns for Women in Rapidly Changing Industrial Societies. In: *Breast Feeding*, 27–33. ed. H. Kato, M. Hirayama, and N. Kobayashi. Tokyo: Medi-Science Co.

Raphael, D. 1984. Supportive Network for success at Lactation. Sunbelt Social Network Conference, Phoenix, Ariz., 18 February.

Raphael, D., ed. 1975. *Being Female*. The Hague: Mouton.

Raphael, D., L. Hale, and A. Breakstone. 1976. Female/ young groupings within mammalian social organization. Animal Behavior Society Meeting, American Museum of Natural History, New York. 9 October.

Registrar General (Sri Lanka). Annual. (1950–1966). *Annual Report of the Registrar General of Ceylon on Vital Statistics*. Colombo: Department of Government Printing.

Reiter, R., ed. 1975. *Toward an Anthropology of Women*. New York: Monthly Review Press.

Resnik, H. L. P. 1980. Suicide. In: *Comprehensive Textbook of Psychiatry*. vol. 2, 2085–98. 3d ed. ed H. I. Kaplan, A. M. Freedman, and B. J. Sadock. Baltimore: Williams and Wilkins.

Richards, B. G. 1978. Hysterectomy: from women to women. *American Journal of Obstetrics and Gynecology*. 131(4): 446–52.

Richards, C. 1969. Presumed behavior: modification of the ideal-real dichotomy. *American Anthropologist*. 71:(11):15–17.

Richards, D. H. 1973. Depression after hysterectomy. *The Lancet*. 2(7826):430–32.

Richards, D. H. 1974. A post-hysterectomy syndrome. *The Lancet*. 2(7887):983–85.

Rist, R. 1978. *Guest workers in Germany: The Prospects for Pluralism*. New York: Praeger.

Roeske, N. C. A. 1978. Quality of life and factors affecting the response to hysterectomy. *The Journal of Family Practice*. 7(3):483–88.

Rohrmoser, H. 1984. Familienplanung und Verhütungspraxis türkischer Frauen. In: *Zwischen Zwei Kulturen*. ed. H. Kentenich, P. Reeg, and K. H. Wehkamp. Berlin: Verlagsgesellschaft Gesundheit.

Romanucci-Ross, L., D. E. Moerman, and L. R. Tancredi, eds. 1983. *The Anthropology of Medicine: From Culture to Method*. So. Hadley, MA: Bergin & Garvey.

Rosaldo, M. Z., and L. Lamphere, eds. 1974. *Woman, Culture, and Society*. Stanford, CA: Stanford University Press.

Rothblum, E. D. 1983. Sex Role Stereotypes and Depression in Women. In: *The Stereotyping of Women: Its Effects on Mental Health*, 83–111. ed. V. Franks and E. D. Rothblum. New York: Springer.

Rowell, T. E., R. A. Hinde, and Y. Spencer-Booth. 1964. "Aunt"—infant interaction in captive rhesus monkeys. *Journal of Animal Behavior*. 12:219–26.

Rubel, A. 1964. The epidemiology of a folk illness: *susto* in Hispanic America. *Ethnology*. 3:268–83.

Rubel, A., C. O'Nell, and R. Collado-Ardon. 1984. *Susto: A Folk Illness*. Berkeley: University of California Press.

Rubin, L. 1981. *Women of a Certain Age*. New York: Harper and Row.

Ruzek, S. B. 1979. *The Women's Health Movement*. New York: Praeger.

Sade, D. S. 1965. Some aspects of parent-offspring relations in a group of rhesus monkeys, with a discussion of grooming. *American Journal of Physical Anthropology*. 23:1–17.

Sanday, P. R. 1981. *Female Power and Male Dominance: On the Origins of Sexual Inequality*. Cambridge, England: Cambridge University Press.

Schieffelin, E. 1985. The Cultural Analysis of Depressive Affect: An Example from New Guinea. In: *Culture and Depression*. ed. A. Kleinman and B. Good. Englewood Cliffs, NJ: Prentice-Hall.

Schlegel, A., ed. 1977. *Sexual Stratification: A Cross Cultural View*. New York: Holt.

Schliemann, F., and G. Schliemann. 1975. Über den Geburtsverlauf bei Ausländerinnen. *Geburtshilfe und Frauenheilkunde*. 35:210–17.

Schnaier, J. 1982. Women Vietnam veterans and mental health adjustment: a study of their experiences and post traumatic stress. Master's thesis, University of Maryland.

Schoening-Kalender, C. 1984. Krankheit im Prozess der Wanderung. In: *Krankheit in der Fremde*. ed. A. Geiger and F. Hamburger. Berlin: Express Edition.

Schrijvers, J. 1985. *Mothers for Life: Motherhood and Marginalization in the North Central Province of Sri Lanka.* Delft, Netherlands: Eburon.

Schultze-Naumburg, R., and G. Scholtes. 1976. Entbindungen bei Ausländerinnen. *Medizinische Klinik.* 71:63–67.

Schutz, A. 1962. *Collected Papers I, the Problem of Social Reality.* The Hague: Martinus Nishoff.

Schwarz, R.A. 1981. The midwife in contemporary Latin America. *Medical Anthropology.* 5(1)(Winter): 51–73.

Scotch, N.A. 1963. Socio-cultural factors in the epidemiology of Zulu hypertension. *American Journal of Public Health.* 53:1205.

Scully, D. 1980. *Men Who Control Women's Health.* Boston: Houghton Mifflin.

Seaman, B., and G. Seaman. 1977. *Women and the Crisis in Sex Hormones.* New York: Bantam.

Seyle, H. [1956] 1976. *The Stress of Life.* Revised. New York: McGraw-Hill.

Sherif, M. 1936. *The Psychology of Social Norms.* New York: Harper Brothers.

Silverman, S. 1967. The life crisis as a clue to social functions. *Anthropology Quarterly.* 40:127–38.

Singer, M., et al. 1984. Hypoglycemia: a controversial illness in U.S. society. *Medical Anthropology: Cross-Cultural Studies in Health and Illness.* 8(1):1–35.

Skeat, W.W. [1900] 1967. *Malay Magic: Being an Introduction to the Folklore and Popular Religion of the Malay Peninsula.* Reprint. New York: Dover.

Sloan, D. 1978. The emotional psychosexual aspects of hysterectomy. *American Journal of Obstetrics and Gynecology.* 131(6):598–605.

Smith-Rosenberg, C. 1972. The hysterical woman: sex roles and role conflict in 19th century America. *Social Research.* 39(4):652–78.

Smith-Rosenberg, C., and C. Rosenberg. 1973. The female animal: medical and biological views of woman and her role in 19th century America. *Journal of American History.* 60:332–56.

Sosa, R., et al. 1980. The effect of a supportive companion on perinatal problems, length of labor, and mother-infant interaction. *New England Journal of Medicine.* 303:597–600.

Spence, D., and T. Lonner. 1971. The "empty nest": a transition within motherhood. *The Family Coordinator.* 10:369–75.

Sri Lanka. 1980. *Hansard Parliamentary Debates, Official Report,* vol. 2.

Statistisches landesamt Berlin. 1983. Melderechtlich registrierte Ausländer in Berlin (West). am 31. Dezember 1982. Berlin.

Stein, L. I. 1967. The doctor-nurse game. *Archives of General Psychiatry.* 16:699–700.

Stender, F. 1971. *Husbands in the Delivery Room.* Bellevue, WA: International Childbirth Education Association.

Stern, G., and L. Kruckman. 1983. Multi-disciplinary perspectives on postpartum depression: an anthropological critique. *Social Science and Medicine.* 17(15):1027–41.

Stevenson, I. 1977. *Colerina:* reactions to emotional stress in the Peruvian Andes. *Social Science and Medicine.* 11:303–07.

Stewart, F., et al. 1979. *My Body, My Health: A Concerned Woman's Guide to Gynecology*. New York: Wiley.

Strange, H. 1981. *Rural Malay Women in Tradition and Transition*. New York: Praeger.

Straus, J. H., and M. A. Straus. 1953. Suicide, homicide, and social structure in Ceylon. *American Journal of Sociology*. 58:461–69.

Strobel, E. 1975. Beteiligung der Gastarbeiterinnen an der schwangeren Vorsorge. *Fortschritte der Medizin*. 93:1301–08.

Suarez, Y., N. Crowe, and H. Adams. 1978. Depression: avoidance learning and physiological correlates in clinical and analog populations. *Behavior Research and Therapy*. 16:21–31.

Sukkary, S. 1981. She is no stranger: the traditional midwife in Egypt. *Medical Anthropology*. 5(1)(Winter):27–35.

Sutlive, V. H., Jr. 1978. *The Iban of Sarawak*. Arlington Heights, IL: AHM Publishing.

Syme, L. S., M. M. Hyman, and P. E. Enterline. 1964. Some social and cultural factors associated with the occurrence of coronary heart disease. *Journal of Chronic Diseases*. 17:277.

Tanzer, D. 1967. The psychology of pregnancy and childbirth: An investigation of natural childbirth. Ph. D. diss., Brandeis University, Waltham, MA.

Taylor, E. E., R. Dirican, and K. W. Deuschle. 1968. *Health Manpower Planning in Turkey: An International Research Case Study*. Baltimore, MD: The Johns Hopkins University Press.

Taylor, R. B. 1973. *Introduction to Cultural Anthropology*. Boston: Allyn and Bacon.

Tedlock, B. 1982. *Time and the Highland Maya*. Albuquerque: University of New Mexico Press.

Tedlock, B. 1984. La dialéctica de la agronomía y astronomía Maya-Quiché. Paper presented in the symposium Arqueoastronomía y ethnoastronomía en Mesoamérica, Universidad Naciónal Autónoma de México, Alvaro Obregon, México. 25 September.

Tedlock, B. In Press. An intrepretive solution to the problem of humoral medicine in Latin America. *Social Science and Medicine*.

Theilen, I. 1984. *Krankheit und Gesundheit in der Biografie von Migranten*. Berlin: Express Edition.

Thompson, J. D., and H. W. Birch. 1981. Indications for Hysterectomy. *Clinical Obstetrics and Gynecology*. 24(4):1245–58.

Thompson, R. A. 1973. A theory of instrumental social networks. *Journal of Anthropological Research*. 29:244–65.

Thornton, R., and P. Nardi. 1975. The dynamics of role acquisition. *American Journal of Sociology*. 80(4):870–85.

Tinberg, N. 1951. *The Study of Instinct*. London: Oxford University Press.

Townsend, J. M., and C. L. Carbone. 1980. Menopausal syndrome: illness or social role—a transcultural analysis. *Culture, Medicine, and Psychiatry*. 4(3):229–48.

Tutelian, L. 1981. Vietnam veteran. *Glamour* 79(June):73.

Tweddell, C., and L.A. Kimball. 1985. *Introduction to the Peoples and Cultures of Asia*. Englewood Cliffs, NJ: Prentice-Hall.

United States Department of Commerce, Bureau of the Census. 1981. Standard Metropolitan Statistical Areas and Standard Consolidated Statistical Areas: 1980. (Issued October, 1981.)

United States Department of Commerce, Bureau of the Census. 1985. *Statistical Abstract of the United States for 1985*.

Uzzel, D. 1974. *Susto* revisited: illness as strategic role. *American Ethnologist*. 1:369–78.

Van Devanter, L. 1983. *Home Before Morning*. New York: Beaufort Books.

Van Esterik, P. 1985a. Commentary: An Anthropological Perspective on Infant Feeding in Oceania. In: *Infant Care and Feeding in the South Pacific*. ed. L. Marshall. New York: Gordon and Breach.

Van Esterik, P. 1985b. The Cultural Context of Breastfeeding in Rural Thailand. In: *Breastfeeding, Child Health, and Child Spacing*. ed. V. Hull and M. Simpson. London: Croom Helm.

Van Esterik, P., and T. Greiner. 1981. Breastfeeding and women's work: constraints and opportunities. *Studies in Family Planning*. 12(4):182–95.

Van Gennep, A. 1960. *The Rites of Passage*. Translated by M. B. Vizedom and G. L. Caffee. London: Routledge and Kegan Paul. (French edition 1909.)

Van Keep, P. 1976. Psycho-Social Aspects of the Climacteric. In: *Consensus on Menopause Research*. ed. R. Greenblatt and M. Albeaux-Fernet. Baltimore, MD: University Park Press.

Van Keep, P., and J. Kellerhals. 1974. The impact of sociocultural factors on symptom formation. *Psychotherapy and Psychosomatic Medicine*. 23:251–63.

Van Keep, P., and J. Kellerhals. 1975. The aging woman. About the influence of some social and cultural factors on the change in attitude and behaviors that occur after menopause. *Acta Obstetrica Gynecology Scandinavia*. 51:19–27. (Suppl.)

Van Schaik, E. 1985. Women, health and culture: The case of nerves. Paper presented at the 85th annual meeting of the American Anthropological Association, Washington, D.C.

Velimirovic, H., and B. Velimirovic. 1981. The role of traditional birth attendants in health services. *Medical Anthropology*. (1) (Winter):89–107.

Vellay, P. 1959. *Childbirth Without Pain*. Translated by Denise Lloyd. London: Hutchinson and Co., with George Allen and Unwin Ltd.

Vietnam Veterans of America. 1981. *The Woman Vietnam Veteran: The Unknown Warrior*. Columbus, OH: The Disabled American Veterans.

Vital and Health Statistics. 1966. *Age at Menopause: United States— 1960–1962*. (DHEW Publication No. (PHS) 1000, Series 11, No. 19), Washington, D.C.: U.S. Government Printing Office.

Vogt, E. 1970. *The Zinacantecos of Mexico: A Modern Maya Way of Life*. New York: Holt.

Walsh, A. C., and J. Simonelli. 1986. Migrant women in the oil field: the functions of social networks. *Human Organization*. 45:43–52.

Webb, C., and J. Wilson-Barnett. 1983. Self-concept, social support and hysterectomy. *International Journal of Nursing Studies*. 20(2):97–107.

Weekend. August 3, 1980, p. 15.

Weideger, P. 1977. *Menstruation and Menopause: The Physiology and Psychology, the Myth and the Reality*. New York: Delta.

Weiss, N. S., D. R. Szekely, and D. F. Austin. 1976. Increasing incidence of endometrial cancer in the United States. *New England Journal of Medicine*. 294(23):1259–62.

West, C. P. 1980. Factors affecting the duration of breastfeeding. *Journal of Biosocial Science*. 12:325–31.

Whichelow, M. 1979. Breastfeeding—keeping up the milk supply. *Health Visitor*. 52:217–20.

Wijma, K. 1984. Psychological functioning after non-cancer hysterectomy: a review of methods and results. *Journal of Psychosomatic Obstetrics and Gynecology*. 3(3/4):133–54.

Williams, T. R. 1965. *The Dusun: A North Borneo Society*. New York: Holt.

Wilson, J. P. 1978. *Forgotten Warrior Project*. Parts I and II. Columbus, OH: Disabled American Veterans, in association with Cleveland State University.

Winikoff, B., and G. Brown. 1980. Nutrition, population, and health: theoretical and practical issues. *Social Science and Medicine*. 14C(2):171–76.

Wittlinger, H., P. Hohlweg-Majert, and S. Sievers. 1977. Schwangerschaft und Geburt bei Gastarbeiterinnen. *Medizinische Klinik*. 720:33–38.

Wolf, E. 1966. *Peasants*. Engelwood Cliffs, NJ: Prentice Hall.

Wood, A. D. 1973. "The fashionable diseases": women's complaints and their treatment in 19th century America. *Journal of Interdisciplinary History*. 4(1):25–52.

Woods, C. R. 1979. *Human Sickness and Health: A Biocultural View*. Palo Alto, CA: Mayfield Publ. Co.

World Health Organization. 1979. WHO Collaborative Study on Breastfeeding. Preliminary Report. Geneva.

Wright, R. C. 1969. Hysterectomy: past, present, and future. *American Journal of Obstetrics and Gynecology*. 33(4):560–63.

Yamada, M. 1963. A study of blood-relationship in the natural society of the Japanese macaque. *Primates*. 4(3):43–55.

Yankelovich, D. 1987. Coming to Public Judgment. The 1987 Frank W. Abrams Lecture Series, Syracuse University, Syracue, N.Y.

Young, A. 1976. Some implications of medical beliefs and practices for social anthropology. *American Anthropologist*. 78(1):5–24.

Young, A. 1982. The anthropologies of illness and sickness. *Annual Reviews in Anthropology*. 11:257–85.

Youngs, D. D., and T. N. Wise. 1976. Changing perspectives on elective hysterectomy. *Primary Care*. 3(4):765–79.

Zink A., et al. 1982. *Ausländische Schwangere: Vorsorge, Diagnosen und Therapie am Beispiel der Versicherten einer Ortskrankenkasse*. Berlin: Volkswagen Foundation.

INDEX

225